praise for lauren berlant

"For Lauren Berlant, to be intellectual is to produce new forms for optimism by being in sync with someone, with something forming up in some rickety damaged world. Work, after Berlant, is a binding to things ideas people smells we don't know. The binding is what matters in the labor of making a more fitting world for the affects we have."—KATHLEEN STEWART

"Lauren Berlant's stunning achievement is that they used not only their uncanny sensitivity to see the affective impact of power over time, to analyze the dominion of neoliberal capitalism's cruelties in daily lives of struggling precarity but also to mine the utopian wishes embedded in otherwise crushed hopes. Their imperviousness helped them put their genre-bending work out there despite not fitting any disciplinary or theoretical mold. Berlant's alchemical trick was to turn the everyday life of difficulty into the dazzling light of brilliance."—LISA DUGGAN

"Lauren Berlant's special contribution to human thought (as distinct from academic knowledge) was the unsettling of 'normativity,' the routine, normal unexamined habits that infect thinking in the mundane spaces of everyday life, the halls of academe, and the corridors of power."—W. J. T. MITCHELL

"Lauren Berlant provoked fantasy. . . . They understood that the world, as a destination, was not the point: it was the attachments generated by making it that mattered."—ELIZABETH FREEMAN

"From the beginning, Lauren Berlant's work exemplified what are now called intersectional approaches to race, gender, and sexuality. . . . They wrestled with the back and forth between having feelings and critiquing feelings, moving in close to felt experience and attachments to objects and moving out to systemic and theoretical analysis."—ANN CVETKOVICH

"Every memory of Lauren Berlant reminds me of their interestedness, their attentiveness. Even their writing on modes of detachment—flatness, withdrawal, humorlessness, suicidal ideation—finds in these means of staying in the world."
—DANA LUCIANO

"Everything I write is influenced by Berlant's thinking. Their work taught me to look closely at the ways people attach themselves to objects (lovers, nations), and to look too at the material conditions from which affect and attachment spring. Their writing led me to psychoanalysis, to feminism, to organizing. In my life and in my work, I try to follow Berlant's lead and to politicize feelings: to see them as part of public, collective experience, rather than as features of private, individual lives."
—MAGGIE DOHERTY

"Lauren Berlant fundamentally altered our sense of how language matters, how language can make and sustain alternate worlds. And they did this with the buoying political lessons of writerly style—style as praxis, as a way of doing political thought by critical worldmaking. . . . As if unstoppable, Berlant wrote toward and not just about the forthcoming and the anticipated."—JILL CASID

on the inconvenience of other people

WRITING MATTERS! a series edited by Lauren Berlant,
Saidiya Hartman, Monica Huerta, Erica Rand, and Kathleen Stewart

lauren berlant ON THE
INCONVENIENCE
OF OTHER PEOPLE

DUKE UNIVERSITY PRESS DURHAM AND LONDON 2022

© 2022 DUKE UNIVERSITY PRESS All rights reserved
Printed in the United States of America on acid-free paper ∞
Designed by Aimee C. Harrison
Typeset in Quadraat Pro and BenchNine by Westchester
Publishing Services

Library of Congress Cataloging-in-Publication Data
Names: Berlant, Lauren Gail [date], author.
Title: On the inconvenience of other people / Lauren Berlant.
Other titles: Writing matters! (Duke University Press)
Description: Durham : Duke University Press, 2022. | Series: Writing
matters! | Includes bibliographical references and index.
Identifiers: LCCN 2021049045 (print)
LCCN 2021049046 (ebook)
ISBN 9781478015819 (hardcover)
ISBN 9781478018452 (paperback)
ISBN 9781478023050 (ebook)
Subjects: LCSH: Queer theory. | Feminist theory. | Interpersonal
relations. | Attachment behavior. | Life change events. | BISAC:
SOCIAL SCIENCE / Feminism & Feminist Theory | SOCIAL SCIENCE
/ LGBTQ Studies / General Classification: LCC HQ75.15 .B467 2022
(print) | LCC HQ75.15 (ebook) | DDC 306.7601—dc23/eng/20211230
LC record available at https://lccn.loc.gov/2021049045
LC ebook record available at https://lccn.loc.gov/2021049046

Cover art: David Leggett, *One eyed poem*, 2016. Acrylic and collage
on canvas. Courtesy of the artist.

contents

a note to the reader

Lauren Berlant completed *The Inconvenience of Other People* in June 2021. Sadly, they passed before the book went into production. As a coeditor of the *Writing Matters!* series, I completed the tasks ordinarily performed by an author during a book's production phase. I reviewed the copyedited manuscript—evaluating suggested changes and corrections, clarifying unintended ambiguities, and answering editor questions—and checked the page proofs. I thank Susan Albury, the project editor, Andrea Klinger, the copyeditor, Aimee Harrison, the book designer, and Scott Smiley, the indexer, as well as Laurie Shannon, Katie Stewart, and Courtney Berger, whom I consulted often. We all worked together to present the book that the author intended.

—Erica Rand

preface **WHAT NOW?**

I am making the final revisions of this book during the coronavirus pandemic. Within a few weeks, a global imperative to kettle bodies in homes shook economies in the home and the world: income streams, intimacies, habituated socialites, rent and ownership, food and electricity, play and education, and demands on attention were all in disarray. Within a few weeks, the anti-Black violence expressed in white state supremacist police practices and limited economic access to health care and work intensified in explicitness the lived political atmosphere. Within a few weeks, the scandal of state-fueled migrant cruelty at the southern border became crowded out, returned, got juggled. Within the year, anti-Asian violence fueled by state xenophobia, straight erotophobia, and ordinary white privilege manifested lethally on and off the streets. Meanwhile the *New York Times* reported surprise that the suicide rate had gone down by 5 percent during 2020, but then it turned out that was only for white people; for urban, rural, Indigenous, Latinx, Black, and Native Alaskans, the rates rose for predictable reasons that are still being culled.[1] This crisis convergence made scavenging and trespassing an episodic way of life for people who were not used to it and for those already exhausted by a lifetime in search of concrete and affective relief. Things heated up. Life seemed closer to death. Hate became an everyday motive for spontaneous and planned violence; different kinds of love organized resistant and reparative action. Mutual care traditions drove pedagogies of survival, which was never presumed anyway for poor, Indigenous, Black, trans, and other unsettling sexed/gendered people in the United States.

People where I live wished for a random bit of luck, like dodging a bullet or some diapers donated to the local free zone. Women were pleading for formula and tampons. There was so much food insecurity that energetic chefs seemed suddenly like heroes to some. People wished for better infrastructures of resource distribution or the end of the social.

As usual, what "we" could be presumed? Numbers spiked and dropped; outrage and numbness set in. Imaginations stopped trying or got massively creative. Many of us burst into demands for an economic and procedural reboot of safety, security, and community, which included defacing the image of the police as the ideal local military. Meanwhile, mental health crises that faced life as well as death expanded into a pandemic with their own structural bases, their own hotlines, their own everydayness, and their own appearance as intimate partner violence *and* as police actions, where qualified immunity protects them from the consequences of spraying out their own roiling emotions onto other vulnerable bodies. Like dust bouncing off a trampoline, active counter-dominant solidarity on multiple and conflicting fronts induced pervasive and desired atmospheres, with their uneven rhythms of efficacy. The inconvenience of other people became a pragmatic political topic: With whom can you imagine sharing the world's sidewalk? What do you do with the figures of threat and dread that your own mind carries around?

This is a book about the overcloseness of the world and how we live it. It is about navigating and generating change from within the long broken and fractious middle of life. Experiencing nonsovereign relationality—the inconvenience of other people—is inevitably a feature of the sensual ordinary of the world. There are many catastrophes: this book circles around the rape and murder of women, both in chapter 1 and in the coda, and tries delicately to separate out devastating violence from our drive to be inconvenienced by each other and the inescapability of being the inconvenient ones.

This concept of inconvenience describes the pressure of the proximity of many different kinds of tension, positively and negatively valenced.

I don't like making statements about the state of the world at the start of transitional eruptions. People read speculations as truth claims and propositions as opinions. Everything needs to be tested with humility and focus. Chapter 1 is mainly, but not entirely, about the generativity of desire and aggression and the kinds of things we do when we are extending a relation that is not about annihilating each other but about trying to find a way to extend a dynamic; it also addresses what happens when we give up the delicate work of moving through the world together and start thrashing around traumatically. The close of chapter 2, on the concept of the commons, speculates about some things that are opened up by white racist self-enjoyment and the pandemic: in particular the question of what's left of the concept of general publics. We know "we" is a problem; also, what is the "it" of "we're all in it together"? Chapter 2 looks at the concept of the infrastructure to ask about how we learn to function in proximity to each other "in it." Chapter 3 turns to suicidal ideation by members of dominated populations. It argues that suicidal ideation is not only or usually a plan but a way of expressing life at the limit. Each chapter thus offers transitional forms that slow and extend ways to live inconveniently with each other: jokes, infrastructure, ellipses. The coda is about art and criticism that uses some cases of rape and murder to explore the critical urgency of refusing the convenience of the "cold case," which allows people to take solace in finitude. It's not over until we relinquish the question, the problem, the event. The alternative is to move with it, to allow the event to be inconvenient to us because otherwise we leave to the past what was merely overwhelming. As the coda argues, for the engaged critic, the unbearable must be borne.

Looking at sex, democracy, and the desire for life in a better world than the one that exists, the entire book tries narrating from the granular ordinary ways to lose, unlearn, and loosen the objects and structures that otherwise seem intractable. How not to reproduce the embedded violence of the unequal ordinary? People say, "You got this!" "We can do this!" But it's more like, "Once you let in the deaths, all that follows is life." A thing to be used.

Hell is other people, if you're lucky.

"Hell is other people" is a phrase from Jean-Paul Sartre's play No Exit, although its continued appeal as a thing people say has little to do with the play. In Sartre's version, characters are sentenced to occupy a room in Hell, exposed eternally to each other's bodily presence and, much worse, to each other's insufferable sameness. When people utter "Hell is other people," though, the phrase confirms more than the miserable effects of the relentless repetition of other people's personalities.[1] Freed from context, "Hell is other people" is an affirmative quip, too, emitting a comic, even courageous, air. Such a blunt cut can generate the conspiratorial pleasure of just hearing someone say it: it's other people who are hell, not you. They really are, it's a relief to admit it.

In other words, along with describing a saturating disappointment in others and expressing a kind of grandiose loneliness that aspires to fill its own hole with the satisfying sounds of superiority and contempt, "Hell is other people" has become a consoling thought.

Of course, some other people are hell, relentlessly saturating situations so fully that it's impossible to relax while being around them—so much so that the very idea of them becomes suffocating. This affective sense of the stultifying person or kind of person also girds the affective life of racism, misogyny, ethnonationalism, and other modes of population disgust that Judith Butler points to in her work on "grievable life."[2]

Mostly, though, other people are not hell. Mostly, the sense of friction they produce is not directed toward a specific looming threat. Mostly, people are inconvenient, which is to say that they have to be dealt with. "They" includes you.

"Inconvenience" is a key concept of this book: the affective sense of the familiar friction of being in relation. At a minimum, inconvenience is the force that makes one shift a little while processing the world. It is evident in micro-incidents like a caught glance, a brush on the flesh, the tack of a sound or smell that hits you, an undertone, a semiconscious sense of bodies copresent on the sidewalk, in the world, or on the sidewalk of the world, where many locales may converge in you at once materially and affectively. It lives on in the many genres of involuntary memory—aftertaste, aftershock, afterglow. It might be triggered by anything: a phrase, a smell, a demanding pet, or someone you trip over, even just in your mind. It might be spurred by ordinary racism, misogyny, or class disgust, which can blip into consciousness as organic visceral judgments. The sense of it can come from nothing you remember noticing or from a small adjustment you made or couldn't make, generating an episode bleed that might take on all kinds of mood or tone, from irritation and enjoyment to fake not-caring or genuine light neutrality. In other words, the minimal experience of inconvenience does not require incidents or face-to-faceness: the mere idea of situations or other people can also jolt into awareness the feel of their inconvenience, creating effects that don't stem from events but from internally generated affective prompts.

The important thing is that we are inescapably in relation with other beings and the world and are continuously adjusting to them. I am describing more than "being affected" and sometimes less than "being entangled": this analysis is grounded in the problematics of the social life of affect, drawing from situations involving genres of the sense of proximity, physical and otherwise, that might involve a sense of overcloseness at a physical distance, or not, and might involve intimate familiarity, or not.[3] It might involve un-clarity about how one is in relation to what one is adjusting to, or not. At whatever scale and duration, "inconvenience" describes a feeling state that registers one's implication in the pressures of coexistence. In that state the body is paying attention, affirming that what's in front of you is not all that's acting on or in you.

Whatever tone it takes, whatever magnetic field it generates, this latter kind of contact with inconvenience disturbs the vision of yourself you carry around that supports your sovereign fantasy, your fantasy of being in control. This state is a geopolitically specific one, too, insofar as its model of the individual-with-intention includes a political and social demand for autonomy as evidence of freedom. The sovereign fantasy is not hardwired into personality, in other words: as US scholars of indigeneity such as Jessica Cattelino, Jodi A. Byrd, and Michelle Rajaha have demonstrated, sovereignty as idea, ideal, aesthetic, and identity claim is an effect of an ideology of settler-state control over personal and political territories of action that sanctions some privileged individuals as microsovereigns. This fantasy, which saturates the liberal colonial state and the citizenship subjectivity shaped by it, is thus seen as a natural condition worthy of defense.[4] But sovereignty is always in defense of something, not a right or a natural state.

As I will argue throughout, the sense of the inconvenience of other people is evidence that no one was ever sovereign, just mostly operating according to some imaginable, often distorted image of their power over things, actions, people, and causality. It points to a style of being in relation and a sense of how things should best happen. People use phrases such as *chain of command* or *the commons of x* to describe what to do with nonsovereignty. The fact of inconvenience is not the exception to one's sense of sovereignty, therefore; sovereignty is the name for a confused, reactive, often not-quite-thought view that there ought to be a solution to the pressure of adapting to "other people" and to other nations' force of existence, intention, action, entitlement, and desire.[5] Sovereignty is thus a fantasy of jurisdiction. It is a defense of entitlement, reference, and agency. Wounded sovereignty is, in some deep way, parallel to the concept of wounded narcissism. For if you or your nation were truly—as opposed to retroactively—sovereign, what then? No submission to or accommodation of another person's or nation's appetites, fantasy projections, regimes of happiness, or control over value? No jurisdictional or ethical struggles?

My claim is that there is an inevitability of the sense of inconvenience that has nothing to do with justice. At the same time, what frameworks and figures do we have available to explain its variety of pressures? This is not a rhetorical question, but a problem that is always being tested out and played with, in this book and generally.

The minima of inconvenience can go under the radar, or not, but it does not register at first as a traumatic or transformative event. At maximum intensity, though, the affective sense of inconvenience is harder, less easy to shake off or step around. In this book the strong version of inconvenience points to forced adaptation to something socially privileged or structurally pervasive. It registers the material effects of inequality's persistent force. It connotes the push of feeling compelled to manage pressures that pervade the ordinary's exercises and disciplines, whether stemming from submission to particular laws or neighbors, or dealing with any of the many hierarchies of difference and distinction that are always jostling one around, demanding one's energies, insisting on the maintenance of one or many supremacist status quos.[6]

We know that, just by existing, historically subordinated populations are deemed inconvenient to the privileged who made them so; the subordinated who are cast as a problem experience themselves as both necessary for and inconvenient to the general supremacist happiness. All politics involves at least one group becoming inconvenient to the reproduction of power; that power might be material or fantasmatic, in the convoluted paranoid way endemic to the intimacy of enemies. The biopolitical politics of inconvenience increases the ordinary pressure of getting in each other's way, magnifying the shaping duration of social friction within the mind's echo chambers and the structuring dynamics of the world.

As an affect, inconvenience can thus encompass all kinds of intensity but still be cast as a mode of impersonal contact that has an impact, opening itself to becoming personal, creating images of what feels like a looming social totality, and making a countervailing social organization imaginable. Think about Cheryl Harris's staging of Blackness as "trespassing" on white consciousness as it strolls and scrolls through the world expecting not to feel impeded; think of the pervasive sexual violence women imagine concretely when they're walking somewhere alone.[7] These sensations of threat are ordinary to the people moving through in the lifeworlds of a supremacist society and its entitlement hierarchies.[8] They can confirm or disconfirm the erotophobia or specific mistrust we have been schooled to live with. The expectation of inconvenience can pull you into a zone where the impersonal opens to genres of viscerally strong yet abstract encounter. It can be an effect of speculation prior to movement that creates hypervigilance, tableaux or scenarios in prefigurative response to potential encounters. It can get people talking to each other about how to change what's deemed structural, even when the only evidence is a sense of things that permeates the social field and is central to the reproduction of its norms of concentrated value. But the threat posed by politicized inconvenience doesn't have to be immediately theatrical or traumatic: a sense of apprehension can arise in any moment, seemingly happening and passing as an irritation. One never knows about effects until this kind of contact becomes materialized in a series. The inconveniences of managing one's own putative inconvenience to the sense of freedom demanded by the structurally dominant is a completely predictable experience, both draining and animating, in intimate and political settings. It forces a constant reassessment of what kinds of impact constitute an event.

In this book, "inconvenience" draws a membrane across radically private experiences of world-receptivity at the periphery of attention and anything people have to face every day—an ongoing labor situation, a family, a politicized infrastructure they may have been born into, the population they've been assigned to, or other people's projected fantasies.[9] When is a body an event because of the kind of thing it is deemed to be, as when they walk into a room or cross a state line? What price and what kinds of price are being paid in order to live a life as other people's inconvenient object? These questions tap into the ordinary of biopower at the same time as they tap into the encounter with being as such. However dramatic the situation of power, it is at its most powerful when it is distributed across the structural, the casual, and the shadowy, as Fred Moten and Stefano Harney, Achilles Mbembe, and Jasbir Puar have documented in their work on necropolitical protocols of the state and related apparatuses.[10] As Puar argues, to maim rather than kill in order to maintain political power is to enjoy enforcing the ongoing theater of the inconvenience of certain other people.

But it's not just bullets that disable living. It's inconvenient to bear the burden of a naming you didn't ask for: there is no getting beyond it, only dealing with it as a form of life you live with. To a structurally and/or fantasmatically dominant class, though, the experience of inconvenience produces dramas of unfairness. Take, for example, the paranoid reversals of "incels" and other entitled persons who experience their vulnerability as an injury of unjustly denied deference.[11] It is predictable that the structurally dominant feel vulnerable about their status and insist that if the historically subordinated deserve repair, so do the entitled. It is as though there is a democracy in vulnerability, as though the details do not matter. From both perspectives, the exhaustion from incessant abrasive contact can produce numbed or intense self-subtraction and the elaboration of massive rage.

At whatever intensity or scale, then, in whatever scenario of power, the sense of the inconvenience of other people in general, and often some other particular kinds of people, is constantly being renewed and reevaluated. Mainly the hit of it surfaces and dives in the ordinary life of being in the world, shifting atmospheres and coordinating stresses without much being memorable. But the ordinary includes the casual reproduction of hatreds and aversions, creating subjectivities powerfully shaped by navigating its entailments, excitements, and tolls.

So, to say that people are inconvenient, that they have to be dealt with, and that this affect is ordinary and profoundly life-shaping in how it generates styles of processing others and life, is not always to point to dramas that feel like melodrama. "Inconvenience" in this sense is more like "attachment": a description of a relation so foundational to coexistence that it's easy to think of it as the whatever of living together and not a constantly pulsing captivation of response. Attachment, one might say, is what draws you out into the world; inconvenience is the adjustment from taking things in. My proposal in this book is that there is an inconvenience drive—a drive to keep taking in and living with objects. The inconvenience drive generates a pressure that is hard to manage, let alone bear. This pressure requires us to reconsider "receptivity" too.

If "inconvenience" is mostly an experience of everyday aversion, adjustment, minor resistance, and exhaustion, it also raises this question: Why are even the objects our inconvenience drive drives us to still hard to bear? We know why threatening things threaten us; it's harder to know why it's difficult to live with the things we want. It can't just be that we fear losing them, we fear having them too. We dread the pressure of constraint, of being with what's ongoing. What makes inconvenience into an event, and not just a state, is the architecture of duration. We know why threatening things are resisted, so as to not be defeating or subordinating, or a puncture to confidence personally or collectively; but it is harder to know why the things we look to for sustenance also induce defenses against what we want from them, especially if one thing we want is to sustain life well while we are working out what to do with it. We know that narcissists and sociopaths and political struggle threaten the pleasure and fact of our and the world's continuity; it is harder to understand what to do when our positive attachments produce queasy-making roils and intimate violence. We know that the mere existence of other people can be a positive fact or negative irritant: it is harder to know what to do with the fact that wanting to be inconvenienced can produce such pressure and threat.

However it appears, the prompt of inconvenience activates the problematic of receptivity to the stimulus and situations of the world. It points to any propinquity that induces adjustment.[12] We are always taking in things like other people. We are always discovering that they have gotten under our skin without an event of choosing to refer to. The fact of this builds pressure to think historically about genres of encounter and their implication in the difficulty of absorbing each other, any object, or the imaginable world itself. It forces the question of the unpredictable relation between atmospheres and behaviors, involving the deracinated modes of gesture and message that we also use to contact each other and anchor ourselves. It raises political and epistemological questions about what we can justly call trivial. Thus, we can also presume nothing about how the friction of copresence will operate in advance of its emergence in a scene, nor how it will take subjective shape given what John Steiner calls the "psychic retreats" that constitute the vulnerability we protect from exposure, expression, and even self-acknowledgment, in defense of dissolving from what's overwhelming and tender.[13]

This means that inconvenience, though intimate, inevitably operates at a level of abstraction, too, where we encounter each other as kinds of thing—but not necessarily in a bad way, because there is no other way to begin knowing each other, or anything. *We cannot know each other without being inconvenient to each other.* We cannot be in any relation without being inconvenient to each other. This is to say: to know and be known requires experiencing and exerting pressure to be acknowledged and taken in, as Stanley Cavell has argued so forcefully.[14] Acknowledgment requires a disturbance of attention and boundaries. Sustained acknowledgment requires self-reorganization. Most experiences in this register, though, are not relations in the robust sense of a drive toward a reciprocal intimacy. They involve the uptick from ordinary contact that is usually processed by conventions, which might have the heft of a microaggression or merely the force of a flicker. They can produce irritation but also kinds of longing—if they produce anything beyond the ding of encounter. To attend to inconvenience is to attend to our constant exposure to stimulations that need to be processed.

In this introduction, the project is first to substantiate why inconvenience is the structure of an affect and a general description of a kind of contact we have no choice but to process. It requires thinking about a whole range of impacts and intensities that may or may not achieve significance, consciousness, politics, or clarity. It also requires thinking about how the vertical hierarchies of privilege capture and recast the tone of ordinary social frictions to naturalize, weaponize, and calcify a self-interested defensive/projective dynamic.[15] To get at this material requires tracking patterns and historicizing the means through which we are trained to live inside many genres of the brush of the world. Citizenship, social membership, belonging, being a neighbor or a regular, being the conveyor of bodily dynamics are some of these genres, but many of the familiar dings are so nonnarrative that they're hard to archive, even in concepts like gesture, because we're talking about actions that dissolve the fantasy that the impersonal is distinct from the personal, the intimate. It is not only the world of other people either—animals, things, and thoughts are inconvenient too. Inconvenience is not just a punctum experience but a measure of the impact and standing of encountered things.[16]

Social theory tends to melodramatize and draw its energy from pervasive social antagonism. Disasters and catastrophes produce concepts that face up to devastation at its most unbearable, as though the problem of the social could best be resolved in the spaces where it most intensively splinters and shreds. But social theory also needs to attend to the difficulty of being with the ordinary not just as a microecology of disaster but a scene of ongoingness that includes catastrophe, comedy, awkwardness, intimacy, work, care work, noticing, dissociating, demanding, shrugging, and working it out in real time. If there is an inconvenience drive, can consciousness of it become a resource for building solidarity and alliance across ambivalence, rather than appearing mainly as the negative sandpaper of sociality? Is it possible to turn ambivalence from the atmosphere of negativity it currently brings with it into a genuinely conflicted experience that allows us to face up to the phenomenality of self-disturbance in the space of coexistence and even the desire to let in particular objects, or to protect them once they've gotten under the skin? This is a key question cluster for this book.

Such an axis of critical attention would help us slow down how we process the situation of encounter and face processes of adjustment, relief, repair, and testing out whether being open to knowing and being known, or just occupying the same space with other people, will be worth the trouble. There's a secret ellipsis after trouble: the trouble to which inconvenience points. The trouble to bother living in proximity to, the trouble to endure or ensure belonging to, the trouble of desiring proximity to, of having reparative dramas with, to seek acknowledgment and recognition from—to live on with. These phrases end with grammatically inconvenient prepositions in search of a linkage. In the chapters that follow, this book's thought experiments pursue the open questions that a focus on inconvenience produces by providing some narratives that clarify and shift how we're taken up in different scenarios and intensities of relation. Sex, democracy, and life-in-struggle are the exemplary scenes of ambivalent receptivity I play out: they stand for scenes that people say they want, are uneasy wanting, try to make do with, try to get at, go in and out of caring about, and want to be okay with. I'm listing here some of the incommensurate wants that constant adjustment generates; *incommensurate wants* is a synonym for *ambivalence* that is technical and does not port with it the bad odor or Kleinian love/hate with which ambivalence has come to be associated.[17]

Thus, the inconvenience of other people isn't evidence that the Others were bad objects all along: that would be hell. The inconvenience of the world is at its most confusing when one wants the world but resists some of the costs of wanting. It points to the work required in order to be with even the most abstract of beings or objects, including ourselves, when we have to and at some level want to, even if the wanting includes wanting to dominate situations or merely to coexist. The pleasure in anonymity and in being known; the fear of abandonment to not mattering and the fear of mattering the wrong way. I am describing in inconvenience a structural awkwardness in the encounter between someone and anything, but also conventions of structural subordination. Thus "people" in the title stands for any attachment, any dependency that forces us to face how profoundly nonsovereign we are. The concept also points to hates and to the danger to our sense of well-being that is produced even by the things we want to be near; it clarifies some things about the registers of power that attach dramas of such disturbance to bodies living approximately in the ordinary.

I have proposed that to study inconvenience is to study processes of receptivity. To study receptivity is to face this idea: when it comes to living in proximity, there is no such thing as passivity. Adjustment is a constant action: the grinding of the wheels of awkwardness and the bargaining with life's infrastructures. This is why the dominant tone of ambivalence tends to be negative. It takes work to live on the arc from minor irritation to threat—and too often people try to resolve the difficulty of being inconvenienced by the world by becoming depleted, cynical, or dramatic fonts of blame. To study receptivity is thus also to study projective identification, the handing off of the responsibility for one's unsteadiness to others, often the same others one resents for being powerful enough to be there to bear and repair what's overwhelming.[18]

Receptivity thus involves styles of processing being affectively disturbed and seeking relief from disturbance, as we will see in chapter 1 on sex and jokes. Its processes force us to study norms of affective proximity, which only sometimes have to do with belonging; more frequently they have to deal with the friction of copresence, as we will see in chapter 2 on democracy and the concept of the commons. Just because we are in the same room does not mean that we belong to the room or to each other. The quality of the affinity is built from the action of relation and the conventions that convince you to summarize sociality as a done deal. Nor is the overdetermination of feeling that we call ambivalence only a relation between antithetical tones; to the contrary, the tones belong together like vocal cords in disharmony with themselves. To study the noise of world-absorption when the world offers inadequate object streams to take in and on, then, often produces fatigue or suicidiation, as we will see in chapter 3, on the fundamental political affect-state I call "being in life without wanting the world." To study the inconvenience of receptivity is also to study living with the unbearable, as we will see in the coda's address to returning to the scene of the devastatingly ordinary crime of the rape/murder of women.

This book's cases circulate some concrete conceptual spaces in which one is drawn to other people, structures, and worlds willingly and with a desire to work with what one cannot vanquish: the friction whose energy is part of the frisson, the intensity that fuels us even while the fatigue of the inconvenience of world-receptivity is pretty wearing. This book is an experiment in working out ways not to think of negativity as the substance of the real, although it is a substance of the real, but rather to see the activity of inconvenience as it tilts variously toward drama, comedy, curiosity, aggressive play, enjoyment, disavowal, refusal, unconsciousness, dissociation, and above all multiplicity, from the slapstick of sex to dissociation for life. It would be wrong to think of these conceptually and often temporally simultaneous movements as needing to be resolved: the desire to make stentorian final judgments according to self-preservational interest is one answer to "where does the misery come from?"—Wilhelm Reich's famous question to Freud.[19] The "ontological misery" of being a person as such comes from the violent pressures to resolve the irresolvable, to underdetermine what overwhelms, but also from the expectation that if things like worlds and people were just, living would be simpler. As I have argued here, and as I do in the chapter-experiments to follow, in theory we would like the world against which we defend ourselves to take less of our best good energy. Life can be different; it can be better or worse. Just not simple, in the sense of resolved once and for all.

In the sections that follow this one, I expand on these claims in small keyword riffs I call "assays." An assay tests things out, tries out various approaches to the object that might change its relevant contexts, associations, and dynamics: its social being. The cases that follow the introduction are also assays in that they involve reading with other aesthetic events for alternative ways of being inconvenient and living with inconvenience. They are assays because they feel out how to create other kinds of social relation from within the world that needs disturbing. The point is not to go from example to example but to use the modular to collect strategies for breaking apart what doesn't work and creating social fields shaped by different, more satisfying dynamics of proximity. The book contains no ranking among strategies; rather, it lays out clusters of actions that become forms of life that shift the pressures of being in relation.

So we need to keep a whole range of object-values and scenes in our head. The sense of inconvenience often erupts in the ordinary of stranger proximity, where people are hanging around the world together. It proceeds even when we notice each other vaguely, not worrying in advance whether incidents will occur. It is a feature of everyday love, of being a regular, and of police side-eye. It fuels the imaginaries that are comfortable with inequality so long as the decisions are "democratic." The pressure of inconvenience pervades how being near each other in time and space will play out, whether in anticipation, in the present, or in the rearview sweep of the retrospect. Pulsating in eruptions and patterns of daily paranoias, speculations, attractions, and attentiveness, these triggers might not reach the level of language, consciousness, or event, or they might stick and amplify, as when the police claim that their violence was justified because they felt fear. Whatever proximity induces associations, which are kinds of relation with histories but not ontologies of cause or effect. From every angle the sense of inconvenience circulates through the body and mind, time and space. It can generate intensities like the awkwardness of an encounter; it can overstimulate a sense of threat; it can just get filed away, stored for later reference; it can appear to be resolved—or not.[20]

Assays

The assays here anatomize the affect called inconvenience to provide different angles on the problem of metabolizing it. Pretty much everything I've written has been modular that way, built through sections that allow a problem-cluster to be both established and transformed through its contact with specific object/scenes or cases.[21] In this book, successive chapters on things we want but not surely—sex, democracy, and a better world for the life we want to be in—stand in for the internally clashing dramas of impersonality, intimacy, and ordinary viciousness that shape the social. They draw out the structural and incidental contexts of lateral coexistence. They continue the historical interest of *Cruel Optimism* in the splintering of the fantasy that there will be a world that rewards one's labors of reproduction: the 1960s fantasy of antibourgeois sex, discussed in chapter 1; in chapter 2, the drawing of lines between the abstraction of the commons and the broken infrastructures of collective existence throughout the nineteenth through twenty-first centuries that people keep trying to patch, especially in the deindustrialized Midwest; and, in chapter 3, biopolitics and dissociation from the 1960s to the present, where the specific vulnerabilities of different populations—gendered, queer, Black—engender dissociation and prefer the inconclusiveness of life in ellipsis. They stage politics as a scene where antagonists are inconvenient to each other in ways that reveal, resist, and disturb the reproduction of structural antagonisms, mentalities, sensual encounters, and properties. They help us stay with different social and political dimensions of the overdetermination that the inconvenience of other people expresses in practical terms. They recognize that one is always in the middle of the broken world, but also that one is learning how to move in it without reproducing the conventional forms of its violence. They offer concepts as tools with which to loosen other concepts. To loosen an object is to make it available to transition. Each chapter seeks to help change the dynamics of association and material practice that can calcify an object/scene. The cases are also just that: explorations that are inadequate to the problem whose scene they stage.

In so offering the pressure of inconvenience as an experience of sociality that overdetermines what counts as the personal and the impersonal, the present and its pasts, and the mutual propping of violence and pleasure in the labor of the reproduction of existence, I join thinkers who represent the contemporary as a zone of life in which the dour realism of an ongoing near-survival scramble is enmeshed with the creative and life-insistent energy that improvises and makes counterinfrastructures for revising what's possible in life. They produce transitional figures for violently unequal normative experience that both make it vivid and refuse to reproduce its worst-case scenario as the Real, using phrases as objects to open the ordinary to transformation by shifting its associations and resonance. They admit that the lived idealized life is still much more inconvenient than its dreamers wished. This mess of divergent directions has been central to the transformative emphases, locales, and attunement prospects described for Queer Theory by many, including Gayatri Gopinath, Kadji Amin, and Siohban Sommerville's *Queer Companion*, whose transnational genealogies and multiple bodies of the queerly embodied, desiring, and located reveal so many varieties of inconvenient subjects gearing up for the present even as the prospect of a general lifeworld fades.[22] Michael Hardt's version of the immaterial in "immaterial labor" reshapes contemporary biopolitics with a counter-logic of biopower generalized across various modes of production, drawing together disparate and sometimes antithetical objects, relations, and institutions into a scene on the basis of their common world-building activity; Calvin Warren and Fred Moten figure Black nonbeing as a philosophical, aesthetic, and political prompt for rethinking relational nonsovereignty; in work in disability studies, queer and Indigenous scholars have also used the boundary drawn between who's convenient and inconvenient to shift the perspective of lifeworld normativity into alternative builds. These associations transform the exemplary object while still drawing connections among problems of the biopolitical drama of getting in each other's way. Madalina Diaconu and Shannon Lee Dawdy look to patina to figure the overdeterminations and ongoing aesthetic generativity of death, life, and history across the material planes of touch; Christina Sharpe configures a version of "the wake" of an object/event's impact that is not a beyonding the inconvenient Black object but a living-, being-, and bringing-with.[23] Our proximities animate and hover near resources for lifeworld reorganization and rebooted transferential projections; they stretch across and rearrange contemporary and historical archives and memorial fields.[24]

Among others, these scholars have generated debates that keep the figural event of the concept of copresence open. They attend to the social consequences of the inconvenience of othered people as the motive for visualizing and reoccupying social form. I write these assays in solidarity with projects of using overdetermined and tonally self-clashing causal dynamics to create better frames for commonly held object/scenes: of course, the question these days and throughout the book is whether and when one can even say that something is commonly held. These assays attempt to create a backstory genre through which we can loosen the world of conventions, spongy norms, and conventional violence—and to provide dimension, texture, and resonance for emergent and ongoing alt-forms of life.[25] To slow the object's movement, to describe its internal dynamics, to shift how we recognize and consider its parts and galvanize their transformation in psychic and social processes require such ongoing expansion, contraction, looping, shredding.

Heterotopias, for Example

Once I called myself a utopian.[26] What I meant by that was that I don't take the insistence of a dug-in world to define constraints on living. In some way, any imaginary situation can be lived in advance. This is partly how realities change.[27] But as an analyst of the historical present, I should have called on the heterotopian, which attends to living in the copresence of many forms of life. The figure here is not of an ontologically radical heterogeneity, though. Of heterotopias, Foucault writes, "We are in the epoch of simultaneity: we are in the epoch of juxtaposition, the epoch of the near and far, of the side-by-side, of the dispersed."[28] At the same time, however, he bisects the heterotopic space into the "crisis heterotopia" and the "heterotopia of deviation," each a transitional space where the social reaches a limit and opens a window to an outside, to new dictionaries and the counternormative.[29] But an object/world transformation does not have to assume a drama of overcoming something leaned against.

Here, to see like a heterotopian is to attend to and elaborate a loose assemblage of emergent lifeworlds.[30] The multiple lifeworlds operating in the heterotopia's heterogeneity provide conduits among the sensual and conceptual, extending according to diverse logics while remaining interrelated. These lifeworlds are related because they are in proximity. Their relation is dynamic and unpredictable, offering as the scene of life discontinuities and decaying holes and loose joints for reshaping. Paying attention to the heterogeneity of lifeworlds that constitute the contemporary social field redistributes the pressure generated by the "it is what it is" assurance of some versions of the dialectic, more regular views of structure, or the confusion of a cultural dominant with history itself.[31] Joshua Clover's "Genres of the Dialectic" is an exemplary demonstration of one way to tell a story about the movement of capitalist form toward overcoming its modes of value generation until it reaches a limit that interrupts structural reproduction entirely and allows for a different dynamic.[32] This image of structural reproduction from within the generative patterns of value chaos has generally been the great contribution of the Marxist tradition; see in chapter 2 the proposal about a destructive use of analogy in my investigation of the commons concept as an unlearning device for conventional ways of denoting structure.

To register the dynamics of receptivity and attachment requires reading across, or scanning, the dynamics of social form and atmosphere, and not just at first. Scanning isn't skimming. The scan-form recognizes that there is always more to see, to process, and to find words for that will point to many potential spaces, pasts, and futures, without adding it all up to an object that can be revealed by two sides of a debate, rigorous scholarship, or the taxonomic assurance of most structural analysis. The scan-form creates frames from the inside of a scene.

It would be easy to go crazy by using the riot and clutter of worldmaking as material to be edited, stored in citations, and trained into tropes and generalizing statements. Establishing smooth systematicity was the training of structuralism and many instances of its posts. After the surprise of reading Jameson's assertion that context is immanent in a text and not a pushpin board securing the present like a police procedural's flowchart of collaborating criminals, my contextualizing practice cracked and changed.[33] Now I see making contexts for my objects as a scene for making concepts, which requires a creative archival practice, a construction of objects from the currents among collected things.[34] It confirms a realist staging of the object's inconvenience to the desire to fix history and meaning by way of a materialist empiricism that sees material as an effect. There are always more things to say, more explanations, not a finite number of things to stack into a predictable shape. Sometimes there are heterotopias in dominance, and sometimes scatter is what attention and narration require. The proliferation of qualities can make you feel desperate, or stop writing, or feel bad when you're doing your small but difficult thing; or it can allow you to craft thought experiments, throw out heuristics that you hope can attain analytic ballast. Through a heterotopian lens, things never quite fit together or manifest all of their potential dimensionality and so deserve a critical infrastructure that can bear the material dynamic that looks solid at a distance while being elastic, rubbery, animated, elliptical, context-changing, and the effect of the drift or clanging of many causes: "the part, that is, of life that is never given: an existence."[35]

In chapter 3 I describe the study of this transformative spatiality as a proxemics.[36] Proxemics studies the closeness and distance among things, and the transformative pressure of the space generated by active organizations of matter.[37] What does it mean to be in the span of proximity, whether perceived as too-closeness, radical alterity, or a vibrating field of objects bouncing off of each other at some perceptible or imperceptible speed, governed by laws and norms but not, as a cluster, predictable in the ways they take and can make up space?

Heterotopias induce historical conditions for situations that will never appear to take shape fully. In them we don't lose our objects but play with their form and test their implications. With them we discover new ways to release ourselves from some forms while remaining some form of ourselves, comic and tragic and messed up as these forms can be. Which is to say that heterotopianism skirts the unbearable. The impact of living its concept might not be fun because it forces inconvenient objects into focus along with the dominating shiny ones, but it might be a relief because it signals the copresence of an otherwise. Because political vision can proceed effectively only if it disturbs the concrete shape of the world it wants to bring into being, the political question for the heterotopian is historical not only in the sense of how we got to this place of many spaces, but also insofar as it generates what else a vision of loose object causality can do. Queer work was all about this from another angle, I thought: a refusal to submit to normative form as though it were good form as opposed to what serves a set of interests.[38] Queer work is skeptical about ordinary modes of attachment, repair, survival, and good objects. It describes the ambivalent position of being in desire while being unsure of what to do with what's overwhelming or threatening in it, and it opens the floodgates about what can be an object of desire: persons, objects, ways of life, a landscape, an angle, pets, ideas, and so on. It usually forces admissions that statements about how the senses, the social, and bodies work are, at best, propositions about the conditions for outcomes. To queer something doesn't mean just to stick an antinormative needle into it, but to open up a vein to unpredicted and nonsovereign infusions.

From this perspective, every heterotopia is a historical fiction, hooked into a distilled version of the world and extending to a yet-unlived plane. It is overdetermined by pressures from the lifeworld that it can bear the weight of while I'm describing them, like the trough of the worm I describe in chapter 2, which inscribes a joinable location even as it changes. Scholarship and riffing, too, create breathing room for alternative constructions of concept and causality, infrastructure and institution. At times I felt, while writing these chapters, that the objects that both hindered and created the spaces of transition in the scene of inconvenience still threatened me. They were hard to describe, and what I wrote about them was insufficient, merely writing; yet the need to stay with the intractable questions about impaired sociality and structural resistances to transforming, and not repairing, the violent reductions that often follow strong ambivalence was enough to fuel my optimism about the generative effects of thinking on affective and purposive judgment. For, like sex, politics, and theory, writing is not a performative performance of the end to violence or ambivalence. It can be a go at shaking up an object/scene to make a fresh fold in time and space, or a new way of disturbing life-disaffirming limits, a generative hetero-topos that is not obliged to, although not free of, any laws or norms. This is what it means to describe the ambivalence of a writing that needs both to fix its object enough that it can be seen and to disturb it enough that it can reorganize its objects. Conventional clauses and the unstable world of contact co-assert the shapes that writers take as facts or fates, and meanwhile we do not just live with contingency but desire its inconvenience.

To be a heterotopian is to live in the disturbing episode but also to recognize that there are multiple discontinuous spaces conceptually adjacent to its presence. It is to understand that even the longest assay is a prompt, a pod full of reactive chemicals waiting to be found, floated, tracked, tested, resisted, and retested.

Overdetermination and Its Affects

This book argues that amid the threat of enemies who want us not to exist, or the intimates who jostle our sense of stability on a solid ground, there sits the threat of objects and lifeworlds we want but in the very wanting are bothered by. This is to say that not only the unbearable is defined by the formal fact that it must be borne, as I propose in the coda. The sense of the world as inconvenient threatens the infrastructures we build out from the very overdetermination of threat, desire, and intensity's shadings that have not yet organized into a genre we want to, or can, coast in.[39] This way of thinking about a social field undermines any linear, mechanical understanding of causality and gives a new inflection to the actualizations we call history, calling attention to the ways in which particular forms and processes associated with diverse lifeworlds are also commonly shaped by multiple factors, in some combination of close together or translocally along a supply chain, in solidarity, and transgenerationally, for example. These kinds of relation are sometimes intimate in the way of a mutuality insofar as personality is involved, but at the same time they are not, because they are governed by the holding environment of a common historical experience with which one will always have been shaped—whether or not one resists or might want entirely to break the dynamic of its reproduction.[40] In my previous work I pointed to this dynamic by way of the concept of the intimate public, but here our focus is on the pressure exerted by any sense of contact, including when it has nothing to do with the material conditions of identification or intimacy.

So, here the intensities expressed in the figure of frictional receptivity requires wrestling with the ongoingness of clash, contradiction, and converging causalities. For example, how does a sex-positive person like me write about sexual violence in its collapse of the personal and the impersonal, of the local incident and its pervasiveness? How does a commitment to radical equality bear the perverse fact that equality must be defined by the impossibility of attaining it, if by *attain* we imagine a steady-state objective condition or a predictable affective one, "feeling equal"? After all, we live heterotopically in so many environments at once that it would be hard to know how the topoi mesh, how to translate across a wide variety of scenes and qualities of attention, how to recognize resources in the real time of the reproduction of life and the ordinary temporalities of capitalist value. How do we write about staying attached to life while living defensively and porously at the same time? How does someone stay attached to life while repudiating the world of bad objects? What's the relation between the uses of an object and multiple processes of object formation, and how does our assessment of its overdetermination affect our analyses of racial and white patriarchal capitalism, with its implication in heteronormativity? Adorno argues that "the shudder" one feels on receiving the aesthetic object registers the intimate effects of an abstract, yet affectively personal, transaction with the world; one could also propose that this very event of receptivity is the event of the inconvenience of the object by way of the adjustment demands it is already making on what is possible to arrange affectively.[41]

If one question of our inconvenient others—that of our inconvenience to others' security or panting desire for sovereignty—motivates this exercise, another question was how to take on inconvenience as an affective sense that has no vernacular emotional correlate called inconvenience, the way the structure of shame has an emotion of shame to anchor its various representations or the way the structure of attachment-love has an emotion called love to organize the variety of linkage styles that can be organized under it, disciplined by the name, and disturbed by the constant sense of approximateness and self-violation associated with it that are supposed to be calmed by its conventions, infrastructures, and rituals. But inconvenience in the vernacular is a state that comes from the sense of having to take in and defend against an object, or of being that object onto whom others project a too-muchness. Inconvenience is another way of pointing to the experience of nonsovereign relationality. It does not always produce a sense of injury but *does* always signify the pressure of what to do with coexistence. Whether or not one has management skills for it, it produces the injury of nonsovereignty.

But, seen as an affect, inconvenience is not the Real interfering with the Sovereign Balloon at its most parade-inflated, although sometimes it takes the form of a drama that feels like drama. The usual inconvenience of being affected assumes the kind of guttural noise that resounds from an impact that one may or may not have asked for but can never be protected from in advance. It's not just what Teresa Brennan describes as the affective discernment one's gut performs when entering a room or a thing that grabs your attention in a way in which you're fully present, but an accommodation that isn't exactly a submission but is a sensed forced entailment, like being drafted.[42]

This introduction to the book's ambition is modular because the affect of inconvenience flows from many dimensions, varying in its intensity of emphasis and the means of mediation. There is no possibility of drawing out this set of problems by addressing them "all at once," if *all at once* means developing concepts from a pretense of knowing what leads from what. We have an ethical obligation to overdetermine our objects while clarifying the scenes of their action. This obligation is why work claiming to be theory must be read as propositional. The animating questions are inconvenient to the thinker's aim; absorbing the transformative implications while reading is inconvenient to the reader. Our inconvenience drive keeps us up, forces fugue states and naps, and distracts us as we try to move some life-entangling problems somewhere by testing them out, rearranging, and supposing.

Infrastructures, Infrastructuralism, Infrastructuring

A heterotopia is an infrastructure. This way of thinking the terms of living across diverse spaces of the personal and the impersonal also encourages us to see what connects people and their practices within a social field. This does not involve establishing the dynamics of a shared, coherent structure that guides thought and action in patterned and consistent ways, but the atmospheres in which infrastructures of inconvenience appear as generative, multiple, and often contested processes involved in the substantive connections among people and lifeworlds. This is why the infrastructure concept is central to the problem of transforming democracy-under-capitalism that focuses chapter 2: having disturbed the conventional object of "structure," I'm also proposing that proffering transitional infrastructures for the extended meanwhile is also a critical obligation of any analyst, writer, or artist, dilating on the long meanwhile of life in the crisis ordinary.

"Capitalism" is often offhandedly designated as the structure that saturates the reproduction of modern life in its lateral and hierarchical forms. But the way it is captured as the machinery of power and origin of everyday life is undergoing many serious challenges and definitional shifts—not, though, because capital's power over life is over.[43] In the current world-national-capitalist theater, the fragility and forced improvisation introduced as capitalist "crisis" is manifestly and incoherently reshaping many processes of value creation, including the protocols of finance and contract: the liberal nation's historic ways of inviting immigration for purposes of exploitation and shunning immigrants for purposes of ethnopride, the capitalist's production of value through the destruction of its/our own lifeworld and resources, the centrality of racial and gendered exploitation to the image of an economic system that figures itself as democratic in its exploitation and not inherently racist and misogynist, and so on. This cacophony of wealth-generating disturbances makes any claim that capitalism produces a plane of structural consistency looks at once as true and banal as the source of figuring a trustworthy world-picture. As I demonstrate in chapter 2, Marxists, anarchists, and realists are now turning to "infrastructure" to reimagine the transformation of living from within the scene of life, replacing focus on the abstraction of what counts as "structure" with attention to what expresses itself most profoundly in concrete social relations—a set that includes ideas about what internally binds the world beyond practices that can be photographed or organized in a spreadsheet.[44]

Infrastructuralism might be called a perspective that looks at the extension of life from within lifeworlds rather than at the dominant causal mechanism for reproducing the world's time, spaces, hierarchies, and relations. As an example: an infrastructure of feeling is different from the structure of feeling to which Raymond Williams pointed.[45] The latter phrase points to an atmospherically felt but unexpressed class-based affect, whereas the infrastructural version confirms and solidifies the sediment of many proximate kinds of sociality, including pasts and futures as they express themselves in the present.[46] To think infrastructure in the context of this book is to focus on the generation of forms of life that broadly bind and extend relationality and the world seen as substance and concept. Rather than seeing the material of lived relationality as epiphenomenal or as merely the present's expressive causality, infrastructuralism focuses on many phases of the activity of poeisis, or world-making.[47]

I am not abandoning materialism by stepping back from "structure." To the contrary, here are some propositions: infrastructure is the living mediation of what provides the consistency of life in the ordinary; infrastructure is the lifeworld of structure. Marshall Sahlins even argues that the superstructure/infrastructure distinction was already tending toward infrastructuralization in the mid-twentieth century. Roads, bridges, schools, food chains, finance systems, prisons, families, and districts link the living in ongoing proximities that are at once material and symbolized.[48] Paul Edwards points out that failure of an infrastructure is ordinary in poor countries and countries at war, but people suffer through its disturbances, adapting and adjusting.[49] This is to say that even ordinary failure spurs infrastructural forces into existence that reorganize life, fueling what Deborah Cowen has described as the creative practicality of logistics in the supply chain.[50] In the best ethnographic work on infrastructure, buildings, roads, economic institutions, systems of norms and laws, and norms that pass as laws are accompanied by ideas and concepts that are generated in the process of keeping things going. The consistency-making, resource-distributing processes are mediations that bind worlds together along with ideas about what the world might be. In chapter 2 this gets emblematized as the wormhole a worm makes while it's moving in order to enable its movement. It may be moving simultaneously within and outside of the normative social: as the work on "evil infrastructures" argues, you can't always tell from the form of it who will flourish and who will have to pay a painful cost. Space- and time-making patterns gain solidity because they represent consistently linked activity, that's all.

The power of thinking the infrastructural mediation of the ongoingness of the ordinary, and the constant copresence of its intelligibility and creative generativity, has been at the core of queer commentary—not just theory, but the very descriptive redistortions that open up gestures, scenes, tableaux, phrases, and demands to at once materializing formations and trans-ing them too. Examples abound, but in the wake of Michael Warner's counterpublics, Jose Esteban Muñoz's utopian horizons, and Juana María Rodríguez's history through gestural transmission, the process I'm describing could be called a queer infrastructuralism insofar as it shares with queer formalism a version of the object/scene that is relational and dynamic, local and utopian, gestural and demanding, situational, labile, internally discontinuous, and yet projected out across fields of clarity and guesses that allow for an inventive longing to amplify what is already here and yet incomplete.[51] It embraces the social labor of attachment, the inevitability of projection, and the utility of speculation as equally strong participants in the infrastructures that shape what's changing. So this infrastructuralism is not focused only on the usual networks of conveyance, like roads and channels; as I have learned especially from Cowen, infrastructural objects are communicative in a lifeworld sense, at once shaped and shape-shifting.

As I argue in chapter 2, infrastructures that manage ongoing relational disturbances can continue indefinitely in their mode or be shocked into shifting their processes fundamentally, yet without stopping. Encounters, episodes, inclinations, patterns become things on the move to return to, concepts elaborated in practice, practices without a concept. Heterotopic, they allow for experiment with teasing temporary practices into continuously lived spaces, topoi to return to and use. Forms of life have an animated solidity that does not have to become calcified in representations, though there's always a danger of it, and often a practice of clinging to them as foundations rather than heuristics. The work infrastructure performs of transforming the temporary into the contemporary can remediate the world. An emergent ongoing form of convergence can dig unexpected grooves. Yet it is important not to get too productivist about it. As Anna Lowenhaupt Tsing argues, everything proceeds under conditions of probability, friction, accident, and uneven transformation, which are not the same thing as determination, nor the same thing as indeterminate lability.[52]

Infrastructure, then, is another way of talking about mediation—but always as a material process of binding, never merely as a material technology, aesthetic genre, form, or norm that achieves something. Mediation is not a stable thing but a way of seeing the unstable relations among dynamically related things. It is in this sense that any formulation of mediation is a heuristic, which is one kind of infrastructure, a propositional one. A heuristic is a thought experiment floated on offer, its logic followed through. As Diana Taylor has argued, when extended as an inflammatory counter-realism or as a counter-power, heuristics alone don't defeat institutions like, say, racialized capital, patriarchy, or the fantasy of the law as justice.[53] But they do spark blocks that are inconvenient to a thing's reproduction.

Think about Fanon's argument about interruption: "I should say that the Negro, because of his body, impedes the closing of the postural schema of the white man."[54] This politically animated impediment is not just a prop for whiteness but an inconvenience to its reproduction. It produces, in Fanon's work, figural and political infrastructures for countersocial organization: not from the determinative force of a violent event but in a war of attrition, form against form—the friction of productive movement, Tsing would say. As Harney and Moten argue it likewise, the undercommons is a heuristic infrastructure. You could say that people live there because the infrastructures change as they travel and become more or less elastic; or you could say that they make an atmosphere of generative movement in proximity to a historical community that may or may not be caught up in liberal "recognition" of identity. Infrastructure points to the inconvenience of a concept that reorganizes spaces and practices in the glitch and suspension it creates, and to the figuration it offers for a collective tryout. Infrastructure can, in other words, loosen the object-world's self-relation while holding on to living, and in this sense it offers the pleasures of an attachment to life from an otherwise arduous space.

As a test, think about the difference between the phrases *the institution of marriage* and *the infrastructure of marriage*. Infrastructures are productive, durationally extensive spaces for the pliable forms of life that people use to make rules and norms and other means of extending the world. Infrastructures do not honor distinctions between the productive and the reproductive because they follow the elastic logic of cluster, of assemblage. Rules are stretchy and norms are porous. In our notice of this capacity for structural distortion and disturbance, infrastructural thought is a way of coming to analytic terms with the complex material and discursive dimensionality, temporality, and use value that constitute the disturbed, yet ongoing, forces of the ordinary. The Deleuzian logic of Jameson's representation of the synchronic or historical present in *Political Unconscious* and the charts in Deleuze and Guattari's *Mille plateaux* figure this: all of these accounts of mediation set the stage for thinking of infrastructure's heuristic genres as radically redefining some definition of *structure* as something other than a kind of smoothness on top of volatility.[55]

Infrastructural affect throws a light onto the generic material kind. The affectivity infrastructure generates is not just in the air or the gut or thrown together or ideology but specifically involves the sensing of the dimension and extension of what we might call organized air, the projected atmospheres sustained by collective practices. For example, Shannon Lee Dawdy and Madalina Diaconu offer "patina" as a slowly moving emerging object/scene made from specific usages that come to constitute historical, political, and potential environments. Patina-spaces are affective insofar as they texture forms of life to one side of hegemonic representations of life in scenes of generative contact. Patina-spaces provide infrastructures through the practical touch that resonates to history and the sense of what is collective and accruing.[56] This means that the very living lability of infrastructure is where actions are located once structure is recast as structures in the space/times where they also operate, have impact, and organize the potential to change. Thus the heterotopic linkage. The perspective it generates shifts how we evaluate the solidity of the world, in order to think about the disturbance that is life as making forms that stand in as structures to return to that are also themselves always disturbed and on the move: adjusting, dilating, and offering new possibilities for causality and experience. This affective dimension of infrastructure expands the gritty version of it to the imaginaries that have to accompany its mediating performance of sociality. It allows us to think not that there will be other worlds later but that other environs are emerging now whose shapes are made by the living.

In a crisis we need to provide a concept of structure for transitional times: I call it transitional infrastructure. All times are transitional. But at some crisis times like this one, politics is defined by a collectively held sense that a glitch has appeared in the reproduction of life. A glitch is an interruption within a transition, a troubled transmission. A glitch is also a claim about the revelation of an infrastructural failure. The repair or replacement of broken infrastructure is necessary for any form of sociality to extend itself, but a few definitional problems arise from this observation. One is defining what distinguishes a transitional infrastructure from the ordinary relational scene that generates the ongoingness of the world through some cobbled-together inventive and repetitive activity; the other is about what repair, or the beyond of glitch, looks like both generally and amid a catastrophe.

Crisis infrastructuralism as an epistemology emerges when we are compelled to understand that nothing from above or on the outside is holding the world together solidly; the emergent threads become manifestly loose and knotty and multiply while still reproducing some aspects of life. In a crisis, what passed as "structure" passes into infrastructure.[57] The glitch of the present that we link to economic crisis, for example, fans out into other ongoing emergencies involving the movement of bodies into and out of citizenship and other forms of being-with and jurisdiction; contemporary anti-austerity politics not only points to new ties among disparately located and unequally precarious lives, but also marks the need for a collective struggle to determine the terms of transition for general social existence. Terms for transition provide conceptual infrastructures for living change as something other than loss, but as part of the protocols or practices that hold the world up.

To attend to the terms for transition is to forge an imaginary for managing the meanwhile within damaged life's perdurance, a meanwhile that is less an end or an ethical scene than a technical political heuristic that allows for ambivalence not to destroy collective existence. This use of writing the long middle without drowning in it is what I take to be one function of Adorno's *Minima Moralia* and also a way of reading the "interesting" and "frenzy" chapters of Sianne Ngai's *Our Aesthetic Categories*. Jeremy Gilbert adapts Gilbert Simondon's concept of provisional unity or metastability for this matter, allowing us to see transitional infrastructure as a loose convergence that lets a collectivity stay bound to the ordinary even as some of its forms of life are fraying, wasting, and developing offshoots among types of speculative practice, from the paranoid to the queer utopian.[58]

Social movement witnesses to the glitch of this moment have included the political practices of Occupy and other anti-austerity movements, as well as antiracist and antixenophobic movements across the world, insofar as they all define the present not just as a fresh slice of settler colonial efficacy, but as a scene shaped by the infrastructural breakdown of modernist practices of resource distribution, social relation, and affective continuity as an effect of capitalist chaos and resistance by communities of solidarity, from the nation-state to the grassroots. Moreover, they all manifest as process philosophies, building critique and distributing self-governance as emergent practices across episodes, without the metastructure of party authority—they work on infrastructural principle. Given newly intensified tensions, anxieties, and antipathies at all levels of intimate abstraction, the question of politics becomes identical with the reinvention of infrastructures for managing the unevenness, ambivalence, violence, and ordinary contingency of contemporary existence.

Crisis infrastructures have already populated our imaginaries of affective realism and material collective life, where we find the affective zone of its collective tone. Tone is what Sianne Ngai calls the "unfelt but perceived feeling" that disturbs our judgment of what in the world is internal and what's external, what's personal and impersonal, subjective and objective.[59] The tone of infrastructure is confident when the present is defined by convergence; when crisis infrastructures point to scavenging as a way of life, the tone is anxious, flailing, emerging from a desperation that's hard to locate but that calls into being patching action in order to maintain the collective movement that joins survival to adjectives other than *mere* and on multiple registers.

But if a glitch has made apparent these conditions of disrupted jurisdiction, resource, and circulation, a disruption in rules and norms is not the same thing as the absence or defeat of structure as such. I've suggested that an infrastructural analysis helps us see that what we commonly call "structure" is not what we usually presume—an intractable principle of continuity across time and space—but is really a convergence of force and value in patterns of movement seen as solid from a distance. Objects are always looser than they appear. Objectness is only a semblance, a seeming, a projection-effect of interest in a thing we are trying to stabilize. I am also therefore proposing that one task for makers of critical social form is to offer not just judgment about positions and practices in the world, and not just prefigurations of the better good life, but terms for transition that help alter the hard and soft infrastructures of sociality itself.

Ambivalence

Along the way to writing this book, many subtitles floated around until I gave up: *On the Inconvenience of Other People: But Not You*—the audience favorite; *Essays on Ambivalence; Essays on Unlearning*. Nothing was alive enough: I'm trying to bring these concepts back from the flat monodirectionality or bidirectionality with which they're associated. One presupposition of *Inconvenience* is that the problem of the world isn't one's alienation from it but, as Adam Phillips writes, its overcloseness, the ongoing pressure of it.[60] See the earlier argument about nonsovereignty. *Alienation* is a technical term for not being in control of the conditions of one's value or ownership of the products of one's labor. It is also an affective state that can be lived in many ways, from the negative sense of separateness from things to a range of feelings from rage to depression. It suggests subtraction, withdrawal, a distance. Yet if the a priori of alienation is the world's overcloseness, then alienation implies a style of response that manages the inconvenience of the world by creating a distance from within the space of relation: in Marxist technical terms, a way of rerouting the body's intimate labor for the value extraction of others. Capitalism fracks the sensorium.

So, brainstorm your own examples of structural and affective alienation.

You will see, I think, that they express not a failure to be in relation but a failure within it. We wouldn't need defenses if relations really failed: defenses are against something or someone that's still there, whether the "there" is just in one's head or appreciable by others or verifiable via research. Creating affective distance in order to make being in relation bearable, good, possible, or just happen is the expression of ambivalent attachment to living on despite, with, against, and in a dynamic relation to whatever's structuring things, both the in-your-face things and the in-the-world things. Jean Laplanche and J. B. Pontalis argue that fantasy is what allows you to bear your ambivalence, not by resolving and vanquishing it, but in the way it fills in the holes left by your incoherence toward yourself, those you love, what matters, your appetites, and the world, whose concept you carry around as a figure in your head and walk through responding in a range of moods—numb, confirmed, and surprised.[61] Fantasy is therefore an infrastructure that points to and protects ambivalence without erasing it. It is inconvenient to genuine transformation insofar as it confuses the world with its penumbra and prospects; it is crucial to the force of social transformation. It is one of the many transformational infrastructures this book will speak to.

When we usually think about ambivalence, it's tilted negatively, as an alienation toward. This book proposes to return ambivalence to its dynamic etymology, as being strongly mixed, drawn in many directions, positively and negatively charged. When I say "I love you," it means that I want to be near the feeling of ambivalence our relation induces and hope that what's negative, aggressive, or just hard about it doesn't defeat what's great about it really—or in my fantasies of it, anyway. This isn't just interpersonal—it's about any affective infrastructure that importantly holds up one's world. If it's important, it names the scene of the inconvenient relation among its threat to overwhelm, the survival it shakes up, the life that proceeds anyway, the confusion about what to do, inventiveness, and, in certain situations, the enjoyment it offers.

This book might be irritating because of its insistence on the many both/ands of attachment. But it is motivated by desires worthy of following through, even if the case study exercises offering transformative infrastructures for being in relation are in themselves too few, too local, too normative, or otherwise unsatisfying. Books are never finished: one just stops writing them. The exempla are beginnings, not hermetic seals.

Unlearning, or Loosening the Object

My argument so far has been that that our task as engaged thinkers is not to replace inconvenient objects with better ones but to loosen up the object to reorganize and extend it, whether that object includes personal or impersonal processes. In *Cruel Optimism* I suggested that our important objects are not things but clusters of promise, projection, and speculation that hold up a world that we need to sustain. They are scenes of attachment that at once seem specific the way a beloved person, animal, or idea can, while at the same time they represent abstractions that allow speculation about the kind of reliable life they generate. That book focuses on stuck or poisonous relations to objects, including ideas of the good life in its many domains, and it points to ways of resisting the reproduction of attachment to diminishing but world-sustaining things. My next book, on humorlessness, is about holding on to the object so tightly one would prefer to bring the world down around it, not in the sense of an addict's auto-consumption but in the sense of wanting to be in relationality yet so in control of its dynamics that they become defined by what is immovable. Inconvenience, though, focuses on the encounter with and the desire for the bother of other people and objects; it's about the problem of wanting that finds oneself wanting in maintaining yet disturbing relations and thus about the problem of transforming objects that aren't only toxic, necessarily, but difficult to negotiate.

How do you change an object from within life? How do you change the kind of inconvenience you represent to others? The concept points to ambivalent relationality that induces elbow room, breathing space, and patience with the contradictory demands we make of our objects—to be known but not too much, to know without presumption, to be real and worthy of idealization, to be graceful but generous when things get awkward.

My commitment in this book is to generate a nonreproductive theory that uses the glitch of the present in crisis to displace the protocols and norms that got us here, as I argue in this introduction's section on infrastructure. Its strategy, which I learned first from reading Nietzsche, is to induce transformation from within relations to the object. I call it loosening the object. You can't simply lose your object if it's providing a foundational world infrastructure for you. You can't decide not to be racist, not to be misogynist, not to be ambivalent about your anchors or fixations. But you can use the contradictions the object prompts to loosen and reconfigure it, exploiting the elasticity of its contradictions, the incoherence of the forces that overdetermine it, that make every object/scene an assemblage that requires an intersectional analysis.

To loosen an object is to look to recombining its component parts. Another way to say it: to unlearn its objectness. This threatens the very way of knowing that brings us to the inconvenience of our objects, to the project of living with them. I learned to attach to the inconvenience of unlearning from Gayatri Chakravorty Spivak's demand for an ethics of epistemological discomfort involving the unlearning of Euro-American monoculturalism.[62] An entire industry of dedicated thought involving unlearning as a project has extended from this work, developing now in decolonial theory: the unlearning of a perspective on the world that reproduces the vertical power presumptions of the West, rationality, patriarchy, white supremacy, and capital.[63] To unlearn the very structuring perspectives of entitlement and freedom that have long sustained settler colonial optimism requires the painful transitional commitment to unlearning the anchoring perspective from which one writes. How to do this? There are many ways to unlearn the object, of which the perspective of unlearning is one that moves throughout the text. This cluster of assays is another formal example of how to do that: to think at once about the many moving parts that would need to shift for a form of thought to come into being and to elaborate their substance, to be a theorist of a process that coordinates without calculating the implications of that shift. A third would be breaking the object, as in chapter 2; refusing its performativity, as in chapter 3; slackening it, as in the coda. In chapter 1, I link and disorganize the conventional relation between disturbance and trauma and then sit inside the overlap of sustaining and destructive sexual desire.

Additionally, as an experiment in loosening the object, and therefore in changing the encounter with its inconvenience, I have attempted to write this book in my parenthetical voice. When writers insert in parentheses material that is not math nor for purposes of documentation, it's sometimes out of laziness: they're inserting something when they think of it. But the parenthetical voice also tends to emerge when, within the parentheses, the author says what they really think. It's an intimate voice, an insider's tonal shift. Its status is confusing: higher truth, gut feeling, unprocessed thought, note for later. Ironic self-undermining, or pseudo-self-undermining. An eruption of frankness in many tones. I have banned parentheses from the writing and tried to be disciplined about limiting the sneaky ways em dashes, notes, and other modes of insertion produce hierarchies among knowledges that distinguish "rational" analysis from other modes deemed less legitimate, more spontaneous, more visceral.[64]

From the moment I wrote my first theoretical preface, I've been flailing in public to find a tone to write in, one that would allow me to bring all of my knowledge to the table that's created by engaging the problem-cause of the writing. The skeptical tradition that Stanley Cavell elaborated allowed him to think that his thinking aloud in the vernacular of world-relation should be the same thing as being philosophically technical: this is especially the case when he thinks with art, where he takes on the limited perspective of limited persons and sees how, whatever mistakes they made, they did what they could do to navigate a world unready for the form of contact in liberty that they could imagine. To show up for the situation of mutuality with what one has is another way Cavell talks about love. "She did what she could do at the time" has long been my comic epitaph, and by comic I mean it enables me to write even from the limits of my ordinariness.

I decided a long time ago that I would write this book in the space of permission opened by Cavell and Eve Kosofsky Sedgwick, too, although they are different in their adjudication of the technical and the vernacular. From Sedgwick I learned that it's not an idea until you circulate it, whatever stage it has reached. From Cavell I learned that showing up with the bruised fruit of one's perspective is what the argument requires to reshape the dynamic processes always on the move from and toward forms of life. These methodological commitments helped me see a way into writing that would be freeing.

To write without parentheses is to avoid the tricky insertions or hierarchies of theoretical, exemplary, aesthetic, or personal value that extend an insider pleasure and witty snob-value to the scene of reading. Proceeding in brokenness, casting heuristic forms for the next phase of thinking, believing genuinely that an experiment extended can become a form of life, it queers the thought experiment, queers form into what's labile, argumentative, and intimate because it's available to the inconvenience of thinking that loosens a question, unlocking its repetitions and releasing its energies beyond coasting. In theory, anyway.

for José Esteban Muñoz

one **SEX IN THE EVENT OF HAPPINESS**

This chapter's original title was "Happiness, 1972–1998," and its ambition was to reexamine the negative effects of separating sexual from structural revolutionary politics, an engagement whose promise is continuing to be abandoned. It derived from a pun about "your happiness and my ha-penis" from *Last Tango in Paris* (Bertolucci, 1972) and stretched to the film *Happiness* (Solondz, 1998). It took *Tango* as a period piece, a restaging of its political moment's insistence on pursuing desire's drive toward the co-destruction of bourgeois economies, nationalism, colonialism, the patriarchal family form, and practices of straight heterosex. It looked at the double logic of revolutionary thought that the film puts forth: where a pop culture consumer style of antinormative love-play competes with an anticapitalist, antitraditional imaginary; where the inventions of intimate lifeworlds contest the built world of national-imperial exceptionalism; and where improvisatory amity resists the familialization of all desire.

In *Tango*, these fresh world-making gestures of "the sixties" were presented as threatening to bring down all at once the whole Euro-normative attachment and value nexus in the hope that having a common project of creative destruction at the level of the couple and the social would allow people to hang with each other while trying out a variety of modes of value and intimacy. Desire would be explosively inconvenient to the reproduction of the normative world. Solondz's *Happiness* emerged from the ongoing catastrophe that ensued from the failure of that political undertaking. It displays as realism an expansive public sex culture that has been largely privatized, casting sex in darkly comedic performances that leak into individual abjection and violent compulsion, and meanwhile implicitly abandoning any emancipatory commitment to the structural transformation of everyday life in capitalist and intimate terms. Bookended by these films, I argued, a history could be told of some things that went wrong when the encounter of sex radicalism with political radicalism became delaminated such that the inconvenience of desired sex disappeared into the catastrophe of nonsovereign relationality. This chapter tries to hold apart catastrophe from the usual jostling and pulling that constitute the ordinary of our interactions and encounters, physical and affective—the tenderness and friction beneath, around, and circulating in the atmosphere of being with.

As revisions went on, I added *Half Nelson* (Fleck 2006) to the mix, another contemporary film about the necessity and difficulty of keeping radical political thought open to the inconvenience of sexual politics and vice versa. What "went wrong" doesn't mean everything failed in the sexual politics/ structural politics conjuncture. A specific political project did: the ha-penis problem, which I take to refer both to the attempted release of a white masculinity from its radical sixties' aspirational armors of invulnerability and superiority, along with the problem of sustaining and remaining with unfinished revolutions whose outcomes continue genuinely to be mixed.

This chapter still uses these films to explore how love and sexual revolution are more than just analogous anarchic situations from which people try to build out relational infrastructures for what they want from the world and each other. Their scenes of practice, fantasy, and attachment focus intensely on how, in desire, they seek to upend and reorganize life in extremis, actually pursuing an inconvenient self- and life-disturbance that would help or even force them to unlearn their unfulfilled ways of being in the world as it is. The desired transitional moment of love and structural revolution, in other words, here involves leaps into insecurity, for the disturbance of normative havens into a disorganized meanwhile requires loosening anchors in the world, including the confidence-sustaining habits of judgment and intuition that have been developed to reinforce them. Such unlearning meanwhile allows for risking inventive flailing and experiments in thought and practice that might lead to something or nothing. This kind of transition has proven to be especially difficult, as the last decade has so spectacularly demonstrated, when conventionality and privilege no longer have confidence about their reproduction and so often unravel into kicking and screaming. In times of radical transition—as people lose confidence in how to be together, uncertain about how to read each other and incompetent even to their own desire, wanting everything hard to be "post-" already, with few skills for bearing transition—their default modes of managing the inconvenience of other people, including themselves, suddenly intensify in awkwardness and generate frictions at all kinds of scales.

What follows, in addition, moves through a kind of darkness I hadn't anticipated, which can be phrased as questions: How is it possible to talk about the inventiveness of pleasure in films also saturated by sexual and sexualized violence? How can a sex-positive person remain thoughtfully so given the pervasiveness of sexual violence?[1] How do we process being receptive to pleasure if it's also always potentially overwhelming in a way that breaks something, like belief in the possibility of trust, a body, or a spirit? Is erotophobia the only or best way to deal with the brokenness of sex before and after "liberation"? How can one take erotophobia seriously without exceptionalizing it, exoticizing it, repairing it, denying its reason, or framing it as other people's failure to be enlightened or adequate? Sex, with its burdens of attachment, optimism, and aggressive need, provides a lens on the incoherence of subjective attachments.[2] Even when it's sex we want or want to want, the disturbance it generates disrupts who one is in relation to oneself and others such that one therefore is unsure to move or to act.

One ambition of this book is to return ambivalence from its association with negativity to its genuine technical state of intensely clashing images and aims: sex intensifies the enigma of the situation of nonsovereign sociality. In proximity to the devastating sexual violence that pervades ordinary relationships, even sex that is wanted bears the difficulties of managing overcloseness and alienation both. In other words, it is a scene whose articulation of the impossible with the survivable and the phantasmatic generates violence and, at the same time, points to yet-uninvented life-genres that might allow for a more capacious social life seen generally. This chapter returns to

Happiness and *Half Nelson* at the end but mainly reads with and around *Tango*, attending to the films' politics and pleasures and asking what they have to do with their rapes.

1. Where Does the Happiness Come From?

Bernardo Bertolucci's *Last Tango in Paris* (1972) is remembered for many things, most of which are related to the way its unprecedented amalgam of high-art, pornographic, and Hollywood style reveled in a sexual explicitness that seemed to express the spirit of France in 1968 and the global revolution of youth against imperialism, capitalism, war, and sexual repression.[3] The film is not known, however, for its jokes. There might be a reason for that: the jokes are not very funny. Whereas the sex in the film transgressed many normative and legal codes, its witticisms, its play-verbal pokes and touchés, are just ordinary irruptions, not too witty or surprising. What they are, however, is intimate.

> JEANNE: I'm a Red Riding Hood and you're the wolf. What strong arms you have!
>
> PAUL: The better to squeeze a fart out of you!
>
> JEANNE: What long nails you have!
>
> PAUL: The better to scratch your ass with.
>
> JEANNE: Oh, what a lot of fur you have!
>
> PAUL: The better to let your crabs hide in.
>
> JEANNE: Ooh, what a long tongue you have!
>
> PAUL: The better to . . . to stick in your rear, my dear.
>
> JEANNE: What's this for?
>
> PAUL: That's your happiness and my . . . my ha-penis.
>
> JEANNE: Peanuts?
>
> PAUL: Schlong. Wienerwurst. Cazzo. Bitte. Prick! Joint!

The lovers at this time do not know each other's names or stories. Without the ballast of biography, history, or whatever would limit their pleasure and freedom to form mutuality, they make their way to each other through riffing. They have different concepts of what freedoms other forms might entail: that is their conflict. Here, the woman initiates the play between them, crawling around the man's supine body and ad-libbing on this and that quality of him. Drawing on a fairy tale they do share, their sex is dirty and crabby, sweet and crude. The lovers are animals, they have appetites. Their hunger is for language, too, and their bad puns fall to the floor like water they've shaken off their fur, transient evidence of a rhythm of call and response that demands only the effort to stay in the game with whatever resources they bring. Plot-wise this passage between the lovers does little: it leads to nothing. It sits there quiet as a passing episode, forgettable as the spontaneous jests that get us through ordinary conversation.

II. The Joke's on Us

Any work on relationality would do well to consider the joke. Dependent as it is on the inferred and intimated, a joke is an intimate body genre. As a performance of aggressive complicity, it seeks also to test and induce reciprocity, mutuality, and affective continuity, whether it occurs between individuals or professionals with an audience.[4] If one is lucky, and in on the joke, the reciprocity is technical, a performance of a sudden interestedness and solidarity. Or, a joke can provoke a painful attachment-break, if the telling is inept or one does not get it, or worse, if the content is offensive and one is bruised by being averse to it or the butt of it, watching from the outside while others enjoy its loosely affirmative holding environment. Freud posits that the effect of the swift intimate sociality made by the joke is not cognitive. Instead, he claims, as the joke works by an economy of surprise and withheld explanation, its effects are entirely affective and social, the pleasure of an available rapid mutuality passing over the surface of language to create the incomparable promise of a shared unthreatening awkwardness.[5] "Every joke calls for a public of its own," Freud writes: the irruption of humor tests the terms of inclusion.[6]

All genres are affective conventions that allow readers to expect to feel held, even for a moment, by a scene: the aesthetic scene they enter to be absorbed by and enjoy, and the world of affective and code-sharing that it suggests.[7] Freud's joke book and many books about humor that have come after it emphasize something specific, though, about the intimacy that a witty act extends: that it's a sexual form.[8] What do they mean by that? Foucault famously writes that sexuality is noisy, that it moves from mouth to ear.[9] This resonates with Freud's claim that joking derepresses the sexually knotted-up subject, less by confessing an unbearable secret or disgusting knowledge that she has encrypted within her than by depressurizing a libidinally overwhelming situation, often sadistically.[10] Ted Cohen extends this view to say that the joke's main task is to organize and provide relief from complexity, one encounter at a time.[11] The Bergsonian tradition sees this task executed in rapid collapses, inversions, and cuts that refuse the comfort that resting in form can provide, while delivering a cognitive delight in assessing and surviving moments of ruffled confidence in oneself and in others.[12] The joke is a form that needs and wants what it breaks, even if what it breaks is itself. And if this is right, then comedy is always comedy of survival, even of something as small as being discomfited by a joke. If this is right, then the impersonality of the joke, its spontaneous takeover of consciousness, is a test of relationality as such.

This is also why joking banter—rapid, witty, hyperattentive conversation that allows for what Stanley Cavell calls "continuous presentness"—is the central genre of screwball comedy sexuality. Cavell argues that screwball comedy conversation, "the conversation of love," performs the possibility of happiness in the couple's forging of claims and openness to acknowledgment of attachment, ambivalence, and presence between them, what amounts to a project of being together rather than of world-building.[13] And this scenario points us back to the happy-sadistic eruption of banter that structures so much of *Last Tango in Paris*: where there is sexual experiment, the promise of joking's burst of inclusivity, mutuality, and affective lightness lingers in the sexual drama whose expression of need, aggression, compulsion, and affective imbalance also hovers around joking.

This is a chapter about ambivalence. In ambivalence, we want and we don't want what we want. Or we want parts but not wholes and resent the added freight. Or we're averse to what we're attached to but can perform neither a reconciliation nor a cleavage. It can be a dramatic state but it's also likely to be a mess of loose live wires that it's hard to put a finger on. This complex intensity within ambivalence extends from disrespect of populations as in misogyny and racism to scenes of love and political obsession. For any important object becomes a source of roiling, confused ideation about who's powerful and who's not, and what the potentials are for cohabitations of the world. Sometimes the internal clash comes from the inconvenience paradox of dependency itself, of needing people or a situation and hating to have that need. Then, being in relation, and forging attachments within it, both threatens and relieves us from our sovereign fantasies and states. The differences among the motives are delicate and vary. In *Tango*, being game for sex, for joking, and for revolution allows the possibility of new social relations between beings who can bear it that relationality is always feeling out for form, for them greedily to manage conflicting assessments and aims. The "experience of continuous presentness" is endurable so long as the mode the couple finds for it performs an okayness with the insecurity of what's ongoing and the difficulty of taking things in without resolving into a drama of ecstasy or subordination and loss. Those dramas will always be there, but the dominant dynamic tone shifts internally and between the lovers.

This is to say that we can learn a lot about desires for and resistances to structural social transformation from the training in strong ambivalence that co-locates the comedic and the sexual. The joke's pedagogy is erotically social in a number of senses. It is a form that induces mutual affective delight if it works, and shamed, deadened bodies if it doesn't; that induces self-forgetting and self-suffusion at the same time if it works, and the weight of being stuck with oneself if it does not; if you're the recipient, it's the scene of a perfect meeting of being you and not you, of being both delighted and untraumatized by a surprise that displaces you from your self-continuity without shattering your confidence, if it works, and a confirmation of a broken attachment circuit with the world and one's own self-idealization if it does not. Likewise, in both cases, even if things work well enough in the moment, you might not feel "good" about the episode later, which, after all, has been technically disturbing. Sex that seemed good enough at the time can induce all sorts of regret and ambivalence, just as a joke often induces a guilty conscience, if it works. I use the propositional *if* instead of the aspirational *when* here to foreground how open to revision being in relation is in each genre of intimate encounter.

But the differences matter: a joke, when proposed, is like an "I love you" awaiting reciprocation, but without most of the pressure of holding up an ego or an enduring world. Still, an incident of witticism asserts a social position. It makes an appeal but disguises it as a dare, a test of perceptual expertise, a gift, or all of these. This range of potentials allows deniability on all counts. The joke can thus be seen, if it works, as akin to the form of good sex with another person. To "work" means to achieve its aim of circulating explicit pleasure in a sociality that induces surprise, delight, being out of control, and a sense of a world that you want to be in, even if for just a moment. It folds into the present a quality that is not meant to be stretched out over every moment of the day or throughout the ordinary but which, by virtue of its appearance, resonates in those other temporalities and conditions of life. But, as Joe Litvak has argued, what if the speaker is a stalker or backhanded, such that his humor might be received by others not as pleasure but as something sour and grave?[14] Like twisted love, aggressive wit that does not cloak its aggression in a performance of friendly affiliation offers mutuality while withholding the relief it can provide. Still, even given those dark scenarios, few genres of social reciprocity are as reliable as the joke form in at once delivering and denying intimacy.[15] This is why jokes are troubling, why they disturb moral certitude, and, because they suck people into the presentness of the disrupted object being joked about, why they disturb memory and self-continuity as well, mostly to delightful, or little, effect.[16] What does it mean to say that a joke works? What does it mean to say that a relationship works? This is clearly a temporal observation, not just a formal one. My emphasis on transitional form points to "working" as the condition of staying with each other or with one's survival beyond the situation of the present, maybe acknowledging the delicacy of a thought experiment.

As they exemplify forces in the scene of encounter, the resonance of sex in the joke and the promise and threat of the joke in sex take on extra performance pressure when we turn to what sex has come to mean in many parts of the world impacted by feminisms and queernesses. As Lee Edelman and I argue in "Sex without Optimism," the problem of what sex does is exacerbated particularly by the social and political pressures to make sex adequate to build a world on, to be like the joke that always works and that distributes the complexities of aggression, intention, and ambivalence amid the noise of normative, romantic, virtuous, stirring, reproductive, or merely affirmative pleasure.[17] Because of its bodily effects and structural utility, sex bears the burden of such optimism: that is its problem. Optimism is often unbearable; so is the fact of openness to life, which is inevitable but often feels forced, coerced, or uncomfortably constrained, even when we want whatever stands for "life." The optimism that sex tends to trigger is for an impossible state of things: the perfect rhythm of being in and out of control, of being open and closed in the right or bearable ways, achieving a smooth, unambivalent holding environment for our own and the world's incoherence.[18] This leads to the relief that many feel upon giving in to a state of erotophobia, an aversion to what's overwhelming in sex that resolves into a strong repugnance or hate.

Erotophobia can be a relief because it resolves ambivalence. It casts sex as trauma and blames sex for disturbing what is already disturbed: the live sensorium encountering the world, and the beings who are trying to keep things together while they're moving. But the disturbance of sex is different from the trauma of sex: that is this chapter's proposition, the scene of its thought experiment. Insofar as we are affected—by the world, by people, by language, by things—we are disorganized;[19] insofar as we take in the impact of encounters with the world, we wobble, surprised, ceaselessly adjusting; insofar as we are members of disrespected populations, this constant process is at once invigorating and exhausting, as even aggressive defenses are always energy-sucking. Then, too, the term *violence* tends to presume self-evidence. As survivors of sexual violence attest, often it is self-evident, except when the harsh impact appears belatedly. Sometimes the drive toward judgment in proximity to sex produces a pressure for which there are no words, no adequate words, too many words, or genuinely mixed feelings, especially if there is bargaining to its appearance of sex generates bargaining to stay in a scene of love or dependency. These complexities can seem so overwhelming that hating sex can feel allaying.

Consider the difference between being sexually assaulted by someone's control over one's time, space, and body, and the ordinary unclarities of the sexual event that induce going with the flow of it from some closeness or distance, and sufficiently enjoying it when a rhythm's established. "Good-enough" sex is ordinary, which doesn't mean that it's always fun or salutary. It just means that the episode doesn't achieve the status of drama, let alone trauma, at the time. It stays around as the possible source of future repetition, pleasant, neutral, ecstatic, or bad. It can later be reclassified, as so many things are.[20] Often it's forgotten. Most encounters, even most mixed encounters, aren't reconsidered, and that's not just because of a failure of imagination or a defense against confronting the ordinary of violence. Most brushes with the intimate other remain story free.

I suggested earlier that a sex-positive person can find writing about rape difficult. How is it possible to be anti-erotophobic, against an image of sex as fundamentally a threat to happiness, while engaging how often sex is indeed violent or diminishes its subjects' confidence or attachment to life? How is it possible not to let the negativity of sex defined by intensities of violence look like the truth of sex, given that, whatever it is, "free" is not a dominant quality of any relationality? How is it possible not to let good sex be defined as dodging the bullet of bad sex, which is for many the apriori assumption?

When one consents to something sexual, one is consenting to a thing that's about to happen, not a thing whose narrative, affective, or sensual shape one holds with assurance. One is assenting to be overwhelmed or disorganized or aroused from touch that happens in the right way, whatever one means by that, and often what one means by that specifically in positive terms is variable, elastic, and imprecisely defined.[21] In contrast, what's negative seems to be pretty clear. But even then the sexual subject frequently becomes a detective in pursuit of the event, scrambling to navigate the lag between incidents and their associated affects. After all, the moment an incident changes its associations, its implications change, whether toward clarity or the impact of cruelty.

It is hard to write this segment without many parentheses, many internal objections and reminders and hedges.

The point here about inconvenience is that the nonsovereign live collectively in dynamics that are at once intimate and impersonal, both intense and passing by. We live in disturbance, cultivating heuristics and processes to move with and within the space of being affected, even when it's bad. An event of trauma is not a disturbance; trauma breaks the ongoingness of ordinary togetherness, defeating our styles of relating openness to defense.[22] This distinction is hard to see, largely because we tend to want the satisfaction of the continuum, which always seems to be most exemplary at the extremes: pleasure on one hand, tragedy on another, and the dreaded grey areas in between, which, being grey, must really be tilted toward the dark. But what if the ordinary of disturbance is one thing and the break of trauma something else? The insistence of the joke, and its capture of affect and time, models anxiety about the relation of the fractured to the broken.

So, too, conventional sex, like theory and politics, usually both seeks out the disturbance of excitement and promises a kind of simplifying, clarifying, or sustaining pleasure, if it is sex that one wants, wants to want, or wants to be game for. Think of the clumsy physicality sex induces, in the body, the voice, and the face; the confusions and resignations of knowledge even in a scene of delight; the small and large breakdowns of concentration and confidence all throughout any episode, and the work of quieting those down so things can proceed. Think of how unreadable the lover is, even when response is well amplified. Think of the sometimes desperate, sometimes bitter, sometimes dejected, sometimes funny rage to stay in sync in the middle of all the internal and external noise, and of the aggressive desire that must be mobilized not just to stay in the zone while keeping the inconvenient other in it, too, but to maintain one's own openness to openness. I'm speaking, of course, of sex that's shared. If no one else is there, one is one's own inconvenient other.

In short, any episode in proximity to sex induces a massive cluster of soft and hard double takes, short ones and long, from neutral and anxious to panicked. Given the self-incoherence that characterizes any being and given the lack of fit between or among any persons, even the simplest sexual pleasure involves a collaboration of tangles. And remember, I am emphasizing here sex that's in some sense desired. I feel the need to keep reminding you of this because our modern training in erotophobic subjectivity, which casts sex as an overwhelming object of fear and threat, tends to make us frame its pleasures as good luck and its pains as the real. I am trying to keep everything in play, to keep the situation open to its variety of outcomes and moods. I am arguing, too, that the incapacity to see the drama of dynamic intimacy as traveling across sex to mass sociality misses an opportunity to refine the problem of distinguishing between the perturbation of being in relation generally and the trauma of it.

Queer commentary has produced two main solutions to this clash between wanting to be disturbed in sex and yet simpler in pleasure.[23] In one direction, it has valorized a zoning for sex that builds ethical and political worlds without requiring the validation of the couple form or the ambition to be recognized in the liberal sense or known all the way through, in proximity to sex. From the work of Guy Hocquenghem and Samuel Delaney to Leo Bersani, Tim Dean, Kane Race, and Shaka McGlotten, this zoning produces concepts of contact and reciprocity that allow sex and sexuality to build worlds without reproducing property relations, while continuing to reproduce other abjecting hierarchies related to class, race, and beauty.[24] But other anti-antisocial accounts of sex, often written from the position of queer of color critique—from Marlon Riggs's *Tongues Untied* to Juana María Rodríguez's account of *Queer Latinidad* and Kadji Amin's *Disturbing Attachments*—have challenged the European tradition's recasting of negativity as freeing because it is shattering, sublime, or impersonal.[25] This perspective insists on attachment, too, on being known, on the sociality and affective thickness of gestures directed toward countering a world of erotophobia and discipline.[26] This version of queer countersexuality tends to focus on recovery from and refusal of the negating disciplines of heterosupremacy. So from all of these perspectives, the sex is zoned for securing unambivalence by way of sex, toward the clarities of being harming or welcomed.

At the same time, there has been a move away from sex to love in the Foucauldian tradition. Many of us were stirred and reshaped by this move in Foucault's "Friendship as a Way of Life," which valorizes the "desire in uneasiness" of "the homosexual mode of life," where "friendship, fidelity, camaraderie, and companionship" preside in contrast to the image of gay ass-grabbing that obsesses the heteroerotophobic imaginary.[27] That tradition has produced brilliant gender and kinship creativity in the idiom of care—see the work of Lisa Duggan, Elizabeth Povinelli, Martin Manalansan, and many others.[28] At the same time, this move can preserve the sense that sex is less important than sexuality, as though sex reduces people to trivial things, or that complexity is "reduced to sex," whereas care is profound and profoundly reparative. Much affect theory, too—as in, for example, Sara Ahmed's *Promise of Happiness* (2010)—has no interest in sex as a thing with promise. José

Esteban Muñoz's *Cruising Utopia* (2009) and Heather Love's *Feeling Backward* (2007) also lean toward replacing sex with memory, hope, longing, and aesthetics.[29]

But there can be no adequate social theory without an account of the desire for the inconvenience of other people. Social theory of course addresses the problem of social conflict, the inconvenience of the Other. But it is not just that the Othered other people are hostile to our desires for proximity, engagement, attachment, and worlding. There are inconveniences that we seek at different degrees of intensity and consciousness, and with various ambivalence dynamics. This is what I called, in the introduction, the "inconvenience drive." It is this convolution within attachment, along with pleasure and the ecstatic negativity of jouissance as such, to which "sex" points in this chapter: and "other people" includes, but is not limited to, one's intimates, as we view them conventionally.

This kind of concern with managing the inevitable disturbance of intimacy, codependency, or the passions is also central to the democratic theory of dissensus from Hannah Arendt and Jacques Rancière to the multitude theorists, neo-anarchists, and some feminists, notably Bonnie Honig.[30] Yet discussions of the antagonism at the center of democracy in political theory too often cleave sex from the commons and other imaginaries of living with social division, if they admit sex to the imaginary of the social at all.

But the very problem of sex as a scene of a disturbance that smudges the differences among care, pleasure, control focus, and harm tests how we imagine being in the world together. As Adam Phillips has written, our kindness is all bound up with an aggressive need to control a situation, and also with our pathetic need to re-seduce people and worlds to be the objects we need them to be and our constant gestural modeling of a vulnerability that we hope will induce a feedback loop of affectionate potentiality.[31] These overdeterminations of intimate proximity are at the core of managing inequality, in his view. Bifo Berardi offers two temporally distinct models that reframe the social problem of managing this mix: a sexuality of connection and a sexuality of conjuncture.[32] Subjects with a sexuality style organized by connection expect attachment to be immediate, knowledge to be instant, and the terms of reciprocity to be transparent near the outset, or forget it; Berardi derives this sexual style from the plug-and-play impatience of cybernetic subjects privatized by neoliberalism and networked communication. In contrast, in a sexuality of conjuncture, one appreciates the strangeness of other bodies and cultivates the emotional resources for curiosity about the enigma they will always be. The uncanny hair on the other's body, or that funny taste in the other's mouth, is not idealized in this view but deemed interesting, worth appreciating. Thus, Berardi argues, conjunctural sexuality allows for the growth of sentiment, the necessary binding that induces the strangeness of strangers into domains of the positive and the optimistic.

By engaging the anxiety and incoherence related to working it out with other people in real time, Berardi and Phillips are trying to account for the affective components of democracy that link being on a crowded elevator, being a colleague, being in communities and publics, and being in an episode of sex. Here, forms of sex and tenderness do repeat dominant dramas of sociality. The theorists are also unusual in that they do not equate the antagonisms of the social with tragic theatrics, as in the Antigone tradition. So, strikingly, they also provide templates for understanding how we are trained to be interested in the kind of awkwardness where, as in the joke, pleasure and aggression meet and dramas of adjustment ensue.

It's not surprising that even radicals need to draw boundaries that manage, displace entirely, or sublimate what's overwhelming in the disturbance of sex. How can one sustain a social theory through something defined by the relentlessness of its formal disturbance? How can one not! *Last Tango in Paris* is hardly an ideal representation of sex in the event of happiness. But it performs the necessity of thinking social, political, and sexual nonsovereignty to social theory; it tries to get inside the mix of pedagogy, politics, and normative incapacities to sustain even the intimacy or equality we want; and, by being located in a revolutionary moment dedicated to changing the terms of the general happiness, it stages as acutely as anything does the problem of how to lose one's object world and the attachment habits that keep it going, while maintaining attachment to what else social relations can do. The transitions are painful, involving mental cruelty, physical violence, and death, amid the other world-generating passions. As it is located at the conjuncture of optimism and cynicism about organized derepression, as it shifts among tragic and comic registers of the encounter with erotophobia and desire, it tests out which processes in proximity to sex might make it more possible to remain in proximity to an atmosphere one could call happiness.

III. Sexual Revolution and Its Genres

Last Tango in Paris begins with Paul and Jeanne, two strangers, meeting by chance and having experimental, anonymous sex for a few days, during which time they come to think that it might not just be for pleasure but could have world-shaking consequences. Critics from Pauline Kael to Linda Williams describe how, by using extreme sex to destroy being intimately knowable and known, the couple shifts its social location. As it develops from the initial hookup, their identifications move elsewhere from bourgeois and existential conceptions of imprisoned, unfree, and isolated personhood. They lean toward a mode of nonsovereign being so radically disheveled that it might well have seemed capable of rippling out from this film to destroy the fetishistic idols of the modern Christian patriarchal family and the colonizing nation.[33]

But this is a bad description of the film, and not just because its staging of sexual nonsovereignty refers only elliptically, in a graffito, to what in France are called "the events" of 1968—at least not compared with Bertolucci's subsequent film, *The Dreamers* (2003), which condescendingly reduces the riots in the streets to symptoms of a frustrated sexual drive that has nothing at all to do with social theory or political claims. In contrast, *Tango*'s couple wants sex to decolonize the world, to produce a present detached from historical determination, but that is not possible. What *is* possible, however, reveals the present as an opportunity for shaping an anachronism in transition.

The historical present in *Tango* reveals four generational, historically saturated, politically ambitious contexts coming into contact in the present, clashing, crashing, and revealing some erotico-political dreams. First, there is the sexual encounter of the protagonists at the film's opening, which emblematizes the sixties' collapse of romance with revolution, fantasy with the ordinary, and depiction of sex as a resource for social change. The lovers' wager is that freedom will be meaningful only if it is wrested from the genealogies of biography and identity, and therefore from inheritance and its logics of reproduction. Each lover wants to be known in a way, but only in a way. Each brings to the situation different evidentiary demands: Jeanne, the melodramatic demand that Cavell describes, to be a known woman with a biography; Paul, a tragicomic inclination to confront and kill his fear of freedom by any means necessary.[34] Each lover takes in the aesthetic of the other's project. Each tries it on for size. Sustaining this affective atmosphere involves not just a dramatic performance of stomaching the unknowns and the unthought knowns but admiring them, being impatient with their threat yet cultivating them, not just tolerating them but being kind to and interested in their risk and weirdness and, as we will see, finding a humor and happiness in the sheer fact of showing up for it that could be called intimacy's great promise and gratification when, as one says of a joke, it works.[35]

This couple's desire for a mutuality that egests the defensive genres of intimacy, however, wrestles with three other generational and affectual styles of tethering sex to making worlds, having a life, and being collaborative with intimate others. The film's whole scenario is embedded in Paul's coming to terms with that week's suicide of his wife, Rosa. *Coming to terms* means resignation to what Laplanche calls the "enigmatic kernel" of their intimate relation, the thing that gets passed back and forth between people to cultivate attachment and even love without the assurance of intersubjectivity.[36] Sitting next to Rosa's corpse, which her mother had costumed as a bride, Paul moves from subject to object to abject supplicant: "Even if the husband lives two hundred fucking years, he's never going to be able to discover his wife's real nature. I mean, I might be able to comprehend the universe, but I'll never discover the truth about you, never. I mean, who the hell were you?"

Paul and Rosa had also been sexually experimental, trying out an open marriage that entailed polyamory and extensive verbal reportage of what they did and wanted elsewhere. That practice itself was a tonic to help him heal from the life of itinerant, vigilante machismo he had been leading, from an isolated and shamed cowboy childhood to the military zones of Korea and Cuba, where he may have been a revolutionary or an agent of empire, or we can't tell, as he was a guy just moving along without a plan. He says he was a boxer and became a bongo player, too, working the vernacular of phallo-bohemian rhythm. He came to his wife's hotel for one night, he says, and stayed for five years. But it turns out, he says, that marriage was another "foxhole." A foxhole is a place where one hides from bullets and strategizes the next aggression. In theirs, the desire for mutual flourishing in a world that would be worthy of the trust they longed to place in it turned out not to protect them from the couple form's own ordinary dangers: where one demands patience for one's own variations and stucknesses but moralizes against the other's; where one's revolutionary energies invert in a flash to the compulsion to repeat what works well enough. In the scene where Paul visits Rosa's lover, Marcel, we learn that with him she tried to reproduce every aspect of her life with Paul, despite her wish only to be original in desire. She had told Paul everything about it, he says to Marcel, and yet it is as though there are enough words for the married lovers but not the right genres for using the instabilities between them to disturb their anchors in the normative ideologies that shape the historical present of their bourgeois attachment to property and genealogical whiteness. They fail because it was too hard not to be a formalist in love.

With Jeanne, Paul remediates the tragedy of his marital ignorance, trying to find new practices to release him from his lifelong loop of acting out against a heteromasculine fear of humiliation, which turns out to be an endless project of proving that he's not only overmastered by his vulnerability. He and Jeanne try to defeat fear by playing with it and dominating it, loosening up and refunctioning conventional form, not knowing what they're doing with themselves and each other while also being paranoid about the improvisation with which they are also in love.

In addition to the couple's experiment in detraditionalism, and Paul's recovery from his private marital experiment, *Tango* folds into its narrative two other perspectives on the kinds of holding environment different sexual genres can provide. The third atmosphere is a bourgeois fantasy that saturates the real estate of the film, aligning France, empire, the patriarchal family, and propriety: it is represented mainly by Jeanne's family. This family story thrives in Paris and its suburbs. It is structured by Jeanne's absent father, the dead war hero. Jeanne's father, it is said, died fighting for France in the Algerian War in 1958; on hearing this Paul comments, "or '68 or '28 or '98," a reminder that the ordinary of European modernity has been defined by the brutal urges of colonial power, and that French pride has a thin foundation in the Enlightenment's beautiful phrases.

In this way Jeanne's father embodies, beyond the colonial regime of distributed death, an episodic but continuous patriarchal legacy. His military accoutrements decorate the family home and provide a living museum of national and familial memory; they also create an atmosphere of casual power and sexual excitement (figure 1.1). It would be easy to miss: the home's very interior aspires to a heavy, wooden, formal respectability. But the respectable home is never secure: it has to keep proving itself. Inconvenient reminders of the colonizer's self-violation of superiority intrude in specific and hoarded things like his guns and his secret-life stash of images of naked African women. These erotics are somehow transmitted to Jeanne's mother, who hugs her dead husband's boots until they make her "shiver." Likewise, the Larousse library

1.1 *Last Tango in Paris,* directed by Bernardo Bertolucci, 1972.

of French high culture lines the walls; Jeanne has used them to learn about sex, about the erotics of Enlightenment abstractions, which she assumes her own marriage will allow to flourish as both desire and discipline.

There's more: the family's vernacular inside voice speaks the settler colonist's casual pleasure: they spontaneously reference "dirty little Arabs" and Jeanne's dead cat "Mustapha"; they play the everyday fun and games around the family estate, involving the harassment of Arab children from the neighborhood who play in the backyard and take defiant shits before they scatter in self-defense. Yet Jeanne waxes ironically about other people's racism, as though that dissolves her implication in state, police, patriarchal, race, and class power.

Yet she also joins Paul as a revolutionary theorist at one with the lifeworld creativity of '68. If, for most of *Tango*, the white-supremacist, imperial pride of France and family structures Jeanne's homegrown counterrevolutionary sense of what she has to play with, and if Paul's existentialist bohemianism stimulates for her another exciting if ambivalent alternative to genealogical reproduction, Jeanne insists on a third perspective that claims to derive from the generative, liberatory action of desire, a practical utopianism that deals with the inconvenience of other people not through denial or jokes but through direct and loving aggression. She calls this new way "le mariage pop"—Pop Marriage.

Le mariage pop is cast as the film's most extended sex joke, providing its own risible, farcical element. Associated with movement culture from the straight, the socialist, the feminist, and the utopian 1960s to the queer contemporary, the phrase stages the radical experiment of rerouting optimism about normative romantic sexual difference into new social modes. This collective demand for freedom from the heteronormative presumption has now become distorted with the noise of many different kinds of revision and refusal, from the ongoing backlashes against '68 that Kristen Ross chronicles to Foucault's scathing rejection of the concept of revolutionary sexual derepression in *History of Sexuality*.[37] We will return to this repudiation at the end. Pop marriage also links Bertolucci's film with the screwball and the romantic comedy, making it an antecedent both to *Shortbus* (Mitchell, 2006) and *Sex and the City*.[38] It predicts, too, contemporary "choice feminism" and other tendencies equating freedom with consumption.[39] But rather than dismissing the force of le mariage pop, I want to take seriously its theoretical demand: after all, its imaginary for sexual revolution has turned out to be more lasting historically than the other aspirational, intersectional, politically radical sexual worlds of the film. More than fifty years later, this flower-power straightness still threatens the pith out of those who are attached to the mommy-daddy-me generational structure. Its association with the feminine and the feminization of masculinity has made it risible, which is a sign that in another register it might have become a revolutionary theory.

Pop marriage describes the situation of Jeanne's romance with a verité film-maker called Tom. Tom has decided to film for television the everyday of his relationship with Jeanne—he calls it *Portrait of a Girl*. Like Paul, Tom makes the rules. He forces Jeanne, without her prior consent, to act within his mise en scène in front of his camera crew, in public. She is never in control of her initial framing. She gets angry about it. But as she is with Paul, she's up for Tom's game, not only submitting to but shaping their improvisation, prompting as much as she is prompted within the situation she did not initiate (figure 1.2).

In contrast to the hermeticism of Paul and Jeanne, the pop couple of Tom and Jeanne has sex in public and in publics. It loves and fights in front of huge, garish billboards and identifies with the ideal couple whose life will be well managed by the cleaning and softening agents the billboards sell. It cultivates a greedy erotics without censorship or loss. Where Jeanne and Paul are conversational, the pop couple is loud; where Jeanne and Paul are focused inward toward the space their actions make, the pop couple is world-facing. It consumes the new French postwar mass cultural prosperity, dressing like hipsters, dandies, and carrying around LPs and portable record players as accessories.[40]

For many people, this is what the sexual revolution looked like: revolutionary play. Jeanne and Tom caption all of this not by imagining the destruction and reconstruction of the world through their on-the-go compositions, but by addressing tradition as another accessory, an entirely private and affective thing with no disconcerting political component. Can it be politics without foregrounding dissonance? The pop couple's vernacular is filled with signs of

1.2 *Last Tango in Paris,* directed by Bernardo Bertolucci, 1972.

contemporary radicalism: Jeanne, for example, blithely projects her identification with the Left by imagining their children, "Fidel" and "Rosa," for Castro and Luxembourg, and also echoing uncannily the name of Paul's suicidal wife. They imagine additionally a revolutionized adulthood, unclear as to its relation to the national capitalist project. Even when something goes awry, Jeanne says, the pop couple will fix the relationship the way workers fix a car.[41] Tom says, "I don't know, [we'll] invent gestures, words. . . ."

Pop marriage skims off energy from familial and national history but throws out depth psychologies, imperial ambitions, and dark philosophies. Its disturb-the-surface gesturing imagines new forms of life emerging. Colonial and racist historical tendencies convert to material for a comic perspective on the present, if we understand "comic" to mean supremacist irony and the dandyish play with gender that, for some, defined the political project of androgyny as a vision of becoming-woman.[42] The racist imperialism of the photographic fetish joins the smooth idealizations of advertising fantasy to become props for a crowing sexual expressiveness; and the wedding they plan joins war as a theatrical thing whose uniforms renovate violence into play, draped and framed by fur, fabric, exuberantly lush sound, and sweeping tracking shots.

In this way le mariage pop remediates singular love as collective life by trying to make meringue from an inherited national/political idiom. Tom and Jeanne's will to flatten history into the memory and performance of pleasures, including by way of frothy yet melodramatic affects, means that in this world nothing is banal and everything can become inflated into an event, too, not just wars and weddings. Melodrama lite should not be possible, and yet le mariage pop takes genres of secrecy, contract, aggression, and pleasure from the conventions of modern sexual melodrama and seeks to make them mobile, visual, aural, public, and not identical to any previous generation's tradition-bound marital bargains with the logics of racism and property. They represent bourgeois transition. Indeed, the soundtrack by Gato Barbieri, richly remembered but used very sparsely during the film, often is heard during their mobility sequences, during cuts to a bridge or a street; it induces and marks affective increase but propels the sense that the film is about the intensities of the drives that circulate less within and between people and more where people encounter them in the formal architectures of the everyday—bridges, bathrooms, hallways, riversides, dance halls, rented rooms, and ancestral, ghosted homes.

In pop marriage there is no historically tangled subjectivity to dissolve, one might say. One can be who one was but must improvise on it in the present, becoming elastic, not torn. Pop marriage idealizes the play of plea-sures and the variations of moods. It can absorb turbulence and ambivalence by theatricalizing them as play, as joke, and as invention. These modes are supposed to stretch out into an intimate space of reliable encounter whose mood and form can never be predicted. It's experimental from within life, but not revolutionary against life as we know it. All sexual experiment in this film has transformative—animating, nauseating, life-threatening—consequences for the participants, whose drama is to want it all: but the task of le mariage pop is to invent an ordinariness for it. In another register we might call that politics.

IV. On Sex and the Event

A politics of the ordinary requires a different poetics of the event. From most theoretical perspectives, the event is a genre that skews the ordinary, whether by interrupting its ongoing reproduction, staging what feels like a break in time that might signal revolution or trauma, actualizing a tran-scendent process or a repetition that comes to pass as fact, or intensifying a predictably impactive reencounter with norms, laws, or power.[43] This is to say that the event is not always anything. It's an aesthetic judgment about the shape and impact of action. The problem for sex is that the inflated genres of the event attached to it overorganize the swift and elastic adaptations, mo-tives, projections, and encounters that cluster inexorably in the scene of it.

The nagging question of how to world happiness where sex appears as an event hangs in the atmosphere of *Tango*'s every scene.[44] The film records what can be released by the elastic rhythms of affective habituation when bodies turn to sex to have an event, and it archives what gets lost when sex-ual formalism begins to stand in for what being in a relation can make pos-sible. So if learning from the presence of the comedic in sex was our first mission, dispensing with the event as the default scale for sex is the second.

Sex is not usually an event, in any philosophical, juridical, psychoana-lytic, or aesthetic sense. It's an episode. To call something an episode is not to denote a mere episode, life reduced to things that happen. It denotes a situation that takes time, that rises and falls in intensity and consequence, that may be forgettable until it emerges later, in a series. It might become an episode. It might become an event that reshapes a life or a world. But it prefigures nothing. It is a scene of temporal demand on your attention, like the punctum, the vignette, and the joke. What distinguishes the incident is the extension of its internal world to other time/space environments beyond the encounter, perhaps through genre, seriality, or the atmosphere, the mood, and the "scene," with its psychoanalytic and criminal implications. Taken together, these minor distributions of condensation provide better temporal models for thinking how the episodic attunement of sex coexists with and can bear most varieties of out-of-tuneness. In concert they also force skeptical attention to reading the object/scene historically without presuming it as a menacing symptom of a threatening cause. Where sex is concerned, such attention to the episode's brevity allows for experiments in thinking about how universal, structural, or singular it is, and what its overdetermined etiology and logic express. The only thing ontological in this model of the sexual object/scene is that, like a joke, it opens you up, at least to asking and shaping what happened and what is happening.

Tango's suspicion of the swollen narcissism of the sexual event is, in any case, all bound up with its use of joking. As the film opens the two are not lovers yet, but strangers converging to rent a space, with all implications of the torn and the temporary hanging in the air. They are shot crossing the same urban zones toward that space, but at first they do not interact, and the camera loops around them up close and from afar as though to measure the sphere of what Bertolucci called the encounter of these "two lonelinesses."[45] Then Jeanne enters the apartment. Their entries into the scene of encounter are always awkward and fraught, the way any threshold crossing can be: not entrancing, but not the opposite, either. Rather, they follow the slow transition from apartness into connection, from different atmospheres of alienation or abstraction into mutually held alienation and abstraction, plus affective, enfleshed interest. No one is assured about anything but that there's an opening whose potentials must be felt for: an unsteady simultaneity mutually composed.

Sometimes a live connection between the two protagonists once they're in the room happens swiftly and easily, and sometimes it does not. Sometimes it's Jeanne who's impatient for attunement, sometimes Paul. Alain Badiou writes that such a continuity hiccup is structural in love: the encounter that breaks the smoothness of time is the event of love at its inception. Something like that structure operates here, although it's not love yet or ever, stuck in an expanded tryout phase. The film wants to break the presumption of love from its conventions of what Badiou calls the "two," and especially from the idea of intersubjectivity implied in his image of the couple bonded in sharing the world they make as an object to lean on rather than coordinate through. *Tango* is skeptical about love as sharing and has a more minimal and physical conception of intersubjectivity; in a film this episodic, scene transitions bear a great aesthetic weight of establishing affective realism about the difficult work of staying in relation without a conventionally cushioning concept or object.[46]

In the first sexual scene, the room is a ruin. Stains loom everywhere, furniture appears abandoned and in heaps, and the blinds are askew, as is therefore the relation of light to shadow. Mirrors and windows mime each other so that one can never be certain of the dimensions of the habitable space. Later we learn that the place stinks, too, denoting not that people have died here but that they have lived.[47] Lived life had an impact on the room, and the atmosphere is thick with the enigma of what it all added up to and why it was abandoned.

Paul leans on the wall in the shadows, one more piece of abandoned furniture. The two play-fight immediately, and we can sense that improvisation will be the default idiom of their relation. At first it is not comic. We know by then that neither of them walks alone in the world lightly. Brando opens the film, walking on the street and talking to himself as though playing both sides in an argument, then yelling: "Fucking God!" At first, Jeanne skips and blows kisses and phones her mother, and yet when she closely encounters strangers she clutches at her body, averse to any stranger's strangeness.

So when Paul and Jeanne meet as anonymous applicants for a space to be filled with life, one feels the weight of their sovereignty, the crowded isolation of their solitude, a haunting exhaustion, and their hunger for relief. The comic potential of all this misery emerges almost instantly, when interior decorating meets the sexual genres. It turns out that amid ruins, one can always play "house"—where should the chair go, Paul asks Jeanne, by the fire or the window? They banter then move into separate places, test each other's desire for the room and glance warily across the decayed enclosures and openings, teasing the architecture into serving as infrastructure for something that goes without saying: interest.

Then the phone rings while Jeanne is on the toilet, seen through an uncurtained window; Paul is physically apart from her then, in the apartment's far corner. They answer the phone together and Paul, gesturing slowly, says in English and French that nobody's there. The shot holds them while they stay silent on the line, performing his truth and his lie: the phone puts them on hold, as it were, facilitating a transfer of affects and a tentative trust, the putting on hold that leads to things in a new attachment. The camera makes sure that we see that the same space becomes many spaces as they assert, defend, and relax across moods of intimation, intimidation, projection, and privacy. When Jeanne moves to leave, Paul comes and shuts the door she has opened and slowly, deliberately picks her up like a bride crossing over a psychic threshold, and they have sex. When it's over, they collapse beneath a sheer white curtain, as though they're both newly bridal.

The bridal uncanny circulates throughout this film, indeed—in the dead wife's presentation in her wedding gown, in this initial tryst, and in Jeanne's bridal fitting for le mariage pop—as though the reenactment of the new beginning emerging from old material that marriage ritually portends might be extended to any bodies and all sociality, forever.

The sex that transpires is wordless, as is the rest of the scene, apart from some Oh Gods, grunts, and groans, soon to be the material for their comedy but here merely phatic, not the kind of communication that calls for the other's response. They are having sex with themselves through each other, but the selves they are having sex with are a relief from what they had been carting around. There is also no voiceover, no soundtrack, just amplified sounds of fabric ripping and the noise of fucking without furniture. The act is awkward. It looks physically uncomfortable, as Paul's body in motion also functions as a chair that Jeanne sits in backward, and there is lots of clutching and shifting around, midair. The tension is both skeletal and sexual, and the shock that they are doing it conjoins with questions about whether and how long they can continue doing it without props, supported by only the muscular infrastructure they bring to the encounter.

All is relieved when finally they fall to the floor and finish—not just letting loose the pressure of sexual desire, but being freed from the aesthetic and affective potential for failure that always floats around sex. They finish when he comes. She rolls away from him, they breathe. There is no other affective valence. The camera cuts then to a shot of them approaching a thick and tinted glass door to let themselves out of the building; the cutaway protects us from any subsequent ordinariness, so that instead of the postcoital evaluative shuffle of "How was it for you?," their spent intensity is maintained and their burst through the door portends a second coming together. When we first see their silhouettes approach the frame rapidly they look like a cinematic shadow couple about to burst out onto the urban streets for a night's entertainment. But as the door opens it is clear that they are not together affectively. Paul looks jaunty and pulls down the sign advertising the room's rental. Jeanne, her face opaque, hugs her coat tight and runs out of the shot, while Paul strolls onto the bridge.

Jeanne runs at full speed to her next episode in the other plot, which feels silly compared with what has just transpired. But the feeling that it's silly reproduces a conventional disrespect for comic relief, about which the film has other views. This encounter is literally an episode of "le mariage pop."

Tom is directing *Portrait of a Girl* as cinema for television, and each encounter between them takes the form of an episode. Tom, like most romantics, aspires to tweak conventionality and call it revolution.

Le mariage pop flourishes only where sex does not interfere with the flow of things. In pop marriage there is sex, but the passion is pretty much all above the belt. The pop plot begins and culminates in cranial carnality, a kiss. "If I kiss you, it might be cinema. If I caress you, it might be cinema" are among Tom's first words to Jeanne. Pop sex is always theatrical and public: the lovers, being filmed by Tom and his crew, meet in train stations, on the streets, in corridors—always in transitional spaces through which people move. Jeanne gets angry that Tom has presumed her permission to be filmed and to be the topic of his work, but she does not walk out, choosing instead to air her resistance to this change to their intimacy within the situation he has set up. She says, sarcastically, the romantic lines he seems to want; she calls him a coward, spitefully. But then she gives in to her unironic need for her lover's hug and kiss, and the ruined first kiss is reabsorbed into a final enfolding of the lovers into each other. The speed of Jeanne's transition from antipathy to the loving cling reveals a central thing about her affective style. She flickers hot and cold, comedic and melodramatic. The men are inconsistent tonally throughout the film, too, but they tend to sustain one tone per episode.

The scene in the train station ends with a hug. The sexual part of the encounter takes place also in silence, as in the previous scene, but is surrounded by the noise of the world. Where there's kissing, there's no talking, no joking, no conversing, but by now we see that all of these modes of flash intimacy express a hunger for a feeling to expand into a world without that world taking on the logic of any richly imagined affective genre or event. Instead, making a transitional space and episodic time, sex is a thing you fling yourself into, a comic apparatus that Paul figures as "a flying fuck at a rolling donut." Sex shapes an encounter but is not an expression of the subject's deep psychic structure, nor an abandonment of it. Before the episode gets to roll around in all of the subjective resonances, something simpler happens: responsivity, like the first beat of the completed joke. The induced response as such is the zero point of the reciprocal rhythm that constitutes the potentiality of any action in relation to attachment. After that comes the atmosphere.

So the opening of the film establishes two experiments in revolutionary sexuality: in the substitution of episode for event, of bodies for language and history; and an interest in what might be taken up and run with. The comedic mood of *Tango* emerges from these scenes of variable mood and digressive encounter, generating the erotic relationship itself as the kind of transitory space that Marc Augé has named the "non-place,"[48] which is different from "the private." In these architectures of intermediacy, people experience the ways that they do not line up with their usual selves or identities. They are in transition: they do transitional things, eat strange food, consume strange media, comporting themselves unusually. They have suspended identities because they are somewhere vaguely amid what David Bowie calls "the stream of warm impermanence."[49] Virtually every sexual encounter in Last Tango in Paris takes place in a transitional infrastructure. These conditions are at once architectural and epistemological: for example, the spaces are rented, and the actions in them are toward not accretion but movement—movement toward things that would generate fireworks, feel like fireworks, while also feeling life out. The two most comic and happy scenes in Tango demonstrate these qualities in the minor genres.

v. Happiness in the Sexual Episode

The two scenes associated most with happiness in Tango are dominated by this awkward weave among intensities. In the scene of bad jokes with which this chapter opens, Jeanne arrives to see Paul standing ready on one side of a new mattress that fits perfectly in the center of the room. The mood music is light cocktail, then strings, then silent. Paul leans on the old mattress propped against the wall and Jeanne sits with her back to him on the new one. The lovers kick off their clothes quasi-comically, silent but for the unzipping noise from Paul's pants that matches the ripping noise of Jeanne's stockings in the film's inaugural encounter. It echoes in the mostly empty room. Paul sticks out his tongue at her, ready for play, the way she was in the previous scene. Even though their sex time begins out of joint, we see that their instincts for play overlap. The camera then cuts to them naked, seated in the middle of the mattress like the figures on top of a sex wedding cake, with nothing but abdominal strength upholding their bodies: this is already the third instance of this couple having to rely on their own musculature, rather than norms, to brave the awkwardness of intense proximity (figure 1.03). Happiness is in the room's relaxed atmosphere. There is no evidence that sex has taken place, but it feels like an encounter has happened, for the lovers' boundless closeness and lightness suggest something sovereign has been disburdened.

PAUL: "Let's . . . Let's just look at each other."

JEANNE: "It's beautiful without knowing anything. Maybe . . . maybe we can come without touching."

1.3 *Last Tango in Paris,*
directed by Bernardo
Bertolucci, 1972.

Paul echoes her and then they throw their heads back, eyes closed, to try. At this point the scene turns into an amalgam of romantic comedy, children's imaginary play, and animal play, the three modes that Jeanne adds to Paul's existentialist drama. "Are you concentrating?" Paul says. Their faces strain, as though defecating or climaxing. They banter and laugh, beautiful and exuberant. Then Jeanne says, "I shall have to invent a name for you . . . ," thus reigniting their battle over what shared idiom will allow them to find each other and to stay in sync.

"Oh god, I've been called by a million names all my life," Paul says. But rather than following into the darkness of his taunting tone, he then offers his "real" name in a series of deep gasping grunts and growls that Jeanne calls "masculine," offering in response her own implicitly feminine animal name, a series of trilling bird sounds. Paul, laughing: "I didn't get the last name," and then more mutual laughing, grunting, and trilling.

The camera moves close to them during this scene, almost as close as they are to each other, then swings back and moves in again. There is barely enough space between the lovers for speech to pass through, and as they talk their lips almost touch, and one senses the breath breathed in by the other. Someone might call these mating calls. But given the rhythms of the previous scenes, there is no reason to think that the grunt is building an Aristotelian plot, life-plot, or embodying desire-release causality of any sort. At stake is finding an idiom of reciprocity without fetishism, without building gene-alogies, kinship, or "a life." As Rosa's mother demonstrates when she rifles through her daughter's purses, after a death we look through the effects. But this is life, improvised, live: its subjects are looking to become worthy of becoming causal; worthy of not being attached to defensive mimesis, defeat, or paranoia in response to the complexities; worthy of the desire for that simple responsivity untethered to the history signified by mood; worthy of allowing disgust and aversion to ripple through the sustaining attachment along with the other tones, perhaps by being interested and curious and not obsessed more with the dark dramas than with the light.

Like the animals they produce themselves as, in their following scene Paul and Jeanne groom at a sink, her putting on makeup, him shaving at sinks side by side. Paul opines that sinks like this keep people together, providing an infrastructure for "bearing" what's "tough" about being open and awkward to that which you depend on but remain curious about. It is a sweet thing for him to say, and the image of the couple at the mirror together—grooming, moving between small talk and big talk, looking directly and indirectly at each other—picks up on the gestural efficiency of the holding environment for which any shared form allows. It is also an image of film's capacity simply to record the intimacy performed by improvisation: little of what happens in this scene is in the screenplay.[50] At stake is a guess at what it would take for two strangers to remain strange without being estranged even as their knowledge grows.

Jeanne had opened the scene searching Paul's pockets to menacing music, and he comes to take out his shaving accoutrements, including the knife with which his wife killed herself. They face the mirror. Jeanne begins to bicker again about his refusal of ordinary biographical handles, but when Paul threatens to break up, her response is to pull back, think a beat, and then say, "Well OK, let's forget it." They start again; she parries by satirizing her curiosity: how old is he? has he been to college? He says archly that he's ninety-three and studied whale fucking at the University of the Congo. Then there's more piercing sexual/racial politics: she asks whether he would like to cut her up like a slave; he says, "I want you free," and she says, "Free?! I'm not free!" Jeanne then puts forth her newest theory, which is that Paul hates biography because he hates women. He gently mocks her bad English but responds that the problem of the sexes is the double claim that the other can be known and that the knowing is always inadequate. She pouts at his disrespect; he shaves. This mode of specular sociality, with its double take, second chance, and reappeal, binds aggression to generosity: the atmosphere holds many tones, is unsure. It is also casual and goes down alleys it does not pursue. It is a recognizable version of intimacy's ordinary; it's also

1.4 *Last Tango in Paris,* directed by Bernardo Bertolucci, 1972.

compositional listening and, in multiple senses, theory. It looks ominous and seems to be headed toward anger, retreats, is sweet, proposes nothing and then something, playing and testing.

Jeanne pouts again, frustrated. Paul teases her amiably, "What's that, what's all this?" by which he means, why have you fallen out of the joke, the insults, the trading, the appeal. Then he picks her up, twirls her around and crows the animal noise sounds that stand in for his name, his appetites, his articulateness, and all the unsaid things (figure 1.4). They loop, weave, and whoop until they're breathless, stumbling and laughing: it's like the sex, the joking, a reminder of why they're there. It seems as though they can get through all the stumbles: in these moments of demand they do not even know what the object that they're investing with the possibility of their happiness stands in for. That's the joke of the zipper, the donut, the sink, all form, insofar as form is not a thing but a relation.

Brando seems at that point to have improvised a line. Paul places Jeanne on the edge of the sink and kisses her lightly: "I think I'm happy with you," he says, just like that. He turns to leave the room; she is still, for a moment, caught in the moment of delight that resolves nothing but confirms that the bourgeois epistemophilias she's been performing are ridiculous. She waits a beat, and then: "Encore! Do it again! Again!" It's the kind of happy moment that cinema can catch, people in character sliding around in what's implied in the infrastructure of their mutual being. Encore, Again: the rhythm extends the mood toward an open clarity that can distinguish the desired affect from whatever dynamic can be made up to stretch it out. But in a minute the scene turns sour. Jeanne becomes angry that Paul won't repeat her script, nor leave the apartment together the way she wants; in their next scene she returns freely but is volubly angry that he assumes that she'll return there. Soon, he is raping her anally. This episode deserves its own section.

vi. Get the Butter

Preceding this section is an experiment in learning from how, in *Last Tango in Paris*, the pedagogy of the joke reframes the close proximity of sexual and revolutionary desires. In this analysis the lability of mood and the jockeying of conversation that make relations into intimacies stand for the on-the-ground expression of lived inequality and the testing out of new forms of life that refuse to distinguish the personal, the social, and the political. These interruptions of the reproduction of tradition act in a variety of ways: they test the lovers' fidelity to conventions of relation; document the ungainly pulls for and against the desire to correlate experience, which is different from holding it in common; separate out intimacy from conventions of knowing or being known; reduce the melodrama of event to the labile tones of living-on associated with the comedic; and lay out the vulnerability, cruelty, and inventiveness in desire. They seek to bear inconvenience, which is to say, the ambivalence of a wanted copresence. "The comedic" here doesn't mean the funny, because comedy stretches into darkness, as we have seen, but it points to the attachment to remaining game for linked life that persists, when it can, even in proximity to lifeworlds of catastrophe.

 Tango is now a museum of these qualities and gestures.[51] This is not because the '60s were a failure but because the decade's experimental letdowns were cast largely in the terms of what Simon Critchley calls tragic finitude, self-evident disasters that destroyed normative forms without offering stabilizing scaffolds for occupying the openness and the loss of confidence that inevitably come during a transition.[52] Without these forms, the aggression in desire and the scalar anxiety that sex provokes about what its episodes mean, might mean, and express have, for many, become the life-form of sex itself.

 Which, sourly, returns us to the comedic. *Last Tango in Paris* is still regularly referred to by a wisecrack, a sex joke that is not a joke in the film. The phrase is *get the butter*. *Get the butter* is what Paul says to Jeanne before he rapes her. *Get the butter* signals straight angst and ambivalence about anal sex.[53] The joke, as we humorless feminists say, is not funny. A nervous joke, *get the butter* signals aroused unease with *Tango*'s collapse of art film–style erotica into a particular scene of sexual violence that can't be rescued by calling it art or legitimating it as an instance of Bataillean radical sovereignty in the form of revolutionary ecstasy.[54] The nervous joke is a blurt we make when we're overwhelmed and feel out of control socially. Here we are focusing on a scene that also begins with joking and verbal sport in a way that is preserved in the rape joke's ongoing life.

As in every other scene of encounter in the film, the rape scene opens with this couple out of sync and searching for a common tone. When Jeanne walks into the apartment she begins joking right away, calling Paul "Monster," seeking his attention, the camera pulls back and glides with her as she wanders the fractured quasi-home space, wanting him freely. Paul sits on the floor of the apartment, eating bread and cheese. He's just come from Marcel's place elsewhere in the building. He's at first harsh, sadistic. Jeanne here exhibits a version of aggressive play that expresses her desire that he acknowledge her immediately and at the right scale of delight: "Why didn't you answer?" Paul becomes game for the activity of mood and bodily adjustment Jeanne initiates, and to be game requires play. The couple crawls around the floor play-fighting until the play falls away.

Over the six-minute arc of the "butter" scene, Jeanne experiences Paul as arbitrary and withholding, and they jockey in search of a common register. He demands the butter, she gets it for him; she puts a red portable record player on the bookshelf, to return to later as her technology for advancing the symbolic order of le mariage pop. In the meantime, they converge over a hollow space in the floor to play a speculative game with it: they wonder whether it holds secrets. Jeanne doesn't want to know: there may be family secrets. Paul riffs on her pants, on the "family jewels." He asks her whether she's afraid, a question he's asked of himself as well throughout the film—a question implicitly about sex, the family, and secrets themselves. The camera moves close to them. She says she is not afraid; he says, "You're always afraid." And then Paul, pulling her and the butter to him, says, "Family secrets? I'll tell you about family secrets." Jeanne is sobbing throughout the scene.

JEANNE: What are you doing?

PAUL: I'm gonna tell you about the family. That holy institution meant to breed virtue in savages. I want you to repeat it after me.

JEANNE: No and no! No!

PAUL: Repeat it. Say, "Holy family." Come on, say it. Go on. Holy family. Church of good citizens.

JEANNE: Church . . .

PAUL: Good citizens.

JEANNE: Good citizens . . .

PAUL: Say it. Say it! The children are tortured until they tell their first lie.

JEANNE: The children . . . are tortured . . .

PAUL: Where the will is broken by repression.

JEANNE: Where the will . . . broken . . . repression.

PAUL: Where freedom . . .

JEANNE: Free . . . Freedom!

PAUL: . . . is assassinated. Freedom is assassinated by egotism. Family . . .

JEANNE: Family . . .

PAUL: You . . .

JEANNE: You . . .

PAUL: You . . . You f . . .

JEANNE: You . . .

PAUL: fucking . . .

JEANNE: fucking . . . family.

PAUL: You fucking . . .

JEANNE: family!

PAUL [coming]: Oh, God . . . Jesus.

Here and in a scene to follow where he has Jeanne penetrate him, Paul explicitly uses anal sex to break their complicity with the reproduction of American-European imperial history and its vehicles for subjection in the Church and the Family. But Paul's takeover of Jeanne's ass in this first instance is not here visible as solidarity, despite the implicit solidarity in his "we." His abduction of her agency involves forcing her not only to be penetrated but to repeat his words, his analysis, and his theory of what needs to be broken for the world to be worth living in. She's compelled to recite a catechism against the Church and the bourgeois family and, two scenes later, she repeats this role as she digitally penetrates him anally. In the latter scene he requests that she accompany him to break out from regimes of distorting fear, and here, too, her response is the perverse marriage vow, "yes I will" and "and more, and more," which agonizingly repeats their comic bathroom moment. Meanwhile, Paul's orgasmic "Oh God . . . Jesus" performs the unfinished business of unlearning his attachment to religious prayer at the moment in which sex moves into the loss of control that orgasm offers as nonsovereign pleasure.

Many other moods are folded into this hailstorm of trouble too. All of them together subvert the view that optimism, sexual or otherwise, always feels optimistic: "more, and more" is again a temporal promise about extending intimacy, not a promise to be in a better or more secure mood. This effect is the film's fantasy of trauma inducing nontraumatic effects. On the first occasion his rage and her tears appear in close-up, in the shadows their bodies make; in the physical climax that comes after the rhetorical one, his drive and her defeat are recorded from the perspective of a ceiling camera, parodying the Platonic position of the two lovers in one body.

Cats are featured in many scenic transitions in *Tango*, and after the rape scene Bertolucci shoots Brando stylized in still life, sleeping deeply in the grotesque twists of a cat on its back and side, as though the chair-seated, leg-crossed, and twisted Lucian Freud bodies that open the film had been knocked off their perch. This return of the grotesque portends the return of the comedic. Jeanne wakes Paul from his post-orgasmic sleep and he's feral in a different way, more alive than he was in the scene before play talk and forced sex were their variations on being in sync. He is frisky again, and willing to submit to her framing of experience. "I have a surprise for you," she says, but it's a double surprise: a pop-music record for him to listen to, her soundtrack, and an electric shock she exposes him to when she has him plug her portable record player into a socket she knows will jolt him. "You like that?" he says, irritated. In her pleasure, she ignores his pain.

Is the lift of being affectively in counterpoint here exposed as a parody, a tragedy, an alibi, harm, and a farce? In this film's experiment in fantasy, the intimate encounter is both play and violence dressed in perverse reciprocity. It raises the question of what reciprocity is. It forces us to ask whether reciprocity is equality or a different thing. Or if the equality effect is really a tableau of reciprocal performances of inequality. It queries whether equality is possible, a good aspiration, a disavowal of the desire to dominate, or all of it.

What, then, is the relation between *Last Tango in Paris*'s ongoing preservation in a rape joke and its enactment of screwball comedy in the electrical contact between sex and revolution? To summarize, this aesthetic question about genre and tone is also a formal and epistemological question about the episode and the event; an historical one about the '60s; a political one involving the desire to empty out so many supremacies—patriarchal, imperial, and racial; and a thought experiment about what democracy looks like when it is mediated by versions of sex that seem to be liberated from tradition and open to inventive forms of being in relation and nonrelation. *Last Tango in Paris* is about what it takes to lose one's anchoring objects not simply by substituting better ones, but through experiments that disturb people's relation to the event of the object as such. Here the often forgettable disturbance sex makes is always in proximity to the experience of trauma, a violence that solidifies into an event that travels through the rest of a life, however it's treated. It is also always in proximity to the comedic, which is generated by the surprise twists of language and failed intersubjectivity. These strongly ambivalent resonances are queasily related to jokes and play: queasily because genuine experiment unbalances our confidence in frames of expectation, time, and causality; queasily because sex and humor rock the boat of confidence in what's ongoing affectively; queasily because even play that's consented to is an opening to uncertainty, which can only always be partly welcome, because uncertainty is rough, whatever else it is.

It would be easier to solve these inconstancies and knots if the eruption of wit in a space of intimacy that may also be a brutal space were really a rape, an inexorable bleed that makes the disturbance we seek in the intimate encounter an unavoidable gateway to trauma. To the contrary, politics and desire are each defined here by the ways nonsovereign instability solicits and breaks their trust in relational form. These lovers seek an end to insecurity in form's holding of power; yet they also seek inconvenience in its pure potential, extending from when the form is what Sedgwick calls a "nonce taxonomy" that can be learned from, played around with, returned to, abandoned.[55] The experimenters hate their intimate experiments and are not able to bear them, though they enjoy them immensely, inconsistently; in the long middle of relationality, they're game to confirm that it's worth the risk to try to do something compositional in the space of intimate contact, but they're also not sure. The scene of the couple in both plots is both extreme and ordinary. In the end, though, they preserve through intimate formalism a cushioning that defends against acknowledging the ambivalence of desire, the complexity of intention, and the disturbance of receptivity, with its mirror in projective identification.

Of course I am talking about a script, a fantasy of causality. But we can turn it to other ends. The transformational infrastructures that are born from within conventional relationality in *Tango* can only hold out so much stability: they're never enough. For people to be "free" to experience the agitation of equality, the institutions and imaginaries that the couple contests need to go through public violation and decomposition too. Le mariage pop and antibourgeois coupling, trying for relational sovereignty in improvisation, attempt in *Tango* to shake the conventions that support the institutions, but the symbolic order of the national-imperial imaginary is too charismatic and engrained for the couples to abandon their use. The rape and the jokes in *Tango* coteach the terribly normal consequences of that.

Conclusion

In the last few moments before he dies, Paul takes a piece of chewing gum from his mouth and sticks it beneath the top rail of Jeanne's balcony fence.[56] The gum reappears in virtually the same place in scene two of Bertolucci's *Luna* (1979). There, it represents the irritating detritus of a teenager's aggressively careless appetite, a goad that also happens to be the last event before his stepfather's heart attack and death, and the beginning of the end of a bourgeois family. If the gesture of the gum is completed in *Luna*, in *Tango* it stands for so much more than a challenge to the bourgeois fetish for appearances and appetitive compartmentalization, so much more than a blot on the new beginning that Jeanne's impending wedding aspires to be. It is also the film's last comic moment. But it is an unshared joke, marking the moment after which no genres of expansive intimacy will be on offer from anyone.

Here, as Jeanne murders Paul, the scene of passion and the crime scene are irreducibly the same, as they have been throughout the film. Every scene in *Tango* expands like this one does, genre sliding among the comic and dark tones of ordinary attachment when the camera pulls back and keeps recording. The rape scene, for example, is followed directly by that slapstick play between Jeanne and Paul, which includes him doing a gymnast's sharp backflip before listening to *Pop Sounds*. Take, too, the train station fistfight between Tom and Jeanne, where she protests his "mental rape" of her. This pummeling takes place in front of absurd billboards making ill-fitting promises about fabric softener, a double take that's echoed later in the play-fight that attends Tom's marriage proposal, which is followed by the image of a sinking buoy. The scene of the tango ballroom that appears in the last act is itself destructured by completely random swerves between comic play, sexual nonsovereignty, clumsy movement, trespassing, and misery.

Even at the moment before his murder Paul is hamming it up in Jeanne's father's uniform, a uniform that, no surprise, seems to fit every white person who wears it, including Jeanne. By then Paul is desperate to keep her near him, and all he has is the bounty of his capacity to improvise whatever genre will do the work: he is sweet and comic, and also drunk. Throughout the entire final scene he chews the gum like a clown or a wiseguy, too, as though commenting on Brando's history as a method actor who can tap into all of the roles he's played to squeeze out authentic emotion in the present that's unfolding (figure 1.5). It is also as though Paul is at once being casual about his need and generating the energy to help them both remain dedicated to the Cavellian project of comic love, which is not to be a certain way but to be generous toward the ordinary awkwardness of incompetence at intimacy and not a tragic failure.[57] They do not want to fail, yet no language exists for what else they want: both lovers end the film moving their mouths with unintelligible sounds coming out, as though incapable of generating sense in the face of the loss of the pop-up world they have generated. And yet they have made sense. Sex opens up the rhythm called conversation, with its generative capacity to interrogate all the moods and make genres for them. The film's other prospect for this, in le mariage pop, ends stuck in a similar ellipsis. All of this potential to be taught by the nonsense of sense and the sense of nonsense is lost when they fall to pieces from their incapacity to find a genre that will sustain them as subjects of their own incoherence.

Like many people during the '60s and since, Foucault disparaged the sexual revolution for its traditionalism and implication in racist biopolitics. He argued that as soon as sex was put into play for world-building it became "sexuality," a resource for making normative and nonnormative forms of life. In this view, then, sex is never merely sex but material for procedures that disturb and organize the controlling and self-cultivating disciplines of sociality. Sex might induce the nonnormative, but that is different than the antinormative, for in Foucault's view we cannot simply transgress what's fundamentally labile and processual, nor can we replace it simply with a better thing. Foucault's *History of Sexuality* ends with a crescendo on this very topic: that we will look back with embarrassment on the time when we thought derepressed libidinal energies could shake up structures, induce freedom, and allow for justice. His claim wasn't that sex didn't need transformation. It was that sex couldn't be freed from making life by being freed for making

1.5 *Last Tango in Paris*, directed by Bernardo Bertolucci, 1972.

a different life, because it was never repressed, always managed. And so the political question he demanded was, Who will manage it, and what will we ask of it, and would it be possible to think about it not just as romance or appetite but as material for new forms of life?

It is not hard to see *Last Tango in Paris* as a participant in the Foucauldian critique. *Tango* shows that seeking out a plane of consistency and ethics for what cannot be correct in advance is also a stupefying illusion, an aspiration to a performative numbness, as demonstrated in Jeanne's final rehearsal for her speech to the police: "I don't know who he is . . . He followed me on the street. He tried to rape me. He's a madman. I don't know his name. I don't know his name. I don't know who he is. . . ."

But what we have seen in this analysis is that alongside the life-and-death event there is an ordinary life made from piles of gesture and episode involving moods and the genre slides they provoke, where people in the middle of a situation are punctured by others' aggression and inflated or controlled by their desire, but also look unsure, uncanny, unlike themselves, unappealing, irresistible, comfortingly predictable, shockingly good and bad, and also boring. One does not have to die or be killed by this variation, and neither do one's radical political dreams. Structural inequality is also expressed and reproduced in this situation, shaping subjects who mistake it for the Real. It is therefore a place where sexual optimism can build genre muscles for the possibility of elaborating one's own and the world's revolutionary resistance to projects of fake coherence, whether antibourgeois, radically pop, or otherwise.

Tango is constantly training us to do this, shifting within the intense hermeticism of the couple fighting, fucking, protesting, pushing, assaulting, and improvising its way through episodes of being inconvenient, interested, attached to each other, and cruel, whether toward offering a project of worlding or just getting through the moment. There is not a flat equivalence among violences or pleasures, but realism about the untimeliness of metabolizing shocks in the middle of intimacy's ordinary.

It turns out that, in life, improvisation isn't within genre but induces genre as a conventional resting place for use when making it all up gets too tough, too exhausting. What happens in sex, therefore, is not just a figure for the social at its best and worst extremes, but a training in how simply hard it is to be in the room with another person, even someone you want there: because it is hard to show up fully to sociality in general, and once there, to maintain an openness toward the objects about which one feels aggressive, has variable confidence, few skills, and little trust that the world will be patient for your self-inconstancy. It is toward building skills for recognizing, explaining, and finding temporary housing for the discomfort of these inconvenient genres of the intimate that this chapter is written. It is toward better assessing the intense proximity of the soul-breaking trauma evidenced in rape to the ongoing disturbances of relation induced by sex and the joke that it also proposes attention.

Coda

A chapter built on one case can do only so much. My aim was to see how a revolutionary moment that looked toward the end of a linked regime of sexually patriarchally heteronormative, bourgeois, and Euro-nationalist privilege evoked the possibility of a new kind of happiness based not on property values and their absorption of the world into nationalist narrative, but on ambivalent scenarios where sex gave its subjects a way to experiment, to try out a range of pleasures and potential norms without being defeated by their unpredicted, weird, and out-of-control effects and variation. It didn't work out too well for anyone in the plot of the film, needless to say. The inconvenience of other people turned into a disaster. But the conceptual drive to place fierce political desire near the screwball comedy in the revolutionary project of '68 and beyond points to the power of trying out forms of life that can be at once decompositional and productive.

John Forrester argues that a case is what we move with when we are proceeding without a theory; it forces us to bring everything we know to the table, to call that material an archive, and to induce a conversation from which can be derived, in a while, more general principles.[58] Sex is a hard case to work with when we use it to ask questions about the infrastructures of social reproduction at the grandest scale. In early drafts of this chapter, it was tempting to make false equivalences among the intensities of unlearning toxic comforts through rhetorics of revolutionary sex and undeniably negative sexual experiments, with x good and y bad kinds neutralizing and overcoming each other. But I believe now that this chapter has something to offer by way of interrupting the impasse between the affirmative and the aggressive view of sex, one that does not minimize or negate the prospects of happiness or violence. It has something related to offer the imaginary of revolution that deals with social antagonism at different scales and in different contexts.

To be sure, the world is broken and breaks people in it. This is the a priori of nonsovereignty, the affective scene of proximity to the inconvenient. But it doesn't follow that substantial social transformation toward a world that puts us on a more thriving footing in relation fixes what's broken. A radical political disturbance, rather than repairing the broken world, rebreaks it on the way. The inconvenience of staying in a rebroken social scene requires its own transformational infrastructures, which is to say, its own defenses against giving up in the face of overintensity and disorganization at the level of ordinary encounters, social imaginaries, and institutions of intimacy. Only in this way can revolutionary projects be cared for and extended. In this chapter the routing of violence and desire into world-shifting strategies produces many styles of staying in the scene of attachment to change while changing how one can remain in that scene. Sex hinges the broken and the disturbed for and against the better world.

Here are another two brief case studies, extending the case for not separating the sexual from the world-changing political.

HAPPINESS (1998)

All of Todd Solondz's films are fairy tales, thought experiments in an alter-realism about the relation of sexuality and identity that presumes a public sex culture, imaginable in the wake of *Tango*, that overorganizes and disorganizes sexual desire and the forms of life that grow from it, but sexuality in his films barely encounters the explicitly political. His works collapse satire about the ordinary of intimate violence and cruelty onto tenderness about the ways people are stuck: they're humanist. Despite a queer relation to the grotesque and camp cartoonishness of anyone in desire, the works maintain enthusiasm for those who continue to show up for life given the austerity of their resources. He allows them to be weirdly self-accepting, even in their violence and cruelty. Solondz's oeuvre is so distinguished by the humorlessness of its comedy. It is marked by an intensity of irony and interest in the persistence of sincerity as a form of grace and aggression, and by its hyper-focus on the hovering presence of ridiculous sexual and affective optimism by people who are also stupefied in the face of it.

In *Happiness* there is a family. There are two parents, Mona (Louise Lasser) and Lenny Jordan (Ben Gazarra). Mona and Lenny seem Jewish, but their kids, not so much. They have three daughters: Helen (Lara Flynn Boyle), the trauma poet; Joy (Jane Adams), the pallid folk-guitarist; and Trish, the housewife (Cynthia Stevenson) who, in her own words, "has it all." They are ruled by habits, norms, and clichés. The second-generation figures are drained effigies from the feminist imaginary, making claims on self-fulfillment and better worlds but remaining attached to encountering the world without risk—which means, of course, that loss is all around. They are also humorless, and the joke of desire is squarely on them. Trish is married to a pedophile who rapes (Dylan Baker). Joy is attracted to men who brutalize and write romantic love songs about longing, including the film's title song, "Happiness." Helen, the poet, has rape fantasies. "If only I'd been raped as a child I'd know authenticity," she says, just before seeking an assignation with the obscene caller (Philip Seymour Hoffman) who excites her on the phone but repels her in person; later she sets up a blind date between this very predator and her sister Joy. "Where there's life, there's hope," Joy says cluelessly, and all the women in the family clink glasses to it, because at this point in history and life all that remain are clichés to keep them bound to optimism.

A cliché is a performance of optimism about truth: that there is truth, that it can be efficiently captured in phrases, and that it will not be too disturbing.[59] The film culminates this attachment to optimism in the empty formalism of its double happy ending. First, all of the women in the broken family attest to being on the lookout for more coupling. This distinguishes them from the suicidal father who loads salt on his food against his doctor's wishes, trying to hasten his death after a sexual experience with a new partner was "successful" but felt like nothing.

Meanwhile, Billy, the twelve-year-old namesake of the now-jailed serial rapist, is masturbating on the balcony of the condo as a huge-breasted blonde woman a few floors below slathers suntan oil all over her bikini-clad body. Billy has spent the film transitioning into adolescence, worrying about his penis size and whether he will ever come. His psychiatrist-pedophile father was warm and unshaming when the child approached him with his fears, and he acts appropriately and honestly toward his son until, debatably, their final scene.[60] But Billy only ejaculates when the buxom woman turns over and he sees her ass: he has some of the same sexual preferences as his father.

Ironically, or something, the child comes on the balcony rail, the same kind on which Brando left his gum to force Jeanne to inherit not only the burden of his death but the remains of his playfulness. Next, the child's dog comes up and licks the cum heartily and then, even more outrageously, the dog trots over to the child's mother, who kisses the dog on the mouth. Billy appears at the brunch table of his assembled family to announce his sexual victory: "I came." This closing line makes the film a comedy. The final shot looks at him as though from the dining room table. We don't get a reaction shot; the audience is left holding the news. This film is Solondz's version of the screwball: the persistence of the appetites in violence and foolishness, the hunger for contact and ecstasy, the inevitable disturbance by another live person, a cluelessness about how we find our objects, what we can do with them, and whether we can maintain a relation to them, let alone to ourselves with them. —

In Solondz's work, characters assault each other to stay near their desires, and at the same time they insist on their tenderness. Like many people, they seem to have no idea why their sexuality takes the form it does, and they just want relief from the pressure of it. They risk the modes of life that are the only modes of life they can imagine living, and they are completely apolitical about it. Omnivorous eating, murdering, raping, coming—these actions don't tell where the sickness comes from. Thus, we can have only mixed feelings about the child's happiness, because it comes from his ha-penis. Distributed across the banality of beauty and niceness, Solondz's world is an effect of the sexual revolution completely emptied of critical ideas about sex, family, or world.

HALF NELSON (2006)

In the final scene of the film Half Nelson, a white man around thirty years old sits on one side of a beige couch in a spare, worn apartment; on the other end of the couch is a young Black girl of about thirteen. The camera is pulled back to middle distance. There's an intimacy in their distance, alienation too.

The man, David Dunne (Ryan Gosling), used to be the girl's Marxist history teacher, but he is indeed done with that because of an unprosecuted sexual assault he committed on another teacher while under the influence of crack. Throughout the film both the teacher and the student are living inside of an urban drug economy. Early in the film the girl, Drey (Shareeka Epps), finds Dunne in a crack-induced collapse on the bathroom floor of the school gym where he had just coached her basketball team; later, he tries to keep her from becoming a courier for the same man from whom he buys his crack. Both characters are always too late to rescue or be rescued. Both characters are wedged into a riven social space—Broken Social Scene, actually, provides the film's soundtrack. But if prevention is out of the question, so, additionally, is repair. In this film there is no such thing as a causal trauma to be overcome. There are life situations. There are episodes. What remains for the characters is mutual care, to help each other lighten the load of consequences and to interrupt the next phase of exposure to a life whose pressures are structural as well as personal. Whatever it is between them, it isn't love: it's the gift and luck of getting each other's affective complexities and bearing them protectively.

Their differences in age, race, and cultural capital are explicit but unstated between them, but as for gender, a suspicion circulates through the film that the attachment is sexual. This attachment is from Drey's end, but it's the man who bears the cloud of suspicion. Drey is trying to figure out how to be expressive without losing her defenses. She wants to be in relation, to be a kid with a bike who is sucking lollipops that do not signify drug dealing and crack dry mouth. She wants to activate sexual difference, too, but not the kind that produces stress and abjection: she plays in solitude, with mirrors and makeup.

But their mutual thematics come from politics. As a Marxist history teacher trying to teach his kids about dialectics, Dunn teaches US civil rights history as the vivid struggle between opposing structural forces. He is also writing and drawing a children's book dramatizing the events, but he's stuck on it. It's as though if he can tell the external political story he will be able to fix something internal as well: it's addiction versus intention aimed toward overcoming the self. The film is more confident about the invigorating effects of knowing that the course of history was once changed by radicals than it is about what needs to go on inside in order for brokenness to be overcome. But it also offers the idea that one cannot ask one genre of question without the other.

Half Nelson is saturated by the white supremacist sentimental history of the race melodrama: here, predictably, the writers give the white guy a last name, while the young black woman has just a first. So it's not staging any version of equality here. Instead, it is trying to imagine reciprocity: in a headlock by their good and bad angels, as the wrestling-related title suggests, they share a structure of disturbed conscience and blocked redemption. At the same time, this film is not a melodrama, either—not in its moral shape or its execution of the relation of intensity to emotional situation. Both characters are defined by a recessive style of acting. There is no easy way to distinguish their openness from their closedness, their self-possession and dispossession, or their toughness and their tenderness. But even given that likeness, their attunement is intermittent, see-sawing. As it is about protagonists who don't know themselves fully, *Half Nelson* has to be a film more about showing up and demonstrating active care than about being known from motive to motion.

At a certain point in the middle of the film the two trade uncomfortable questions about personal life that neither can answer free of shame. There's silence and the specter of relational defeat. But the gaps work and allow for some breathing space. Dunne teaches Drey about the Free Speech

Movement and historical turning points. And she teaches him that women are seduced by jokes, by the comedic.

DREY: See what you need is some jokes. Women love jokes . . .

What do you call cheese that's not yours?

Nacho cheese! . . .

It's yours if you need it.

The bad joke idea leads Dunne to a good seduction of a colleague. But the teacher is too addicted to stay cleaned up and is asked to leave the school. As the film closes, he has completely bottomed out, and Drey pulls him out of a classically disheveled, smoky hotel room to which she's delivered drugs. Their encounter is tense and awkward. It leads to the final scene on the couch that is not a therapy couch, as they attempt to stay in relation without referring to heavy things. He breaks the ice of wordlessness by telling a joke.

DUNNE: Knock knock!

DREY: Who's there?

DUNNE: The interrupting cow.

DREY: The interrupting cow who?

DUNNE: Moo.

DREY [laughing]: That was horrible.

DUNNE [grimacing]: Yeah.

End of film. The scene is shot intimately, with the camera pulling in toward the cocked heads, two people relaxing into their old banter, as in a comedy of remarriage. The joke substitutes for whatever real they could say, but it's a real exchange in its own way because they're reaching back into history and pulling out an alternative trajectory. She's getting what she needs, to feel chosen by her expertise in the joke; he's demonstrating what he's only half-believed, that the teacher is teachable. The joke is also that he messes up the joke, which he's heard earlier in the film from another woman. Comedy is tragedy plus timing, it's been said.[61] Dunne is out of sync. In that knock-knock joke the interrupting cow is supposed to say "moo" while she's saying, "The interrupting cow who?" but he neglects to interrupt, to be inconvenient. They have a good laugh because a knock-knock joke is a parody of consent. The person who answers the door of the joke always consents to the verbal pratfall to come, even if they know better, because they're curious. They're interpellated into manners, into showing up for the encounter.[62] The two have a good laugh because his timing, like all timing, is off. The unsayable magic of the affective infrastructure between them makes that OK. The low-bar demand to show up for the joke makes that OK. It's a form of social generosity. So if history is the study of change over time, one might say that comedy is the study of changes in timing, and that's something they can work on, no joke.

These films demonstrate some of the contemporary complexity of putting sex comedy and sex violence in the same scenario that involves the disruptions of capital and citizenship. The copresence of comedy and violence is revelatory about why it's hard to sustain fidelity to the very transformations that might find form, systematicity, and revitalized structures when people wriggle out of the norm, redistorting it. The problem is at once scalar and subjective, but it is also about the devastating effects of an impasse between the perspective of the political and the perspective of the sexual. Each film operates logics for managing ambivalence about the forms of life and fantasy that are available at their historical condisjuncture. Each has its way of making messes and cleaning them up without dispensing with the problems of having and not having the forms of life and intimacy you want, but not entirely. This chapter sits in the mess their impasse makes, for it is only from here, in the zone of multiple wrecked defenses, that "new relational modes" are made.[63] If only new relational modes could be freely, unambivalently chosen, let alone imagined. But the incorporation of new forms is the disorganization of others. At the same time, there is no choice but to use the structural productivity of ambivalence in order to make better forms of life, which is one of the reasons that sex violence and sex comedy have become so enmeshed—the other one being a desperation not to be defeated by the disorganized affects and effects of a demanding and ungiving world.

What if slapstick were understood to express the dominant affective mood of democracy and not comfort, peace, antagonism, or recognition? Would this help explain to our greater satisfaction the contemporary carnival of longing and aggression in proximity to the political, and increase our efficacy there? Would inhabiting this help us open better imaginaries for jolting the good life into being, beyond antidotes to the nonsovereign, like ownership and control? None of these questions is rhetorical; all of them are propositional. The case of sex in proximity to happiness demands an archival discipline around questions such as these, and more, and more, upsetting the politically stentorian ones that see the tragic as truth and the comic that is also there as ephemeral, ridiculous, subconceptual, mainly a weapon, and low, an unworthy resource for sustaining the event of the social. But revolutionary desire takes up the body, and so its theory must also take up even what's inconvenient about it.

This chapter is dedicated to José Esteban Muñoz, who kind of hated it when he heard it—"It's not my favorite of your papers . . ."—but liked it more when he read it, and who pushed me to sustain the motive of its initial vision, which was to address how the impossibility of distinguishing being known and unknown in attachment affects the shape of revolutionary thought. This drive toward what can't be known feeds the need to control safety and risk in world-making desire, and thus activates all kinds of defenses, experiments, and aggressions without neutralizing the drive to be inconvenienced by the world and by others. He allowed that these aims did not have to be imagined only beyond the lifeworld of the present, where they are being violently, adoringly, and awkwardly navigated, even though the utopian leap out of the mess into queer futurity, in gesture and thought, was his very favorite thing.

we are geometric problems
in the slots of loveliness
— SEAN BONNEY

two **THE COMMONS**

Infrastructures for Troubling Times

The previous chapter explored the inconvenience drive that produces the adrenaline of an intimate attachment that feels personal, whether or not it's among people who know each other personally. The pleasure and risk of being with a new relation comes from the desire to be exposed to the friction of collaborative life. Still, a degree of vulnerable openness increases during any encounter, whether it's brief or enduring, memorable or nondescript, or one that flashes and crashes on repeat.

To sit with this generative and degenerative potential, *Last Tango in Paris* turns to the couple form to stand in for a double image of the social: first, the specific couple as a laboratory for becoming different together through what the intimates perceive as their revolutionary strategies and ideas; second, the couple form as itself a figure for a social movement where individuals become transformed by working together to induce a sea change structurally. These models are not scalable into each other: as Spivak argues, there is a lack of fit between the personal and the structural standpoints from which the world is imagined and acted on.[1] So the question of revolution involves assessing the resonance among models of reciprocity. From either perspective, one cannot be sure in advance about the outcome of the social's extension into experiment, ideation, and trying things out.

This is why, during an encounter that vibrates, there is always an accompanying fear that inflames the defenses. *Tango*'s couples imagine that they embody revolutionary social registers in which people actively embrace their nonsovereignty and go for it—"it" being love and social change—"without guarantees."[2] But as they discover, it's not only that you can't guarantee consequences in advance. It's that you can't be certain how you'll feel about or be able to live on in the disturbance you created, that comes from the substantial challenge to subjectivity, reciprocity, and worlds that, in some sense, you desired. Conflict is inevitable, reciprocity is always negotiated, all objects remain enigmas, and ends do not usually provide a sufficient summary judgment of a project's value.

In any case, during the stretch of attachment-testing, people can only think they know what they want or what they don't want. They find out later that their desires were proposals. They find out later that trust is hard, jolted by the surprises of the unfolding situation. What was behind the leap into amplifying the mutual? Are they trying to lose a habit of being, unravel and restructure an unequal social field, or build something out of actively shared energy to feel more optimistic about the world? Are they trying to make things simpler by calling it love or justice? Are they up for surprising complications, and which ones? Does having gone through it before make you better or worse at adapting and refusing to adapt? Is the aspiration to reorganize what sociality can be limited to a moment, a movement, a room, a feeling, a scene, an institution, a figure, an atmosphere, a life, or a world? What if the politically or intimately allied are just throwing themselves into an imprecise transition because the other way was not unbearable but no longer to be borne?

All attachment opens defenses against the receptivity one also wants to cultivate, in short. A whole world can wobble when that openness ignites insecurity about how to live otherwise. Such is the uncertainty that accompanies the inconvenience drive. Such is the ambivalence especially directed toward revolutionary movements that hit internal and external limits. For the past half-century, the "sixties" have taken a lot of the heat for false promises and disturbances of the conventional world by student movements, Black power movements, queer and feminist liberation movements, and the anticolonial struggles that upset the standing of the nation form. Many people and classes remain attached to, furiously resistant to, and emotionally all over the place toward freedom imaginaries and the effects of these counterpower movements and demands.

Unsurprisingly, then, in the memory of the popular culture of Europe and the United States, the explicitly political contexts of *Tango* lose out. The film is reduced to its scandalously rotten sexual encounters and failed love stories. Anchored in the couple during a time of global and European revolution, the embodied and phantasmatic drive toward an alternative world somehow comes to begin and end between individuals, seeming merely personal even as the protagonists fetishize military uniforms, perform thoughtless racism, and take up legacy positions within the hierarchies of imperial and colonial life. Like many bourgeois who think life should be smooth, they end up asking the police to protect them from themselves.

But if, in the end, the logic of vertical, traditional power wins and clots what else was imaginable politically, in the long middle's moments of radical unlearning, things got pedagogical. Those of us who attend to the film's narration of Jeanne's styling of le mariage pop and Paul's will to induce an anti-imperialist, anti-Catholic, antinational, and antibourgeois upheaval at the granular level can tell a different story: that the personal here is both where structural and sensually endemic violence materialize and always a potential conversion space for not reproducing capitalist, imperial, racist, and patriarchal lines of descent. Here's the thing: that the both/and turned into the neither/nor does not mean it was a bad idea to try.

In this chapter the commons concept is akin to the long middle of *Tango*. It denotes an experimental scene of practical life and "affirmative speculation."[3] But the focus is impersonal because it is about what the world generates for the beings in it and is not generated by them. The common is not on offer here as the solution to the problem of psychic or structural social antagonism, nor as a visionary motive for toppling the state and capital, nor as a synonym for belonging better and social healing. If anything, the chapter holds in suspicion the prestige that the commons concept has attained in the United States and the theory-cosmopolitan context. One might think of the encampments of Occupy or of assertions like the knowledge commons or the affective commons, as though the genre is a fact about the relation among things and not propositional or worked out in real time, as genuine equality must be.

Take as counter-exempla two figures, beginning with Thomas Hawk's narrative image of the Detroit Public Schools' abandoned book depository (figure 2.1). Any library or depository is a public resource of sorts, but a public is not a common: institutions narrow access to what circulates through the patronage norms of philanthropy, the ownership norms of most publishing institutions, and the obligations of the membership card. If you saw this image in color you'd witness so much dead analogizing between the "priceless" value of knowledge in the book depository and the beauty of the building: now all of it in negative, through the abandonment of a space's upkeep demands, and the image of use as the destruction of resources. Carnegie's aesthetic pride in the glorious interior décor shines: copper, gold leaf, marble, and so on. For all the signification of pricelessness, however, the Public Schools' holdings create material and abstract scenes of crime for which one can be arrested—from knowledge theft to the building itself, which has been so abandoned that what's valuable to the public now are not the collections of books but the sought-after metals that can be stripped from the infrastructure and converted quickly to scavenged cash. Property, theft: the "public" commons is a mangled fantasy.

Think also with Stephanie Brooks's insertion of police tape into the zoned-public space of cultivated nature (figure 2.2). In her performance series called *Lovely Caution*, the camera goes around enclosing open spaces. Her spaces force the common into view as a distraction, a pastoral episode, a whiff of the unreal that is also just what there is. What is the "lovely" that blots out the "caution" usually printed there on the yellow plastic? Can we

2.1 Thomas Hawk, *Detroit Public Schools Book Depository, June 13, 2010.* Color photograph.

2.2 Stephanie Brooks, *Lovely Caution*, 2010. Color photograph. Printed with permission of Stephanie Brooks.

see a park now without the shadow of white hatred of genuine publicness and the police standing ready to rescue from it?

To Brooks, lovely is a quality, the common sense of the beautiful. It performs the conversion of a nonspace to a form realized in the common atmosphere, in the power of a caption to shift what it captures: a nonspace that is perfect because it's there to be witnessed, fenced off, and not ruined by habitation, by other people. No people exist in either the nonspace or the fenced off, captioned commons: they are inconvenient to the concept, and also to the problem the concept tries to solve. It's an idea whose material basis is the urgency that generates it. Private property, even as figure, is a policed space. At the same time, enclosure itself is a figure of a different kind of crime. Not of trespassing but of property as theft, of citizenship as a holding cell with unpredictable openings: a lenticular space.

Police surveillance is already within us, our conscience and our doing. As the title *Lovely Caution* suggests, at this point in time yellow tape needs no caption; it's become performative, a truth held in common, that all lovely spaces remain lovely when they seem open for the kind of business that asks people to honor the common spirit of the common. It turns out that this trust has no object to sustain it, that any place in ordinary life might convert in a snap to an event in which something alive or held close to life has been massively transgressed.

The main point here is that when the commons comes into representation, it cannot not represent the inconvenience of other people, even when the representation turns its eyes away toward something beautiful in an enclosure. It also can't turn its eyes away from the struggle against the law and other networks of congealed power that can both make you crazy and want anarchism to organize the transitional space; I learned to think the formal use of the commons as such a political tool while reading with the love and anarchist ferocity of Sean Bonney's The Commons and The Commons II, which radically take up, document, and shreddingly counter-hate the ongoing destruction of life by the hegemons' insistence that their rebarbative chaos is an achieved order on behalf of the good. There, and here, the commons concept serves as a preserve for an optimistic attachment to recaptioning the potential for collective nonsovereignty and as a register for the gatekeeping and surveillance that organizes still so many collective pleasures.[4]

So, if the commons claim sounds like an incontestably positive aim, I think of it more as a tool, and often a weapon, for unlearning the world, which is key to not reproducing it.[5] The commons concept in the contemporary context threatens to cover over the inevitable complexity of social jockeying, belonging, and perspectival conflict it mobilizes by delivering a confirming affective experience of a smoother lifeworld that derives from a pastoral past or present. In the United States and some global contexts, the more recent hope was that a democratic proceduralism would flatten the frictional encounter of different interests.

It's understandable to desire collective attunement or attachment that has been emptied of the dynamic of possession and dispossession that saturates property relations and the forms of desire that it cultivates. With theorists like Silvia Federici, I argue that the attachment to the common is too often a way of talking about politics as a means of resolution more than as a path through struggle. It too often stands as an aspiration to consensus that tries to make affectively simple the nonsovereign relation that is at the heart of true equality, where status is not worked out in advance but in real time.[6] I understand that many indigenous struggles claim sovereignty as a fact and aspiration against the genocidal incursions of settler colonial states. As I argue in the introduction, my view is that sovereignty is at root a defense against occupation or dispossession, which is why it's become central to antagonisms about jurisdiction, and not anything like a natural right or natural state.

In this chapter I propose an alternative use of the commons object insofar as it has become something of a false performative. I use materials mainly from the United States, and from some white people's desire to create a commons free of the common. Although it's implicit in their work, I am arguing that they use the commons concept to dissolve their world from under their feet. The chapter closes by addressing contemporary crises of the "we" associated with orchestrated resistance to anti-Black state violence and communities of care that have been mobilized to keep life going medically, economically, and emotionally during the COVID-19 pandemic. It thinks constant transition not just as a fact but as the effect of the inconvenience drive: a life texture involving loss, contingent mutuality, and a desire to mobilize the resources of tradition and the work of having each other's backs. It functions not just as a care common filling a general need, but a zone of attention in which heterotopic forms of life might build out.

It looks to Muñoz's and Harney and Moten's undercommons of queer, Black, and Brown study and prefigurative solidarity, but not as a solution to the devastating faults and blows of the Euro-white idealist tradition. Instead it moves with the situation they describe to ask visceral questions about how the common as an idea of infrastructure has provided for settler colonial subjects both mystifications of freedom and a pedagogy for unraveling the corrupted world, while at the same time offering affective scenes and methods of living regeneratively and revolutionarily. It shows how some thinkers use the commons concept to move away from good-life fantasies that equate frictionlessness with justice and satisfaction with the absence of frustration. Broken analogies and live infrastructures are offered as transitional mechanics for dissolving the world from within the world. As with the previous chapter, it also asks how a bodily practice can provide "glitchfrastructures" for inculcating unlearning.

Second Introduction: The Common Sense

This desire for the public to be a free, indeterminate space is embedded in the history of the common. We are tracking here uses of the commons concept to break the consensual historical present, not restore a collective's sense of sovereign right. What follows rehearses types of the commons and the affect called the sensus communis. It tracks their status as a placeholder for the scene and fulfillment of belonging; it recasts the imaginary infrastructure of the public commons in a pedagogy for unlearning normative realism and rethinking structure as something in constant transition. It closes by addressing contemporary crises of the "we." It thinks constant transition not just as a fact but as a life texture involving loss, smudging, contingent mutuality, and literally having each other's backs, among other things.

The recently "resuscitated" fantasy of the common articulates many desires for a social world that is unbound by structural antagonism.[7] "'Common' has a multitude of meanings," writes Peter Linebaugh, "common land, common rights, common people, common sense."[8] The concept is so overloaded you might think that it's empty, but you'd be wrong. *The common* usually refers to an orientation toward life and value unbound by concepts of property as constituted by division and ownership. It reframes *public* as something generally accessible for use. It also points to the world both as a finite resource that is easily depleted and spoiled and, in addition, as an inexhaustible fund of human consciousness or creativity.[9] At the same time, at the moment of this writing, the proclamation of "the common," what it works to manifest, is always political and invested in being inconvenient to the reproduction of power, with aspirations to decolonize actual social and economic spaces that have been weaponized by empire, capitalism, and power over land rights.

This means that the commons is incoherent, like all powerful concepts. Under its name, across the globe, communities tap into legacies of occupation to contest normative jurisdictional ownership rights and resource justice, and under its name, people often project a pastoral social relation of mutual attachment, dependence, or vitality. Concepts of the common attached to "the common sense" also point to irreducibly different affective angles: from the most normative view of how things are to the Kantian sensus communis. For Roland Barthes and Ann Laura Stoler, "common sense" is merely the bourgeois order of truth standing in for the universal, what Stoler calls "a folk epistemology."[10] For Raymond Williams, it is a "structure of feeling," which locates affective mutuality in the atmosphere of the common historical experience of class antagonism.[11] In contrast, for Kant and Arendt the sensus communis involves nothing so referentially specific as the capitalist good life.[12] It refers instead to a sense of judgment about an intersubjective experience that is common above and beyond visceral responses to the material world and other people; the "sense" in this tradition of common sense is exercised in the capacity of humans to achieve the free movement of their faculties toward disinterested, impersonal, nonrepresentational, and yet "universally communicable" judgment on the model of an aesthetic attunement to something like beauty.[13]

Steven Shaviro argues that the Kantian concept of beauty or attunement looks not to any normative sense of symmetry or elegance as a ground for principles like justice or freedom: attunement is a perceptual event that bypasses cognition and hits the subject the way a song does, as a singular perception all at once that is, at the same time, universal.[14]

This is to say that, in all of its traditions, the sensus communis is deemed to be a higher gut feeling, if you will. It involves the recognition of normative or universal principles of being; it organizes a potential world around them; it moves the body away from satisfaction with the horizon of conventional experience toward a visceral self-experience of freedom that ought to govern the activity of all being in common.

So, too, the universal appears in political fantasies of the common that structure much contemporary political theory and action: as Žižek summarizes it, it involves protecting "the shared substance of our social being whose privatization is a violent act which should also be resisted with violent means."[15] To clarify, three kinds of vulnerable referent tend to motivate this urgent vision of the commons: (1) the struggles of disenfranchised citizens and migrants, whether in the undercommons or in contested indigenous habitations; (2) the substance of immaterial labor that taps into and depletes the world- and life-making activity of humans and by analogy all species;[16] (3) the being of nature as such, which includes but does not prioritize humanity. Adding to this collection of defensive and generative associations is a fourth kind: the depressive uniformity Paolo Virno imagines, associating the contemporary commons with an actual, immanent, and already affectively felt global homelessness.[17] The apriority he names as the sensus communis isn't just a sense but a specific feeling of being affected: the condition of displacement.

In the early 2000s, these senses of the sense of the common helped to shape a politics of precarity in the global Occupy and the ongoing European, Latin American, and South Asian anti-austerity and counternational movements, which ask various questions: Should society be organized to expand wealth or to support life, and not just human life? How do we think about the redistribution of resource vulnerability in relation to the distribution of rest, strength, and enjoyment? What roles should political institutions have in fomenting collective life, or do we need a different structural imaginary to organize the figurative and material political complexities of stranger intimacy and interdependence? What's the relation between structural violence and that which is physical and emotional, and how do we keep more disciplined protocols of control from masking the endurance of legitimated force? In 2020, as we shall see, these questions of resource and publicness, of ideologies of protection, exposure, and care, reignited into some tangled social debates about how to deal with the inconvenience of other people facing anew dissolving and looming infrastructures of life and death.

You will no doubt note the unbalanced load of desire that the commons claim now carries. These perspectives mark a new phase of a serious collective rethinking of what, if anything, attention to the commons can contribute to producing alternatives to the wreck of the persistent good-life fantasy that "we are all in it together."[18] More on this phrase at this chapter's close.

Commons talk, like precarity talk and austerity talk, in other words, tries to develop a generative counterformalism within and against national capitalism. In contrast, the commons projects of fugitive utopian performance associated with José Esteban Muñoz and the cowriters Stefano Harney and Fred Moten extend this problematic not only from the position of universal singularity, citizenship, common sense, or a like injury within a scene of violence, but also toward temporally different understandings of collective belonging and plural being in the historical present. How to develop, from a violently unequal historical inheritance and institutional experience to this very moment, a space where the collectivity-so-far can be extended and developed enough to change the referent of the world?

Harney and Moten's undercommons is what Marc Augé would call a nonplace, which is to say a space of time where the subjects of history en masse do not line up with themselves as individuals: it's lenticular, and in the gaps between who you were and what the space releases you from, you're a fugitive.[19] Just as you don't eat the same food in the airport, on vacation, in the hospital, or spontaneously because you're not the ordinary cruising you you've developed, in the undercommons the condemned can figure out another way to make collective space through movement. To be in those difficult and loving timespaces at one time requires using a strong tactic of aesthetic scenicness in order to extend Black study beyond social reproduction or correction; this undercommons mobilizes the material and speculative senses already pulsating in lifeworld solidarities beyond the space of faithfulness that the university or any dominant institution of social order delegates to its members as conscience, vocation, and managerial accountability, and tweaks of reform.[20]

For Muñoz the scenic aesthetic is similar but oriented more toward the future in the present rather than, as in Harney and Moten, the being-present from which a mutually attentive and caring heterotopic space-practice can come. The surplus of Muñoz's "brown commons" begins in an already realized affective commons that confirms the good life for a minoritized belonging in a way that gives a taste of what's possible at the scale of lifeworld confidence for a concrete, yet indefinite, common "we."[21] "We" is an orientation, an attitude. It is a name for critical queer of color and punk negativity that turns getting negated into acts and attitudes that move the future around. Muñoz writes: "I contend that the clinamen, or the swerve at the heart of the encounter, describes the social choreography of a potentially insurrectionist mode of being in the world."[22] Choreography isn't in lockstep but attends to dynamics. The encounter as the place where the flint hits steel makes love and potential insurrection. Muñoz thinks with Jean-Luc Nancy's image of the touch that preserves the specificity of the Other in the register of a common form that's apprehensible but not representable except as a sense. A sensus communis from which an undefensive infrastructure can extend. A commons that begins with being-with.

The commons concept here is reparative against the world's destruction of the life whose labor sustains it, the exploited and negated humans who deserve a future that can only be found in organizing the courage to be more interested in than threatened by the commonality of difference. How does one stay attached to life given the constitutive experience of nonbeing or negative social value? The inconvenience of other people in the good sense is the ground on which the brown commons generates resources for a collective attachment to life.

This chapter comes to the form of the common from another side. It argues that what's best in the commons concept is its capacity to retrain affective practical being, and in particular in its power to dehabituate response and displace certain normative continuities and conventions. Instead of redirecting what is, the "we" we already have, it looks toward dissolving some institutional grounds that establish our continuity. It's not annihilative, as it involves care for the world and for beings whose conditions of flourishing are exploited and stolen, but its potential focus on specific undoings loosens up, disrupts, and reshapes registers and planes of existence. This chapter's cases focus on unlearning the overskilled sensorium that is so quick to adapt to damaged life with a straight, and not a queer, face.

In other words, in contrast to the universalizing yet concrete affective abstraction of the Kantian or the insider/outsider sensus communis, this chapter's political version of the common requires a transformed understanding of the shared sense not energized by the shared world of a traumatic history, nor an achievement on which to build. It is something other than a rage for the reproduction of an already cultivated sense of likeness. This chapter's common is as an action concept that acknowledges a broken world and the desperate need for a transformational infrastructure. It begins a compendium of getting out. It uses the spaces of alterity within ambivalence to regenerate what can be done with the inconvenience of relationality.

This includes the pleasures of estrangement itself. Stanley Cavell comments on "Wittgenstein perceiving our craving to escape our commonness with others, even when we recognize the commonness of the craving; Heidegger perceiving our pull to remain absorbed in the common, perhaps in the very way we push to escape it."[23] Many philosophical traditions in relation to the ordinary converge in Cavell's thought: what's important here is that the movement to be together better demands confidence in an apartness that recognizes the ordinary as a space at once actively null, delightfully animated, stressful, intimate, alien, and uncanny.[24] Rei Terada makes even a stronger claim about aversion to the given world, arguing that some thinkers respond to the "endemic normative pressure on thoughts and feelings" by turning away toward a relief in abstraction or dissatisfaction that she calls a kind of queer phenomenophilia.[25] With these thinkers, this chapter turns to the desire for displacement or separateness from the inconvenience of other people, from the overpresence of the world, which is not the same thing as not loving or wanting the felt relation as such.[26]

Crossing Boston Common: Or, Emerson's Worm

Boston Common exemplifies the nonexistence of its own concept (figure 2.3). The oldest named common in the United States, it carries in its various monuments an American archive of racial and economic crimes against human flourishing along with the affective promise that, even within capitalism, public premises should exist on which to develop a sensorium for the sense of a common.

The vicious ironies of this fantasy have not gone unrecognized. In "For the Union Dead," for example, Robert Lowell presses his face against the black iron of the Boston Common gate, exiled from experiencing the freedom of relationality that any common holds out to a public, a respite against the world of property values and enclosure.[27]

During his childhood, he writes, there was an aquarium in Boston, now in the same looted and abandoned shape as the Detroit Public Schools' book depository: "Its broken windows are boarded. / The bronze weathervane cod has lost half its scales. / The airy tanks are dry." It used to be that young Lowell melded "like a snail" with the glass tank that separated him from the fish there, as if being in spatial sync enabled him to breathe in the air of the

2.3 Boston Common. Courtesy of Wikimedia Commons.

Other, "the bubbles, / drifting from the noses of the cowed, compliant fish." It was as though there was a common air despite the separation of species being and knowledge from tactile transmission. This low-bar national naturalism appears throughout commons talk, insisting that one has had to move through nature to return to a sense of a "we" that is bound together politically. The nostalgic "I" of Lowell's poem still sighs for the image of nature persisting and decaying in the same time and space as he was emerging, compared especially to the "yellow dinosaur steam shovels" of modernity "grunting."[28] He's intent on revealing the thinness not only of this so-called collectively held public surface, but of the ones scattered throughout the area, too, in "a thousand small-town New England greens" that celebrate the Revolutionary War. The "green" is an idea of the common without the utopian promise.

Meanwhile, in Boston proper, the city is building near the park a parking structure for passing occupants that embodies more of what white national capitalism offers: the rental of temporary space. This model is that of modern property, defining the fungible status as always fluctuating value. This is the model of US citizenship. Boston politics seeds the temporary and calls it "public" if that's where the funds come from. Looking around, the poem thus sees the whole system of belonging in shambles, the statehouse held together by scaffolding, monuments propped up by planks, the nearby grass providing no cushion.

In other words, it is not a fantasy of the affectionate body politic at leisure that keeps Lowell returning to the park space. Instead, he focuses on how belonging is given an aesthetic density in the space where the green provides a distraction or alibi for the ongoing, violent nationalist history also monumentalized there. "For the Union Dead" focuses on the Saint-Gaudens monument to General Robert Shaw's Massachusetts 54th Regiment, a white-ruled regiment otherwise composed entirely of Black soldiers that was decimated during the Civil War (figure 2.4). Most scholarship on the poem focuses on its monument to white sacrifice in the heroic body of Shaw, and the irredeemable American crime of using racial genocides to prop up the ideality of its national concept.[29]

This 1850s monument was planted there to honor that sacrifice, Lowell writes, but also to establish the very pastness of white supremacist violence. But the 1960s poem refuses the story of Northern racial blamelessness. Lowell's version of the Union fought over what forms of limited sovereignty capitalist democracy could bear: encountering a celebration of this low-bar settler imaginary is sickening. The Boston Common houses the performance of separateness, of apartheid and death. In General Shaw's claim that anyone

2.4 Augustus Saint-Gaudens, Robert Gould Shaw and 54th Massachusetts Volunteer Infantry Regiment Memorial, Boston Common. Photo by Rhododendrites, November 13, 2019. Reprinted from Wikimedia Commons under Creative Commons Attribution-Share Alike 4.0 International license.

might "choose life and die" for the nation, the monument tries to demonstrate the centrality of sacrifice to settler "democracy"; even the lost are the partial persons of the Constitution.[30]

The Common's monument in "For the Union Dead" triggers the poem's processing of Hiroshima too: that act of US imperial violence that had not at Lowell's writing, nor has yet, been monumentalized in the physical or imaginary collective common.[31] Hiroshima hangs in the poem as an event that is apparently not yet displaceable enough into the past that mourning's convenient screen memories obscure the racialized costs of liberal freedom. Outer "space is nearer."[32] No First Nations history is entered into the lyric record. This model of the common presents the New England lifeworld as a mass grave of many styles of complicity. It appears too much to pretend that all of US history and activity isn't a choking destruction hidden by a green screen of episodic and limited freedom.

In that sense, in the battle of antimodernity Lowell wages, and in his disrespect for civilization and its minor mystifying sites of refuge and relief,

Lowell's turn toward and against the common draws on the precedent of Emerson's "Nature," which also takes place famously on the Boston Common. There Emerson, too, struggles to both occupy and depart from complicity with the US American appetite for dispossession. But while Lowell uses the common against its historical function of distracting public attention from the ongoing violent flesh-effects of settler and imperial practice, in "Nature" Emerson adopts a materialist strategy for ridding the Common of what's become common. You could call this an anticapitalist rather than antiracist argument, but that would point to a collective politics that doesn't attract him in the present of the writing.[33]

For Emerson, choosing life in the common abandons the historical body: the sensual and politically saturated body, with its inculcated wants, is a false front, not a "natural fact." He also brackets the collective intellectual and political ballast of his own transcendentalist life in Boston, as well as anything that is an inheritance. Inheritance, in his view, blocks "an original relation to the universe": it interferes with the sovereign. Always the Spinozan, Emerson seeks the joyous increase of his powers,[34] and like his heirs Hardt and Negri, he looks to the inexhaustible activity of universal singularity, that part of being which cannot be generalized nor made normative, as a resource for remaking the world. But whereas in Hardt and Negri the "commonwealth" of singularities called "multitude" can organize itself in commons-like alternatives to national-capitalism, Emerson uses the singularity to generate a route out of the world entirely, toward life on an abstract plane. These two heterotopic styles are born from within conventional life but move away from it. Emerson moves through, then away from, the body; through, then away from, the natural object that offers to consciousness a revolutionized idea of spirit.[35] Opening up to receptivity is his sovereign act.

The aim of Emerson's method in "Nature," then, is not to reproduce or clean up the ongoing world, and it engineers a Boston Common that enables one to discover in oneself the sensus communis that is not tied to a representation. Breaking the environment that produces a false-positive common of national unity is not his main issue, as it was in Lowell's translation of the common into a national-political graveyard. Rather than providing a material for a social movement, Emerson sets out on a thought experiment that could provide perspectives that redeem the world. If "you conform your life to the pure idea in your mind" then beings and infrastructures in the world will be redeemed, and "disagreeable appearances, swine, spiders, snakes, pests, madhouses, prisons, enemies, vanish; they are temporary and shall be no more seen."[36] Prisons, enemies, the things of national grandiosity, are of the same scale as any other disagreeable things: only idealism can restore a true relation to the lifeworld.

Emerson concocts a multistage project to achieve this end. It begins with going to the Common not to be in common with others but quite the opposite, to push the noise of the world from his head. "To go into solitude, a man needs to retire as much from his chamber as from society. I am not solitary whilst I read and write, though nobody is with me. But if a man would be alone, let him look at the stars."[37] There is no solidarity here, no subtracted space from which he speculates a return to a populated utopia. But why would a man go to the Common to be alone? Why go to the public space of episodic democracy to subtract all that from it? The Common is a place he goes not to possess but to be possessed, to submit to being dispossessed of property in the self by the immediacy of a nature that is what it is, dissolving the attachment to sovereignty and base instrumentality. Typical men, with their gross materiality, false assurance, and confusion of capitalist wants with rationality, get in the way of the judgment of the universal common sense. Capitalist subjectivity is too clogged with "pseudo-activity" to acknowledge the vital relation among things.[38] The noise and flesh of other people are inconvenient. In shedding that he thinks he becomes more himself. He thinks he can show how anyone can molt being if they're willing to receive the idea of spirit rather than dominating what's in front of them.

Men in the flesh, here sensed as flesh, do not create relief from themselves or respect for the presence of the flesh, as in Lowell. As Lawrence Buell writes, Emerson never welcomes the appetites except when they are oriented away from worldly ambition.[39] Not surprisingly, it is said that on this very same Boston Common Emerson exhorted Walt Whitman to desexualize his poetry. Whitman, Emerson is said to have said, should write about man, not men; ideas and language, not bodies or anything bearing "mean egotism."[40] Or as "Nature" puts it, "The high and divine beauty which can be loved without effeminacy." Emerson has wrapped the Common in moral police tape. Perhaps, figuring himself on the Common as a "transparent eyeball," he wants to separate the receptive disturbances of desire from the penetrations of the spirit. In his version of unlearning the body in the world, the flesh can't become confusing.

A transparent eyeball mobilizes the senses as channels of the world's impact. Seeing subjects as fundamentally permeable to, rather than fundamentally possessive of, what they apprehend is a way of talking about affective knowledge: Marx calls this turning the senses into theorists.[41] Emerson uses these intensities to experience a mode of embodied abstraction that frees his spirit into a state neither personal nor impersonal: full of sensation, he becomes a "nothing." From that figural position one no longer confuses sovereignty for the form of appetitive nonsovereignty that treats the world as a cupboard of things to grab at and fetishize. One no longer confuses freedom with the merely formal and forensic status of the political subject, nor wants to possess the chosen intimate: "The name of the nearest friend sounds then foreign and accidental: to be brothers, to be acquaintances,—master or servant, is then a trifle and a disturbance" compared to "the perpetual presence of the sublime."[42] This self-dispossession does not feel like loss, therefore. The presence of the sublime tells us that to break the world and open access to the universal sense, we have to shatter how we know.

At first, achieving a reoriented sensorium comes in the form of a new habit: moving through, then away from, nature. Cavell amplifies Emerson's desire to destroy the fallen common on behalf of the sensus communis through a practice of reinventing natural analogy: "the analogy that marries Matter and Mind."[43] Mind, or the idea, releases the body from its feedback loop errors and allows the subject of the Boston Common not to imitate himself and call it freedom, but to practice a mode of world acknowledgment that does not calcify singularity in a representation. This means, counterintuitively, that the analogical marriage of matter and mind is not a matter of synthesis, mimesis, or the extension of likenesses. It involves seeing in analogy a chain of discontinuous continuity secured by movement at once destructive and generative.

Turning from men, Emerson would rather think about worms. The epigraph to "Nature," a poem by Emerson, reads,

> A subtle chain of countless rings
> The next unto the farthest brings;
> The eye reads omens where it goes,
> And speaks all languages the rose;
> And, striving to be man, the worm
> Mounts through all the spires of form.[44]

On offer here is a logic of proximity that looks like an infrastructure, but an infrastructure of association, unrepresentable except through figuration's intensity of displacement. The eye reads prophetically but without narrative assurance; rings on a chain resonate with nearness across extensive but not saturated space; the movement from eye to rose inters human perception in a wrenching enjambment and metaphorizes "speaks" beyond the limit of the sign. Then, the worm. The worm strives to be man simply because it is generating form, not because it shares anything like tradition or organs: only nonsubjective intention. This association is presumably a reciprocal one. To be free on this Common also requires gliding through the mud: an expression of materiality in continuous movement that's uninterrupted by possessive ego performance.

Branka Arsić claims that such a streaming movement is what Emerson means by "thinking": interrupting the ego distortions of "reflection" with dynamic projection "carve[s] out . . . paths on the earth-brain so that its vegetation starts growing."[45] This new configuration is linguistic in "Nature," structured by the rhizome of analogy that pushes out the conventional to make room for an original thought, figured in enjambment, lyric leaps, and evocative speaking.

To become worm, then, and so to renew becoming man, Emerson's man must take up a position as a formalist following out movements that become forms defined by direction, not their idealizing tableau. In this version form is not a thing to be rested in. The worm creates a space of movement that becomes form. If it is form it becomes social, that is, of the world; at this stage it is movement and singular. In the wormhole the worm creates an infrastructure to hold itself in the world: the hole fits the worm, but only as it moves. It reveals an ontological flatness of all matter, but more vitally such recognition induces movement into new proximities. This transduction of the natural symbol into a revelation of ontological resonance in movement through analogy makes Emerson "glad to the brink of fear."[46] For the form of the analogy is not a brace or foundation but a sign of scene-making action and exposure to risk, what Juliana Spahr calls a zone defined by the sliding that happens in it.[47]

Toward a Poetics of Infrastructure

Alone, then, the Emersonian man looks at the stars to embody the sensus communis that can grasp the world in its immediacy. But the stars do not return the world to Emerson in the shape of a distilled something that is held in common. Instead they provide for him a spatial opportunity to experience an impersonal affective immediacy from a distance that is also ever to be traversed. For the possibility of accessing the common that subtends all being requires him not to inhabit or possess it but to desire it—to have, one might say, a crush on it.

We will remember that he says to look at the stars in order to achieve the common sense. He continues: "The rays that come from those heavenly worlds, will separate between him and what he touches." That sensual "separation between" suggests an important foundation for Emerson's sense of what analogy can induce for a social theory of an infrastructure that would afford the inconvenience of other people: a new apprehension of the proximity of things to each other. It does not work by way of metaphor's conceptual figuration; nor by anaclisis, the propping of x onto y that reveals the chain links of investment in a psychic economy; nor by parataxis, a catalog; nor by what the flesh feels immediately as touch and impact. Analogy's special gift to him is the separation within the nonsovereign relation that makes linking possible.[48]

In other words, the separateness between, the dynamic of difference within relation, has to exist in order for Emersonian common sense even to be conceived of. We would not, after all, need a concept of the common if alterity weren't moving through the wormholes that structure intimacy, itself a sensed but unrepresentable figural space graspable only in the reflexive movement of bodies, moods, and atmospheres. The commons concept foregrounds the ellipsis of difference in which a common historical being and separateness-in-relation resonate with and push each other formally, transmuting inconvenience into practices called intimacy and democracy that the overcloseness of othered beings requires. The space between and the spaces among involve distances created by the disturbance of being close without being joined, and without mistaking the other's flesh for one's own or any object in the world or object world as identical to oneself. Nonsovereignty is not, here, the dissolution of an expected boundary. It's the original experience of an affect, of being receptive, of being.

The word Emerson uses for the experience of the natural immediacy among things is not *belonging* but *detection*: "Not only resemblances exist in things whose analogy is obvious," he writes, "as when we detect the type of the human hand in the flipper of the fossil-saurus, but also in objects wherein there is great superficial unlikeness. Thus architecture is called 'frozen music' . . . and [a] 'Gothic church' . . . 'petrified religion.'"[49] He thinks of metaphor as a subset of analogy, a kind of disturbance within a figurative relation. Even if the Emersonian natural symbol integrates processes to produce models of a world unbound by mortal distortions, the work is to detect and therefore to create spaces within the image that can assume an unpredicted rhythm, one recognizable but sensed, not of a "likeness."

In the common of the "separation between," then, a sense of worlding is unimpeded by an economy of loss or a worry about the destruction of what is finally an indestructible singularity. Paradoxically, by putting things into analogical relation, Emerson interferes with the mode of likeness that embraces the narcissism of sovereign-style subjectivity. He enables nonsovereignty to feel like a relief from the reproduction of heavy selves. This nonsovereignty does not bind relationality to any specific shape. To the contrary, this positive version of dispossession makes the world bearable by projecting and receiving a collective, but not mutual, movement in practice.

We have learned all this by following the becoming-man of the worm. As its track is an infrastructure of continuity across the surface of things, the concept helps us to see analogical figurality as a conduit for social infrastructures as well. Susan Leigh Star, the great ethnographer of infrastructure, describes it as a relational and ecological process of sustaining worlds that is mostly visible in its failure. Star, more a formalist, argues that when systems of social reproduction stop working, you can see the machinery of the separation that has induced relations among things and the dynamics that kept them generating the energy for worldmaking: when infrastructural things stop converging, she writes, they become a topic and a problem rather than the automata of procedure. So, we can see the glitch of the present as a revelation of what had been the infrastructure of the lived ordinary. When things stop converging in the reliable patterns of social and material reproduction, they also threaten the conditions and the sense of belonging, but more than that, of assembling.[50]

This way of thinking infrastructure-making gathers up many processes: the convergence scene of various value abstractions, material protocols for metabolizing resources, and the socially distributed experience of making and sustaining life, to start. It resonates with David Harvey's view of the local disturbances that capital makes to protect infrastructures of interest to the dominant class.[51] It suggests that disturbance is what allows for collective work to be done in order to build out zones of return for alternative lifeworlds. But this is not the same as building new institutions. The liveliness of world-making activity distinguishes infrastructures from institutions, although the relation between these concepts and materialities is often a matter of perspective. Institutions enclose and congeal power, resources, and interest, and they represent their legitimacy as something solid and enduring, a predictability on which the social relies. Institutions normalize reciprocity. What constitutes infrastructure, in contrast, are the patterns, habits, norms, and scenes of assemblage and use. Collective affect gets attached to it, too, to the sense of its inventiveness and the horizon of dynamic reciprocity it entails. This is what it means to invent alter-life from within life, what I called in the introduction the heterotopian impulse.

In contemporary left commons talk, social institutions that deliver mass resources are deemed worthy only if they provide an infrastructure for the common rather than privatizing it, along with delivering something like what the state does, an exterior-looking focalizing point of material and imaginary survival for its often desperately at-risk members.[52] These proximate modes of counter-organization include the practices of mass social movements, local cells, alternative supply chains, phone trees, petitions that disturb beyond opinion-strutting, and pooled ideas, for example. Whatever is sustaining grows from exchange.

Institutions generate the positivity of attachment and protocol even while destroying the lifeworld of the lands and lives attached to them for survival. The notion of structure as calcified, as a thing, also negates ordinary continuous adaptation and adjustment by casting them as epiphenomenal. The very figure of infrastructure, too, can block seeing its contingency and creativity, establishing tableaux that bear witness to the formal regularity of movement. But it's worth the risk. We live in a time of massive institutional failure that has led to infrastructural collapse: of bridges, economies, health systems, practices and fantasies of intimacy, ideas of what equality can look like, and what the state has to do with it. The old logics or analogics that make collective life collective seem to be loosening and collapsing.[53] Protestors push the analogical breakdown, which is a version of destroying confidence in causality, in what leads to what. See, for example, the centrality of broken analogy to contemporary abolitionist movements. X is not like y in relation to security: see the ordinary violence of policing, prisons, universities, and, though not in this exact terminology, antiracist, feminist, queer, and trans antiharassment and pro-rights movements. Then sometimes x is like y, but you need to read the revised caption. The disturbance of material and conceptual infrastructures is a radical opportunity.

Emerson modeled a common without movements, on which other people could not jostle his idealization of a universal spirit made possible by "the separation between." He achieves his ambition to represent by taking up strings of figuration that, like the wormhole, are not residences. He floats an affective trail and trial more powerfully than a map for method. Yet if seeing worldbuilding as immanence and infrastructure-making starts where the universalist fantasy provides a primary location for flourishing, it is here that the Spinozan tradition finds its limit. As the Spinozan transcendentalists and their heirs in Deleuze, Hardt and Negri, and, from a queer project perspective, Lee Edelman and Leo Bersani demonstrate, it is very hard to move through symbolization without becoming overattached to a primary analogy or figure.[54] It is hard not to read signs as though they are slogans.

Writing the common from the Emersonian tradition has been central to Juliana Spahr's practice of the past few decades. Her work's discipline is processual, labile, and mobile, like Emerson's, and politically lyrical, like Whitman's after him. The intensity of her habits of figuration also expresses the sensuality of being in a common movement without attaching it to a particular shape to serve as a foundation for a better likeness. Like the worm, she converts feeling things into feeling things out. She receives the world and metabolizes it so that its troubles look moveable.

But Spahr's work does not begin with the serial perfectionism of singularities or other lyric modes that proclaim singular "I's" and "we's" in the wishful performative. After Lowell's use of the historical faux-Common against the idea of the common and Emerson's protection of it by using analogy to deontologize, Spahr's work adds a third approach, using it to enact and unravel settler imaginaries of the common by beginning with the ubiquitous manifestations of the nonsovereign. There's no travel to that common and no escape from it: it's where people live. Spahr's work performs instead an aspirational mutuality among the inconvenient, who are always a bit uncoordinated in time and space, falling into and out of each other's way.

Here are some examples of how the making of a common through analogical destruction has worked for Spahr. The effects are not merely rhetorical or subjective. Her autobiography, *The Transformation* (2007), takes place in the intimately and politically collective timespaces of structural violence that cross the Hawai'i of 1997 and New York City in the penumbra of 9/11. The text spans these timespaces by charting the erotic and intellectual love of three people for each other. But Spahr writes of an ambition not to see "relationship" writ large as "a feedback loop" of desire or something clarifying like a triangle.[55] You cannot make a stencil of this transformation. You cannot copy the form or carve your life into a likeness of it. The question is of the scalability of attachment and what can be done with how you use it.

The lovers seek what she calls "a Sapphic point" of impersonality that would allow them to think of themselves as a "they," avoiding the way a two-person couple conventionally thinks of itself as an "it." This formation cannot be skimmed or lived as a shortcut. The "they" is the first beat of a transformation, as the title predicts. Spahr looks not to the common of singularity to keep herself safe from engulfment in the "we," nor to an abstract solidarity that allows for self-heroic inflation, but begins where the bodies are in a dynamic to which they must pay attention that is critical, loving, and persistent.[56] That's one thing it means to hack normativity.

The affective scene focuses on receiving and metabolizing the world while unraveling its presumptive solidity. The lovers personify themselves as a collective, which ruffles and proliferates analogies:

> They just wanted to talk to each other the way that humans talk to each other when they go on long car trips in the country and they have nothing really to say after the first hour in the car but sometimes in the hours that follow they might point something out or talk some about what thoughts came to them as they drove along, mesmerized by the blur of space passing by them. They wanted to be they the way that humans might be they with a dog and a dog they with humans, intimately together yet with a limited vocabulary. They wanted to be they like blood cells are compelled to be a they. What they meant was that they were other than completely autonomous but they were not one thing with no edges, with no boundary lines.[57]

Whereas some critics disparage Spahr's association with experiment as lyric vanguardism and bourgeois play without risk, I take the Spahrian project of describing the textured dynamic of an ongoing nonsovereignty to offer the affective idea of worldmaking as infrastructural improv, churning out a space as the worm does, through situational generative movement that requires an ethics and a politics.[58] To read Spahr executing this aim is to enter the production site of a sensus communis that must remain disoriented: the eyes are receptive and aleatory, but not unfocused. Its task is to take in, feel out, be historical, be speculative: to keep moving while assessing. The bodies autonomously signify things that must be acknowledged and folded in.

Meanwhile, the glue that binds the floor of the world that privilege enjoys dissolves in her version of flat-toned affect. Intimates, peoples, and structures crash into each other, at once overclose and distant. To break analogy is to break bad habits of responding and relating, freeing the inconvenience drive to try out alternative linkages. Avant-gardes attack, and Spahr is a good polemicist and historian of literary activism when she aspires to it.[59] The commons-work puzzles things more intricately though, worries them from the inside where existence is more felt than verified. "And when they thought rationally they felt that being they in this awkward time should have made them feel more safe."[60] Of course it doesn't, because, as we saw in chapter 1 in relation to *Last Tango in Paris*, plural form is not only a wish for a refuge or cushion; it is also social, an exposure, a mediation, a conjuncture of moving parts, and a launching pad in relation to which beings can find each other to figure out how to live. It is as though their kinetic movement takes energy from the term *movement*'s political resonance. Or maybe it's both/and. Movement changes how space works too.

As a poetry of infrastructure, *The Transformation* stages enclosures that are located outside, and when inside there are always open windows and screens, such as on the computer. It connects mediations and spells out what's going on there. In short, if the infrastructure of the social emerges within predictable life, Spahr releases it into an open plan. But it is not a flat plane, because the language through which the book generates a narrative image of their life is a bumpy surface, like life is: a neglected side road for bodies and the histories taking shape. One has to make language do what it cannot yet do. How the lovers use it matters because they want to be like what they are not yet like.

Through an aesthetic that collects streaming observations, then, Spahr's work aims to circulate a new common sense from analogy that does not redeem the world, as in Emerson, or condemn it, as in Lowell: Spahr sees the analog as a material infrastructure starting with the body that can anatomize, dismantle, disturb, and make possible living in the world that is always, for good and ill, intimately touching from near and far and therefore changing what proximity does. The "they" begins in contact. The common of contact produces plans for structural transformation from where the bodies and lifeworlds are. To say, then, that Spahr is a poet of infrastructure, a queer infrastructure, is to point to an aesthetic zone of perverse undefensive expansion in multiple dimensions that risks speculating about everything, placing a flattened voice near what's threatening, aversive, and inconstant in attachment's vibrating action.

This practice does not become a formalist fetish in her later work. *This Connection of Everyone with Lungs* (2005) is a different kind of queer reboot of the common, testing out what's converging in the plural, using a practice of hypernaming and indistinction to shake out of hiding and necessity a whole range of things from the lifeworld of US empire, privacy, and whiteness.

You can't shed history performatively or by decree. In italicized passages preceding each section, she describes having to take in the wars in Iraq and Afghanistan while living far away in a never-postcolonial Hawai'i where US military operations are also ordinary, intruding as the white noise of the day. All of this is in proximity to aural and visual mediations of world destruction, beauty, celebrity scandal, birdsong, human friction, many racisms, love, and the ocean. Such a willful poetic seems, sometimes, not to be opening up beyond its desire to be good and do good. But the formal practice installs a glitch in virtue.

There are these things:

cells, the movement of cells and the division of cells

and then the general beating of circulation

and hands, and body, and feet

and skin that surrounds hands, body, feet.

This is a shape,

a shape of blood beating and cells dividing.

But outside of this shape is space.

There is space between the hands.

There is space between the hands and space around the hands.

There is space around the hands and space in the room.

There is space in the room that surrounds the shapes of everyone's hands and body and feet and cells and the beating contained within.

There is space, an uneven space, made by this pattern of bodies.

This space goes in and out of everyone's bodies.

Everyone with lungs breathes the space in and out as everyone with lungs breathes the space between the hands in and out as everyone with lungs breathes the space between the hands and the space around the hands in and out

as everyone with lungs breathes the space between the hands and the space around the hands and the space of the room in and out

as everyone with lungs breathes the space between the hands and the space around the hands and the space of the room and the space of the building that surrounds the room in and out

as everyone with lungs breathes the space between the hands and the space around the hands and the space of the room and the ·

space of the building that surrounds the room and the space of
the neighborhoods nearby in and out

as everyone with lungs breathes the space between the hands and
the space around the hands and the space of the room and the
space of the building that surrounds the room and the space of
the neighborhoods nearby and the space of the cities in and out. . . .

In this everything turning and small being breathed in and out
by everyone with lungs during all the moments.[61]

Did you skim? It is hard not to let the incantation fuzz out the demands of
staying with what's changing in a rhythmic common.

Close reading close breathing, Spahr turns everything into a holding
environment that articulates the common in common but reshapes it too:
other verses scale up, moving across mesosphere, stratosphere, islands, cities, rooms, hands, cells. Not identical, not joined and spaced in a regular
net, but copresent, singular, general, and dynamic. A space of collectively
encountered information emerges that is not necessarily collectively or co-
herently comprehended information, performing the speed of encounter and
the reality of constant processing. Chanting is access to hearing, to assuming,
and to not hearing, too, a force toward and against listening. Unlearning is
not the replacement of a cartridge.

There is something romantic and humanist about this version of a process aesthetics; there may be insufficient friction in the proclamation of
mixture at the political, productive, and cellular levels. Then, too, the historical fact of bodies repairing and disappearing in relation to the universe
of things that include each other in sync and in counterpoint involves taking
each other on and in but never collapsing the distance that allows for attention. This comfort in distance may be veiled by the "we" and the "everyone."
To take something in is to be nonsovereign in relation to it, but "we" already
were that: to be exposed to one's exposure is not equal to being destroyed by
it. Intentionality minimizes loss. Facing a liberalism that can't account for
its moral comfort with national-capitalist dispossession, the poem nonetheless imagines dissolving its own floor in the histories of colonization that
include the present. If we can distinguish mode from method, Spahr's mode
digests and extrudes an infrastructure of evenly distributed attention that
notices discrete disturbances in the sensual and cognitive fields to squeeze
out a "connection," an infrastructure without attached directions. This is
how the paradoxical relation of rhythm and flatness works.

Rhythm turns out to be key to Spahr's analogical aesthetics of the common infrastructure in resistance to punctuation's orchestration. This is not the common as a regularity but the induction of history. Rhythm is a whiplash, a double take, a retrospect. But the discovery of a pattern also involves listening beyond the situation, speculating beyond the object, and following the disoriented body out to unsealed relations. Here flatness is not the opposite of what's dimensional but turns out to be the environment of relationality itself. "How connected we are with everyone," she writes, not just because we have ridden the same catastrophe and the same built environments but also because we have breathed in their dust particles.[62] Dust is the effect of the contact between skin and the world, the universe and the world, and also what buildings release and the ground gives up. Pinged and hurt and inflamed by contact, we've become disoriented together, and breathed the dust out jointly, even when we're overwhelmed by what's too hard or too embodied.[63]

This dust, that sand, that perturbing grain, and the smooth surfaces and soft air, too, affect people differently. They are in us, but the space they make is in a new alien zone of inexperience that might become something if we follow its tracks. The tone of the work varies, from a discourse of the common as the space where being connected meets being collectively doomed, to the practice of an aesthetics of interruption where any observation releases a pressure both to stay there forever and to refuse to become absorbed in the mirror of a suspension that refuses time.

This description of the variety of nonsovereign relations brought to the surface through the continuity of the life in breathing and the universality of infrastructural physicality understates the presence of internal resistance and glitch in This Connection of Everyone with Lungs. The work can be funny in this way, maybe unintentionally: its willful mixtures create the breakdown of the machine of sense on the way to expanding it; its desire to witness complicity sometimes feels like alchemical hygiene:

> In bed, when I stroke the down on your cheeks, I stroke also the carrier battle group ships, the guided missile cruisers, and the guided missile destroyers.
>
> When I reach for your waists, I reach for bombers, cargo, helicopters, and special operations . . .
>
> Fast combat support ships, landing crafts, air cushioned, all of us with all of that.[64]

The desired point seems to be not to use form as self-defense, nor to achieve beauty as attunement to a visceral sense of elevation and fairness. Nor is it to homogenize the world as disaster: This Connection of Everyone with Lungs is neither Adorno on the lyric nor The Waste Land.[65] The desire in this text is to convert idioms of sensed impact into a scalar patterning that can become a scene of live collective being. It is sometimes graceless, absurd, or willful, but the risk of not trying for the common of awkwardness, complicity, and intimacy would be even more ridiculous and deadly. The work is about trying to stay in life gladly extended to "the brink of fear" without creating more enclosures or refuges.

Acknowledging pattern, with its constitutive interruptions, as a process of communing is extended in Spahr's Well Then There Now (2011), whose title is at once an admonition, a call to attention, a performance of therapeutic caring, and another cataloging of the common as a scene for the settler's destruction of her own historical structure and syntax. The ambition is to stage what she variously calls "sliding" and gliding, shifting, and "slipping the analogy of the opening of things."[66] Here the problem of analogy transformed becomes a project. In this book's version of the common, the Emersonian analogy of the "separation between" is acknowledged, but rather than shedding the world or flattening difference, as in This Connection of Everyone with Lungs, Well Then There Now "approximate[s]" the "shapes of things I saw around me," loosening the attachment of figuration to its traditions.[67] The work does this by putting things next to other things in ways that emphasizes discontinuous yet ongoing experience.

Like This Connection of Everyone with Lungs, Well Then There Now is located in Hawai'i, but where in the former work the land and language expose a common vulnerability in the register of the permeability of "all" to violence and desire, the latter book intensifies and denaturalizes the noise of one infrastructure using a translation program to move the languages of Hawai'i back and forth into each other. Still, standard hegemonic white English remains the setting in the end. Does this mean the unlearning of a settler screen-memory register can't or won't dismantle its ground?

Well Then There Now exposes its desire to be an archive and a counter-archive. Its mixtures of love and complicity recall the field of precarious documentation that Paige Sarlin put forth in her work on structural vulnerability, where

> whatever grows, is produced, aggregated, created, or amassed within a space of sharing (outside the logic of market exchange) is vulnerable to the logic of the market & market forces, especially in relation to debt. . . .

This concept describes the way in which practices of connection, sharing, and being-in-common breed a kind of transformation in those involved in the production of a collective space/practice/mode of sociality/movement/resistance. This transformation and change is porous, messy and hard to quantify or evaluate, but it is a crucial aspect of these forms of sociality and therefore needs to be recognized.[68]

What Spahr envisions as the vulnerable language commons is defined by glitch: a glitch she makes in the reproduction of colonization, migration, occupation, reproduction, nature, and capitalist circulation.[69] Spahr thinks of this enmeshing as in the tradition of ecopoetics, but in this version of it repair also looks like a will to disrepair.

> what we know is like and unalike
> as it is kept in different shaped containers
> it is as the problems of analogy
> it is as the view from the sea
> it is as the introduction of plants and animals, others, exotically
> yet it is also as the way of the wood borer
> and the opinion of the sea
> as it is as the occidental concepts of government, commerce,
> money and imposing
> what we know is like and unalike
> one stays diverse with formed packages
> that is what the problems of the analogy are
>
> . . .
>
> analogy from analogy
> analogy of analogy
>
> . . .
>
> it cannot be of another way
> it cannot be of another way[70]

The problems the glitchfrastructure of the text performs are three: the container as a figure for the material means of distribution, which is what an infrastructure does on the ground; the institutions of structural domination; and the formally normative model of analogy, which, broken, gives way to radically different linkages. "It cannot be of another way," repeated, does not mean that the form of things is fixed but that there are so many ways to forge strings of attachment in and to the world.

The multiplication of indices even in these stanzas lets us begin to see through Spahr's eyes the diversity of infrastructures of belonging. Belonging intends property, sovereignty, politics, tradition, being obligated, and sharing qualities: belonging is someone else's judgment about "fit"; belonging is a sense and an aspiration, an appetite, recycling the world. Belonging also points to something simpler than belonging that I have been calling "proximity." More on that in the next chapter. The kinds of proximity that matter here are made by practices of attention not defined by dissensus or agonism but technically, by atmosphere-generating juxtaposition. This proximity dilutes what we called structural by shifting the force of the normative infrastructures from the state and commodity capitalism into the ordinary that also includes local plural intimacies and the associations that make life sticky and interesting.

Spahr's tactic in *Well Then There Now* is, then, to take up a position within her colonial/racial/patriarchal/class inheritance and from there mess up the tracks of forms in movement. The function of the bot, I think, is to do more of what intention never does fully, to break likeness without protecting anything, to play with analogy randomly, with unpredictable effects. It's a deliberately naïve use of the mechanic to mess up the image of the world one carries around.

That's significant. For Aristotle, analogy originally pointed not to "an equality of relations" but a mere technicality about the repetition of key terms.[71] But analogy has become a broader vehicle than for establishing likeness-in-relation.[72] Spahr breaks apart this model to refuse the presumption that equality involves the distribution of the affective comfort of equivalency in any register: but this does not mean that she is not interested in equality. This poetic performs how difficult and demanding it is for a being who has taken up a position in life within imperial/capitalist infrastructures to figure equally valued social being. Attempting to decolonize and deprivatize the visceralized, invested archive of likeness creates a different form to return to, putting the flat ontology of being in the world near the materiality of raw exposure and extreme risk that Virno argues is the ordinary of the contemporary common, a dispossessedness in its awkward, convoluted, observational, comic, noisy, general, and diversely manifest vulnerability.[73] Nothing is archaic in a crisis politics or poetics. The settler colonial presumption is alive, as are the not-mere gestures toward making its presumptions useless. At its best, Spahr's poetry is a technology of engagement in which all objects are granular and regenerate their relation to difference and distance. The ongoingness of this dynamic is what I mean by infrastructure.

Spahr's work slides consciousness of all of this into suspending its judgment without evacuating judgment, absorbing the noise of the world, and breaking the world into noise. This training in unlearning the world through reading it across many profoundly malfunctioning genealogical machineries produces an infrastructure of patience and appetite, an unusual pair. But if there is a flatness to what's evoked in her broken figuration of what also continues, and if the poetry refunctions the violent voice of indistinction as a way to reconfigure democracy, it is also haunted by the universalist desire to mechanize change rather than to stop for or be stopped by what's inconvenient about it. The machine absorbs the friction while playing with its destructiveness. A regressive poetic, in the best sense. Of course, this state was the liberal world-wish, too, imagining the extension of the common through inclusion, without loss. In the end, every moment of unlearning the world and reference has to bear the transition of fantasy, desire, and material exchange no longer governed by possession. We write out of where we write from.

Unlearning the Common

There can be no change without revisceralization. Throughout this chapter, this summary statement has been indicated in terms of the incitement to break open habits and naturalized norms of association, for example through the use of the commons concept to dispossess the normative analogy of its force. Such change involves all kinds of loss and transitional suspension of our confidence about how things work. It also releases creative energy for worldbuilding.

But it's not simple to move from fight and release to a generative freedom. The transition requires reconditioning what pass as instincts, triggers, gut feelings, true feelings, presumptive ties, the whole default world of emotional and affective expectation. In the affective common, that reconditioning is often what gets in the way of staying with who you're with while also nursing many small and large scars. I flagged this part of the process earlier in the term unlearning, which is another way to lose your object. Infrastructuralist perspectives experiment with what can generate ongoing life. So far in this chapter they have used the common to generate tactics for change that are fundamentally conceptual, experimental in the way they're lived. Such a focus on the transformational infrastructure is central to the anarchist tradition that begins with building from what bodies can do together on the ground, in the weather, through ideas manifest in material practice and living concepts, and not just to get through the ongoing moment but to generate forms of life in resistance to an Oz horizon that doesn't hold up close up. The aesthetics of kinesthetic performance beginning with the body can provide tactics that might grow new proprioceptors. I close with two examples focusing on the sensuality of learning in the middle of the dehiscence of unlearning.

Liza Johnson's film In the Air (2009) is about her hometown of Portsmouth, Ohio, although she doesn't name it: it could be many postindustrial US landscapes, except it's predominantly white. The two dominant affects "in the air" are distraction and boredom: the film's central question, posed in different forms every day, is whether the burned-out and "wasted" parents, who spend time drunk and antagonistic in cars and bars, will leave for their children what Patricia Williams describes as the inheritance of a disinheritance.[74] The disinheritance isn't just familial or financial. It's about the exhaustion of language: the heavy silence of what goes without saying sustains this world.

The town in this film has been abandoned not only by its elders but by capital. It seems to have one industry, a junkyard (figure 2.5). The junkyard's aspiration seems to be to avoid events: a sign announces the string of days without accident. But the feel is as though the world of this town is one punctured membrane away from becoming the scrap it now organizes. The buildings and streets are empty: it seems to be being maintained as a ghost town.

The film is from the perspective of the kids of the town, its current crop of dreamers: they are protagonists in training. The training comes from the only live collective space we see in the town, a circus school that is called, in real life, but not in the film, Cirque d'Art.[75] We see the circus teacher dead serious at the front of the room, getting the group in sync to do tricks. The kids

2.5 In the Air, directed by Liza Johnson, 2009. Printed with permission of Liza Johnson.

are in many kinds of transition: in late high school about to be sprung and testing the world, still at home living with and against their families, and as student performers veering between kidding around, flirting, and admiring each other's skill and the focus of people in training.

The kids are learning to spin and to fall. They are learning to lean on each other (figure 2.6). A little light romance might be starting, but autonomy and abs are the focus. You have to be able to hold a whole body in the air while it swings. None of this feels like the pre-enactment of fantasies of stardom or love. It does not feel at all phantasmatic or allegorical: learning to be awkward, to be graceful, to leap, and to fall is a training in attention and also in revisceralizing one's bodily intuition. It requires making and breaking habits of response. It involves rethinking gravity. The air is not the common, as in Spahr. Training in collaboration is the thing that collapses breaking forms with making a common life.

This training includes ordinary physical dynamics themselves. Disturbing what threatens and what comforts, the circus schooling shifts what Virno calls the dread and the refuge that shape contemporary ideas of the commons as a relief from life.[76] It does this by foregrounding the difficulty and pleasure of maintaining footing during conversations, in the world, and during performance that requires people to show up for others' bodies.[77]

The high point of the film is difficult to describe because it's so simple, but the point of rebooting relationality through remaking visceral response is that in order to reinvent the lifeworld in the present, one must transform what reciprocity can mean.

In the final scene the high school kids want a ride somewhere. The parents have been working, fighting, or drinking, appearing wasted and exhausted, sometimes aggressively deadpan. Finally, they track down a mother while she is doing her job. For a living, she sweeps an empty building by herself

2.6 In the Air, directed by Liza Johnson, 2009. Pegi Wilkes teaching Christa Castle Benson, Brian Rushford, Jon Chandler, and Heather White Chandler. Printed with permission of Liza Johnson.

(figure 2.7). She is a maintenance engineer for an abandoned architecture, hired to preserve the hoarded infrastructure of capital just in case it feels like returning for some more exploitation, resource extraction, and real contribution to the atmosphere an abandoned town can only remember as live.

The kids approach her. She barely looks at them, repeating, "What do you want? What do you kids want?" They refuse to speak and assume an expressionlessness interrupted only by the relay of side-eye. These lateral glances shift the film's genre. As though rehearsed, the kids respond to the mother's query by surrounding her and making her flip over them backward, as the music begins. They take their schooling out of the school, but they do not become teachers. No longer tracing the decay of the harsh real, where the remaining fantasy is getting through the day, the magical-realism musical that emerges in this scene derives life from whatever it is that brings people to the situation.

Everyone who has been in the film comes out of an imaginary space of the shot. Collectively, the dispossessed self-possess. Entrained or untrained, they do circus movement. Launching and landing pads mysteriously appear. For the most part the performers are white and working class, but not entirely. For the most part they are strong and skilled, but not entirely. Johnson doesn't stage them as biographical subjects with names and desires, or as stars with untapped auras of magnificence: the elders join the kids as they all learn to use their bodies in sync, which includes counterpoint. Their coordination not only counters the saturation of everyday defeat by work and the absence of work, but also stages a becoming that might lead to belonging. If it works, the revised bodily habit of nonsovereignty creates a collective orientation, a shared subjectivity. It does not erase individuality but creates a mutually transforming affect-sphere where it has no "right" to be. In the

2.7 In the Air, directed by Liza Johnson, 2009. Sue Stevenson. Printed with permission of Liza Johnson.

hollow spaces of abandoned capital defined by coordinated movement, we are in a different world from the "rights" world.

For the most part their faces are still and composed, so muted as to be inexpressive; they have the stiff bodies of workers entrained by work's rhythms. Johnson isolates only one participant, a young plump woman who makes a victory sign with her arms when she achieves a glorious split, celebrating a victory not over but through her body. Mainly everyone is focused on being in step, but not rigidly: both actors and audience, poised for next phase of movement.

The group embodies, then, not socially necessary labor time or normative intimacy, but something simpler and often inconvenient in ordinary time: socially necessary proximity looking for a way to be. Who would be there to receive a protest? No one: that's how abandoned they are. They turn toward each other without metastatements. The analogy they perform among all persons in a world of people and architectures abandoned by capital becomes the condition of this convergence that isn't a merging; and the propertied space that someone owns becomes a pop-up common defined by skilled, patterned movement that could become a transformational infrastructure. "Space is a practiced place," writes Michel de Certeau.[78] Practice acknowledges the imperfect, the impermanent. As I have argued, the episodic common is not a form of mourning for the loss of the collective ordinary; it's a test to see whether a future can be built through episodes, and what kinds; it's a sensual experiment in breaking down what the body has learned about being in relation. Here, squatting in a space, the people become potential heterotopians.

The soundtrack to this scene is a 1998 song by the group Alice DeeJay called "Better Off Alone." The song's only two lines are, "Do you think you're better off alone?" and "Talk to me," a rhetorical question and an imperative phrase. "Better off Alone" has had a substantial life in clubs and has been remade and remixed a number of times. There's little to it other than the desire to convert the rhetorical into an actual question.[79] Usually it appears in a space where people are alone together, singular and various, intimate and mostly anonymous, looking for a minor release from the solo burden of managing their pseudo-sovereignty. The song delivers the core message of popular culture, that "you are not alone," and challenges its listeners to use their proximity to sense a better lifeworld and build toward it together.[80] In this sense the song is air and provides one.

What is "the air" in In the Air? As though joining Spahr's inquiry into the common air, the film asks us to wonder about what's the matter with the air,

2.8 *In the Air*, directed by Liza Johnson, 2009. Anita Skaggs in front of Misty Windsor Graham and Eugenio Perez. Printed with permission of Liza Johnson.

as it recirculates the scrap from the junkyard and the humidity from the lake into lungs and muscles. There's pollution. There's energy for making new genres of convergence. Is there something in the air that might protest the nervous fraying and self-numbing medication of the body politic? How can a discipline of the ordinary body toward pleasure and kindness create an atmosphere for a new economy's good life that does not begin with where the wealth is and judgments of who's deserving?

The film's older figures appear too beaten down to protest the exploitation of supply-chain capitalism, and the abandonment of working populations by the wealth hoarders seems to produce less a politics than rampant and depleting nervous conditions, from irritation to short fuses and numbness (figure 2.8). The receptive posture of aesthetic attention helps the youths to loosen or unlearn their defenses against taking each other in. They train each other, then the adults, to reoccupy existence in a chilly place. Individuals may be exhausted, but as a whole they've not yet given up on the world.

So in *In the Air*, collaboration clears space for the common, which has no form but offers a point of return through the creative use of proximity, improvised synchronicity, and spiky kinships no less intimate for the ambivalence. In its recessive way the very purposiveness of gymnastics in this final scene makes for a brilliant postwork and antiproductivist performance,[81] with the musical number serving its traditional function as a placeholder for living otherwise. But the number is in the air while the bodies are quiet and on the ground. Not in the register of the manifesto, the film points to what's there, not proclaiming the reparative solution that is part of the promise that the political holds out. Another use of flatness: to put a wedge in causality. Here the liberal world picture crashes to the floor as the group stands still in the absence of confidence about connection, causality, and building out the world. The first step becomes literally that. No abstraction can provide resources for bearing each other and life's long middle. Unlearning the exhausted gimmicks of normativity, the bodies pause in the space without a satisfying outcome in sight.[82]

And this is where we are: the "we" who are not one.[83]

Those who desire to invent a transformational infrastructure to shape the world that is always in transition often look for something to appear more solid than it can be in order to anchor what's emerging.[84] Charismatic authority is one example of something solid-seeming frequently called on.[85] The commons concept takes up that texture, too, insofar as it stands specifically for cosmopolitan struggles against national-neoliberal privatization strategies such as the massive wealth grab by the 1 percent and "public-private partnerships." These displacements obscure accountability for the offloading of debt, dispossession, and direct violence onto the already structurally vulnerable and violated.

In terms of sloganeering, too, the twenty-first-century translocal cosmopolitan assertion of the commons as the ground of radical democracy became an aspirational performative, acting as a thing that can be collectively asserted, held, achieved, and occupied. New analogies were tried out in its name in the United States. The organizing rubric of the commons of Occupy became a way to point to public space reoccupied for constituent power and a trial balloon for the bodily copresence of direct action or "assembly" in the ordinary.[86] It signified something like affective mutuality and feel of what Jonathan Flatley calls a "revolutionary mood."[87] It replaced the uncanny sensation of "the touch of the state" with schooling in respectful social distancing and patience for rhetorical protocols that amplified solidarity and sometimes became intimacy.[88] It proliferated so quickly and intensely through allied cells of Occupy that within a few years it began to irritate some of its early users: "In late July, [Sandy] Nurse pleaded on her Facebook wall, 'Does everything have to be called "Occupy"? Come on, y'all.' A commenter on a similar post a few weeks earlier put the matter succinctly: 'Burn Occupy on a funeral pyre and move the fuck on.'"[89] Such processes of revision-in-association have tended to link concepts of political voice, atmosphere, proximity, and the public sphere to specific sensual qualities of the common as such: the toggle between the affective and political infrastructural imaginary creates space beyond itself. *The commons* still serves as a mere synonym for *public park*. At the same time, it is usually temporally specific and geopolitically local: the resource and spatial common of Occupy Sandy, Occupy the Hood, Occupy London, Occupy Nation. In the meanwhile, occupy/common has changed into a way to describe collaboration and careworlds more generally. Critical work on ecology, states, indigeneity, political movements, knowledge, and research itself blazon Occupy to ally with the desire to transform infrastructures that organize specific resources and concepts necessary for life. It's a kind of dog whistle addressed to a movement dream.

It is hard to avoid making a powerful concept all-absorbent when all you've ever known is how to own, possess, and use action concepts in defense of your existence.

But if the imperative Occupy and ideas of the common have become virtual siblings at this point, their political association during the 2008 economic crash with protests against the reproduction of economic inequality has also been changing. Its legacy endures, for example, in Occupy City Hall, a pop-up common protesting the New York City Police Department's extreme funding privilege and ordinary violence against people of color and the poor.[90] Triggered by the video-recorded police execution of George Floyd in Minneapolis on May 25, 2020, this appropriation of a zoned "public" space as a political common also mobilized the archive of anti-Black murders captured on video with cellphones, already on regular display, to dispersed and local publics. It explicitly created and reanimated knowledges of the genocidal and often barely extrajuridical extermination of Black, Indigenous, and Latinx life in practices such as lynching, as Ken Gonzales-Day has demonstrated across many media.[91] This revision of the Occupy commons also takes energy from the video archive of weaponized joyriding that includes the police and took form in the white supremacist enjoyment-murder of Ahmaud Arbery in Satilla Shore, Georgia, on February 23, 2020.[92]

Writing from the multiple crises of the present in 2020, I resist the desire for performativity for which the commons concept so often stands. Crisis hastily generates multiples of the "we." There have always been bullying, thin, and nostalgic "we's," of course, used for good and ill. Leading to projections of a unity of experience onto a mass, the imperative to posit the atmosphere of belonging works either as assertion or as a hope that if you name it, it will come. During the COVID-19 crisis, before the phase of antiracist protest, corporate and individual pronouncements proliferated with smileys, balloons, and exclamation points. Street corners, posters, shop windows, and TV ads proclaimed phrases like "We are in it together!" Who is "we"? What is "it"? Fantasies of democracy as the experience of collectively equal exposure to vulnerability tried to establish a ground where there is no ground.

At the current conjuncture, the "we" arises in contexts of structurally induced suffering-toward-death from anti-Black police torture and murder, food insecurity, medical bankruptcy, drug price inflation, the widening militarization of state tools for control and domination, the racist carceral habit, and so on. These are crises in the ordinary, but not probable and en-grained: as Spahr catalogues, as Johnson presumes. Failed state democracies, racist ideologies, life-shattering pandemics, and ordinary fatalism about the suffering of the "essential" worker join the mass refusal to allow the ordinary of racist police violence and specific anti-Blackness to seem like a fate. These conjunctures have multiplied questions about what a life is, what targeted death does, and where and whether any "we" can be said to stretch across communities, bodies politic, epidemiological populations, sets of people with analogous feelings of exposure and vulnerability, consumer addressees, and citizens of the local now defined at all scales: neighborhoods, cities, states, regions, and nations.

All of these "we's" are projections from specific visions of a zone of col-lective experience. The plural is always local but often masked as the name for the general. The same goes for the universal, which always ends up being specific, a failed abstraction. Is "we" ever more than a heuristic coupled with a desire? When is it a way of talking about the effects of a history of defin-ing experience? What does it have to do with liberal and illiberal concepts of "the public"? Is the common effective or a shortcut in generating the plural beyond the moment of the "we" of historical community? None of these questions is rhetorical. No mass politics or any politics exists without some attention to the building out of the "we." This is the power of feeling-with crossed with solidarity in the political sphere.[93] But the very fractures of in-equality are also affectively and materially amplified during crisis, in the reg-ister of life and death.[94] As the next chapter argues, *life* comes to mean many things. And still there are "die-ins" on the Boston Common, making a bad copy of a literal and pervasive death (figure 2.9).

Peter Linebaugh proposes that "it might be better to keep the word [com-mon] as a verb, an activity, rather than as a noun, a substantive"; he wants us to think about commoning land, life, history, and memory, rather than presuming them, so long as it doesn't serve to further divide the world into local enclaves of value, as it mostly does.[95] Massimo de Angelis argues that the commons is always a doing that is a decoupling from the reproductive ener-gies of a normative life's standards of value, and not a replacement for capital-ism.[96] This chapter is in sync with these claims. Again, we are talking about the aspirational use of the concept, its destructive function, and not the tradition

2.9 Die-in at Boston Common, June 3, 2020. Color photograph by Brian Snyder. © Reuters.

of lifeworld self-protection in which culture and economic clashing mark a war for a genealogical or an Indigenous community's survival. Linebaugh and de Angelis refer to a rhythm of worlding that resonates with this chapter's project of tracking the growth of an affective infrastructure whose very existence acknowledges the inconvenience of other people in the midst of the struggle to transform life economically and subjectively. Embodied tactics are required for heterotopian praxis. The frictions of counternormative affective infrastructures can bring structural political imaginaries to their knees.

One might respond to my infrastructuralism with the idea that any specific address to transforming the aspiration called the sensus communis is at best a mere episode to hang a wish on. But that's what an episode is: a goad to rethink seriality, continuity, analogy. Every transformative example implicitly disturbs an analogy, decouples coupling. Every broken analogy releases affectively bound energy back into the world. Andrés Green writes that when discourse stops binding "word-presentation, thing-presentation, affect, bodily states, [and] act," the unbound affect might "snap the chain of discourse," inducing a "qualitative mutation."[97] The commons concept requires infrastructures for sustaining the mutations that emerge from the chains that are breaking in the popular resistance to austerity regimes and anti-Black and patriarchal capitalism.

I've argued in this chapter that the inconvenient gesture of breaking analogy, rather than hastily, anxiously, or needfully asserting it, is a prime device for opening up the figural world of what's held to be common. Ian Bogost writes, "Sometimes there is nothing more refreshing than a startlingly
bad analogy. It's like a crisp cucumber bursting from the dip of a bad day's
sphincter. Like a restorative rain drenching the vomit of last night's bender.
Like a cool breeze tousling the blood-matted fur of roadkill."[98] He doesn't
mean this in a positive way. I do. The commons produces riffing on the other
side of assurance: What isn't mixed? The political and epistemic problem for
the politically autopoetic, which is what all world-creating subjects in coordinated struggle are, is that the placeholders for our desire can too easily
seem solid and ironed out rather than affective figures for delivering a convergence process we can cling to and with which we draw lines of belonging
in the sand, in the air, on the streets, in liveable spaces.

What remains for the pedagogy of unlearning that we derive from the
aspirational commons, then, is to build affective infrastructures that admit
the work of desire and the work of ambivalence as the tactics of commoning.
What remains is the potential we have to common infrastructures that can
absorb the blows of our aggressive need for the world to accommodate each
and all of us and our resistance to adaptation, and, at the same time, to hold
out the prospect of a world worth attaching to that's something other than
an old hope's bitter echo. A failed episode is not evidence that a project is in
error: by definition, forms of common life are always going through a phase,
as infrastructures do.

Three minutes before certain death,
I probably still would laugh.
— HANNAH ARENDT

three **ON BEING IN LIFE WITHOUT WANTING THE WORLD**

No World Poetics, or, Elliptical Life

This chapter has an indefinite number of sections. One is a conceptual introduction proposing attention to a poetics of dissociation. There is already in
contemporary theorizing an account of dissociative poetics associated with
Tony Hoagland and Stephen Burt. For them, a dissociative poetics is located
in a lyric poetry whose style is distinguished by lists, episodes, and an observational tone that merges the practiced casualness of stand-up comedy and
the personal essay with the formal self-reflexivity of the romantic lyric. Hoagland and Burt characterize this style as involving compulsive cataloging,
reflective banality, and lightly condescending aloofness. The depressive and
hollow defensive detachment that we associate with dissociation is not the
dominant mood of this proposed poetic kind: techniques are what matter,
insofar as they allow artists to observe from a distance a world in which they

are also manifestly embedded. Burt and Hoagland claim that because this kind of poetic language is prosaic, so ordinary and seemingly offhand about situations and events that matter, the dissociative aesthetic is at once realism for a world in crisis and yet, at the same time, entitled and shallow. In other words, their critique both honors and rejects the lyrics they choose to exemplify the shape of their historical moment. The critics also foreclose the wider range of implications for thinking and feeling historically when, in their view, a person or poem takes on a dissociative form.[1]

So let's try again. Dissociation is at least five kinds of thing: (1) It is an ordinary mode of cognitive delay in the wake of any affective impact, which usually goes by unnoticed. (2) It is a state, like that of disbelief, that registers the disruption of the experience of being affected, a beat of belated self-encounter that is not fundamentally, necessarily, or usually pathological. A typical example of this dissociative kind is a thought like "What just happened?" that arises after an improvised interaction. (3) Dissociation can be a standard clinical referent: an unconscious process that manages potentially self-disintegrating intensities by separating them out so that one does not feel, for example, an overwhelming conflict among one's needs, vulnerabilities, aggressions, appetites, perceptions, and habits of being.[2] Were it not for this displacement and forgetting, this chapter would be about anxiety, the copresence of all that I just catalogued—but this chapter is about dissociation, which keeps inner conflicts at bay, until it doesn't.[3] Again, in its contemporary psychoanalytic scenario, this state, which protects the subject's survival, is not necessarily pathological, and its relation to the shock of trauma that splits the subject internally is the *exception*. (4) It is also a condition of dispersed, multiple awareness states that can present in any number of ways, but crucially are present in ordinary managerial situations, like driving or teaching or giving a lecture, in the sense that one has normative performative obligations to focus on that demand bracketing the many on behalf of particular vortices or perspectives. Being trained as a professional, for example, is a training in dissociation. (5) Finally, I will argue, dissociation is a predictable effect and nonexceptional experience of living with, in, and under biopower's structural disciplines and historical aggressions, even when they're enacted in the register of care or life-affirmation.[4] I am referring to racism, misogyny, homophobia, xenophobic and class disgust, and not just as structures but as lifeworlds, where the impersonality of structural violence becomes personal, as it is both projected onto the persons who are members of populations already deemed deficient and internalized as a fact that shapes, without determining entirely, the forms that being deemed a kind of person takes.

The biopolitical perspective on a dissociative poetics attends to life taking form from within an ongoing difficulty felt in the body as a demeaning displacement. Frantz Fanon's demonstration in *Black Skin, White Masks* of explosive self-fragmentation in response to a proliferation of anti-Black projections onto him that stick, yet do not add up to him, is a classic example.[5] More recently, in their crucial and powerful book *Racial Melancholia, Racial Dissociation*, David Eng and Shinhee Han offer the phrase *psychic nowhere* to describe the nonground of desperation and stressed adaptation on which recent East Asian migrants to the United States have lived. *Racial Melancholia, Racial Dissociation* locates these affective states not only in the effect of departing from family and homeland but also in the strain of managing familiar and unfamiliar forms of success, sociality, and sexuality that entangle ambition, pleasure, self-doubt, and self-loathing.

In Eng and Han's telling, the individualist project of using the university to organize becoming a self-integrated person with manageable inner conflicts and an arc of life that students look forward to forging fails dramatically, often tragically.[6] The students' defenses crumble enough that, against pride and tradition, they seek clinical help and diagnoses. Melancholia's twisting attachment styles and dissociation's multiplication of conflicting self-states shape their lives as zones of defenses against the world. The authors cast Generation X as burdened by a struggle with melancholic attachments to lost contexts of the monocultural life to which, as migrants, they have erratic and ambivalent access; they cast Generation Y as burdened by a desire for forms of freedom from the past and family by way of the inevitable self-reinvention migrancy forces on its subjects-in-displacement, a situation that generates hoards of secrecy like sexual closets and other contradictions that are difficult to bear. Melancholic life turns toward suicidal hopelessness; for good and ill, the deracinated life produces dissociated subjects. Blocked from full-throatedly cultivating affirmative forms of fun, play, and speculation without dread, Eng and Han's Asian-racialized clients, students, and populations are unable to engage in satisfying self-development.

Eng and Han's insights laser in on a very specific set of disruptions and symptomatic dissolutions from pressures exerted by ethnicity, race, sexuality, and geopolitical, economic, and psychic displacement. They achieve this by powerfully and persuasively gathering historical, structural, and autobiographical forces that express traditional and neoliberal logics. Yet in *Racial Melancholia, Racial Dissociation*, the toggle between individual case studies and structural generalization, and the emphasis on styles of disorder that lead to illness and diagnosis, focus on turning these affects into curable dramas by way of reducing symptoms through therapeutic explanation. My focus on aesthetic cases allows for feeling out the moments of living the inconvenience of being an imperfect and flailing subject, whose debilitating and desiring moods force them to generate alternative forms of getting through episodes and existence that allow for continued attachment to life. My focus is on biopolitical displacement from and injury by the normal and the privileged within a convergence of many structural inequalities, and on how inventive alterations of receptivity can generate spaces of alternative life *alongside* threat and breakdown. This discussion of dissociation will elaborate on the affect state's pervasive cuts and creative heterotopian builds. The frantic creativity toward survival in atmospheres of threat and distress wears people out, creates at once useful and terrible defenses, and fuels lives scrambling and planning to thrive in resistance and desire.

Dissociation under such conditions of structural hazard often involves an overwhelmed subjectivity vibrating with extreme defensive hypervigilance, a multiplicity of speculations and thoughts about what threatens and who's to blame, and a variety of intermediate states ranging from the numb to the acute, the heavy to the frenzied, the shrugging to the furious, and the rational to the ranting: the affective stations of biopolitical realism. So, to call dissociation a structure of *discontinuity* would underassess its contribution to self- and collective persistence and disregard its profoundly social and historical character. It would preserve its conventional association with manifestly flat expressivity and dramatically split consciousness and reproduce the association of reasonable performance with psychic self-integration. It would too often bracket the beyond-survival imaginaries of those deemed inconvenient toward reconfiguring the world. This chapter emphasizes the structure of continuity within this condition of affective shifting along the nonlines of life in ellipsis.

Thus, dissociation can be a tragic or stunned-tasting state but it does not have to appear as a symptom that looks or feels like a clean state of detachment. It can be affectively sensed as a gap in some places and an event complete with a saturating image in others. But usually the subject in dissociation fears its multiplication of loosening attachments and compulsively reenlists in the drama of seducing the world in the way she knows how, and she does this literally without thinking.[7] By trying to remain clotted with the object of desire, by insisting on having an object in a particular way, we can refuse its contingency and our fragility. We can remain in a drama we know. But in our particular cases, the subjects move through life with a kind of diffidence or openness as to what might be converted to a hook, an anchor, or a direction, and how. In the cases I address here, the prolific splits of affect and attention in the face of disturbing events and insecure objects provide opportunities to hold out for life detached from the damage wrought by the usual ways that making up a life can use up a person.

For purposes of exemplification, I read with the supertext of A Single Man, involving both Christopher Isherwood's 1963 novel and Tom Ford's 2009 film, and Rankine's lyric Don't Let Me Be Lonely.[8] Both of these works sort dissociated life with something like a state of disbelief about what it takes to have a life, and not just in the historical and geopolitical present. They figure life as a bodily experience in proximity to desire and death, especially within the sexualized and racialized ordinary of many saturating inequalities that have to be lived at some closeness and distance: dissociation is both.

Here the subjects of suicidal ideation are considered by the powerful and the supremacist to be the inconvenient ones. But whatever politics emerges from the bodily intensities from the below that is also an outside and too much inside also expresses a version of the inconvenience drive that insists that the world owes them a different register of the ordinary and the structural in order to have a life worth staying in and pursuing. The aesthetic worlds of the Black, gay, sick, and laboring that are occupied in this chapter keep generating strongly felt experiences of vulnerability and threat, over-closeness and distance, and pleasure in the register of suicidal ideation, which often is itself a mask for an affective sense of the radical incoherence and impaired action that subordination produces. Both works also entertain suicide to imagine healing the fissures in the collective sensorium that Adorno called "damaged life."[9] Both works insist on cultivating the necessary life force of the heterotopian alt-world imaginary.

Take with you, for instance, Ntozake Shange's For Colored Girls Who Have Considered Suicide / When the Rainbow Is Enuf. Shange locates her survivors in economic, sexual, affective, familial, and political life contexts where survival is under pressure and fight is exhausting and confusing. She then moves the survivors she creates from the proximity to overclose suffering that produces their suicidal ideation as a relief from a seemingly foreclosed life, to the glorious space she calls "the ends of their own rainbows."[10] This is to say that she designs for them ways to use their physical and emotional energy to create alternative arcs, tableaux, and atmospheric colors in infrastructures for encounter, performance, and collective development. Racialized, gendered, and sexual flesh become firestarters that burn some narratives and inflame others. The title of the book, a poem with a line break, is also its dedication: to the "colored" survivors and more-than-survivors who resisted the story of impossibility handed to them from becoming their only story. She gifts them the formal "meanwhiles" of dissociated life.[11]

Biopower asserts the proximity of some kinds of life to a living death. Yet if the pressure of autopoietic death saturates the atmospheres of *Don't Let Me Be Lonely* and *A Single Man*, no one kills themselves. Suicide is in the air as potential, as a looming consoling and threatening event. It is political in the sense that Huey Newton's "revolutionary suicide" is: a radical refusal to reproduce the calcifications of power in bodily and practical acts that affirm collective life.[12] It is lyrical in that it uses personal narrative to exemplify living as a "kind" of thing.

In other words, the very specter of self-induced finitude appears in a dissociative poetics when life as an x keeps on hitting the limit.[13] This shift between suicide and its ideation makes a difference. As Foucault argues, biopower not only forces individuals in its targeted populations to appear in life in a certain way; it also associates them with death and a proximity to death yet unfulfilled. It justifies racialized, gendered, and class mortal injury as somehow what these populations have already experienced or are imminent in their experience. It normalizes suicide as an option and casts its recent rise as an "epidemic" as something to be expected in a suffering community that is living out a bruising history.[14] In this chapter's archive, living, thinking, planning, and scrolling through suicide becomes a way of life for the subordinated in exhausted submission and resistance to wearing out.[15]

Suicidiation under the discipline of biopolitics, then, is neither an expression of identity nor a plan. It is a register in which the labor of managing the work of living uneasily as a social problem or as a being battered by the ordinary of contingency and crisis imprints itself on consciousness. Sometimes suicidal ideation is executed in suicide. There are many reasons for the contemporary swelling of such events of self-cancellation, from exhaustion from being targeted by the predictable lived frictions of white, hetero, and national supremacy to the shock of insecurity and loss of standing for people who had believed that they would be cushioned by their intimate and economic statuses and fantasies.[16] Sometimes, too, "life" is chosen through suicide, as in dramatically political sacrificial acts of performative immolation. But usually, and here in this chapter's archive, suicidiation marks the sense of the unendurable that is endured, and the work of holding things together while feeling that they might not hold and that life, as it is known, might not either.[17] Suicidal death can tie up life in a tragic narrative package: triggers of suicidiation show the desire for life and the effort it takes for it to be affirmed and extended, even while raveling and unraveling.[18] Suicidiation requires its own concept. It is not defined by the success or failure of an intention.

In each of this chapter's aesthetic cases, an exhausted, historically saturated being moves around life without unconscious fantasy or compulsive symbolization filling up "the hole in the real."[19] The protagonist's dissociative sensorium sees the world and is in it, and at the same time has turned elsewhere—because it must, because it needs to, because it did, or to test out ways of flourishing. I argue that there are reasons to literalize such thought at the limit of life and that there are political forces shaping the direction of the ongoing pressure of that thought. The artworks record this disturbance as an affirmative disorientation through aesthetic modes that register an affective experimentalism. The tone emerges from the internal frictions of being in life without wanting the world. Life proceeds as the world recedes as an object/scene for desire. Even the distinction between life and world is a political one in these contexts: life, a technical scene of animated and dynamic embodiment; world, the sensed, physical, and extensive context for social being and collective life that is saturated by norms of the relation among action, effect, institution, and event.

Dissociation, in these works, is crossed over by many affects: the subject's discovery of a relief from losing the world that had rarely, in any case, been welcoming; a beleaguered atmosphere that generates a version of suicidiation that holds open a place for stopping the reproduction of loss; and a proliferation of tones and gestures toward seeding new forms of life. When scholars talk about political subjectivity or the social life of affect and emotion, we tend to focus on a dominant tone, one at a time—shame, happiness, or trauma, say. It also might be none at a time: a pulsating noise, interrupted signals, or split off attention. It might be multiple, in ambivalent arcs or proximate disorganized tendencies. When we talk about political emotions, we often tie them up to the most calcified version of events, in the exceptionalizing language of catastrophe or scandal. But, most importantly, affect also inevitably marks unincorporated domains of experience that have not, and may not, become event, scene, or anchor.

The loss of a project of reinfusing the threatening world with the optimism saved for the attachment to life is therefore not always catastrophic, apathetic, or even curious. Here is another way of thinking about object loss: when an ordinary form of life is radically disturbed such that a subject's or people's sense of continuity is broken, what results is the release of affective enmeshment from its normative attachment habits. In other words, when one's attention is bound to something that organizes one's energy or interest, that very relation, for good and ill, provides an infrastructure for understanding and moving through a situation or world: think the nation form as an object of desire, or the concept of your own goodness or trustworthiness, or just something that's been around as long as you have, say the sun, the earth, or a parent. The previous chapter discussed the effects of unbinding from a constitutive object in terms of the energy released from a broken analogy. The aim of protecting and extending self-infrastructure had organized the intensities of your need for specific objects that seemed to contribute to a world you wanted to be in; the loss of the sustaining object returned this organizing energy to you. The freed energy and attention can be inconvenient, even frightening, because without the object organizing your inconvenience drive or your fantasies of the stabilizing object, you're now at loose ends that are threatening; at the same time, those energies are available for recomposing the world, causality, and possibilities. This is how dissociation can be at once a blockage and a defense whose cleavages can threaten and protect the attachment to life.[20]

It is this relation between negative and affirmative dissociation on which I focus in this chapter. As with all of the case studies with which this book works, the question is not how to lose an object but how to loosen it, how to make it available for different kinds of attachment, use, form, concept, scene, world. These works offer us some resources for paying attention to disintegrated existence as a thing in itself, an effect of subordination, a necessary transition, and sometimes as a confirming mode of being in a world defined by a menacing threat that is structural, if by "structural" we mean the activity of predictable life within complexly knotted fields of force, resources, and activity that shape our imaginaries of value and of what it's possible to do about them.

I call this interim state of life-affirming world loss "being in life without wanting the world." To anyone structured by political consciousness, being in life without wanting the world is a common and recognizable affect: I'd say, a fundamental political affect. It occasionally gets pointed to as a symptom: of trauma, depression, or anomie, a kind of thing that's gone wrong and produced the senses of brokenness I have just described. But it need not be defined only or mainly in negative relation to normative paradigms of integration and fluidity. It need not be romanticized either. It could be better understood as a state in which the drive to stay attached to life is met by a world of inadequate objects. As a political sense, it need not only be defined as a response to dramatic damage, passivity, or defeat. It also involves subcutaneous or fleeting experiences of aversion and the desire for something else. In these artworks, the protagonists are always testing the world to determine if the energy absorbed by transformative projects is worth the absorption of their best creativity.

To document this end, this chapter offers living in ellipsis as a structure of dissociated continuity loosely bound to symbolization, a way of life that is not a project or anchored to norms of explicit fantasy.[21] In Deleuze's work on pure immanence, the word *life* itself is often followed by an ellipsis. "What is immanence? A life . . ."; "A singular essence, a life . . ."; "One is always an index of multiplicity: an event, a singularity, a life. . . ."[22] Grammatically an ellipsis signifies both that which can go without saying—inside knowledge, withdrawn or withheld, but in the collective assurance of "you know what I mean"—and its antithesis, that which fails or breaks in the phrase, a petering out leading from knowledge to the punctuated unsaid. Elliptical life then emerges in the place where what's known meets what's unknowable and what goes without saying meets what fails to reach meaning. Whether or not a sentence shaped by its ellipsis insists on what is already known, lapses into failure, or follows multiple tracks, it always sets off speculation and interrupts realism. If it has a shape, it is the shape of, in Derrida's phrasing, "wandering without return" to building on form in the usual sense.[23] This wandering incites Jean-Luc Nancy to cast the ellipsis as the placeholder for the lost body that finds sense anew, displaced from fantasies of its origin—a sense that can encounter itself only as absurd, always out of context.[24] This pervasive lostness and displacement can sound tragic, and indeed the ellipsis can be cast as the dissociative diacritical mark that is rhetorically rendered as a falling apart of meaning and connection. But its collapse also releases affective potentiality into the very process of lapsing: the loss of the narrative line to component parts; the scatter as a call to connect the dots differently, or not, to devote them to play.

This elliptical self-division is what allows the pieces in this chapter's dissociative archive to spend long stretches as comedies, defined not by what is funny but by scenes of satire, irony, and falling apart without ceasing to exist.[25] Propped near the tragic but seeking out life, the protagonists, defined by how they feel out the world, find that there is no tone, no dominant structure of "feeling in solution" for an imminent class formation, to smooth their unsteadiness, distance, and restless rhythm. Rather than fleeing the dissociative state, they prefer its ellipsis to any other.[26] They shrug, they rant, they pursue life, they eat, they're political and distracted, they move. Their exemplary force is in how they embrace dissociation both as an affirmative state and a pathological one that is also a political one, not to be overcome by coveting objects, reinstating normatively meaningful worlds, or achieving seriousness. In the state of withdrawal that can lead to pleasure in abstraction, they point to particular ways to live in negativity, located in the continuity of belonging to life across a whole range of tones rather than to the world's echo chamber. Thus this is an exercise in thinking nonreproductive continuity. How do we stay in life without reproducing what's diminishing in it? If unlearning it isn't an explicit project of loosening one's and the world's anchoring objects, how else can one inhibit going along with things because of the sour realism "it is what it is"? Here there's an offering of how to construct and occupy the historical present.

I am, then, neither selling the dissociative state as an aspiration nor idealizing it as a counter-world heterotopia. In thematizing the idiom of suicidiation, these works figure the limit from which they retreat and with which they move, living on in a space that associates "freedom from" with an openness that also brings dread, revenge fantasies, disavowal, and speculation. I am proposing the dissociative as a common condition that brings with it a clarifying resource for thinking about what to do with a life that is defined by what is out of joint in it.

11. Interlude, *A Single Man*

Toward the middle of Tom Ford's 2009 film adaptation of Christopher Isherwood's *A Single Man*, the protagonist, George Falconer, plans to kill himself and fails (figure 3.1). Ford invents this plot, which is not in Isherwood's 1963 novel, to demonstrate what it's like to hit a wall that cannot be scaled by optimism. Multiple negations disclose the world in front of Falconer as an impossible place for happiness. Some of them are structural: in the novel and the film he rants passionately against a United States that is still familiar, fueled by fear of communists, gay people, African Americans, and other nonnormative immigrant strangers whom he analogizes as "freckled."[27] At the same time, his injuries are radically personal: the political rage with which he moves is all bound up with mourning his dead lover, Jim, the beautiful boy who appears to him as evidence that he's been loved and that he's lonely—and to the film audience by way of gorgeously textured flashback, fantasy, and soundtrack eruptions that arise disconcertingly within the already disturbed space of the cinematic biographical and historical present.

In the novel, Falconer's politically and erotically complex darkness is accompanied by a pervasive sense of abstractness, as though he lives one thin-

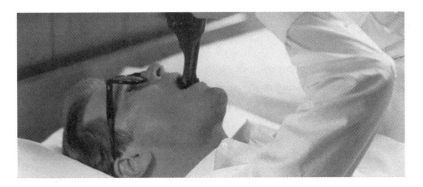

3.1 A *Single Man*, directed by Tom Ford, 2009.

walled apartment away from the events in which his body is fully involved. He imagines throwing himself into situations, but every scene is infused with the noise of alterity, indecision, defense, distraction, and appetite. Dissociative life is the definition of life in A *Single Man*. This is how it opens: "WAKING up begins with saying am and now. That which has awoken then lies for a while staring up at the ceiling and down into itself until it has recognized I, and therefrom deduced I am, I am now. Here comes next, and is at least negatively reassuring; because here, this morning, is where it has expected to find itself: what's called at home."[28] This is, in one sense, ordinary subjectivity, the ordinary self-composition of the subject upon waking. Movement precedes consciousness, and architecture confirms identity. The provisional unity of the "I" is a thing in the room, like the ceiling, and it locates the subject minimally as an effect of sequences of actions rather than biographies or other histories.

This is not a scene of being thrown together and becoming integrated for the day and for life. It is a process of self-organization whose ongoing dynamics constitute the ordinary work of being a being that most people do habitually, or don't much notice. But it is more than that too. Falconer is an English professor who monologues about the loose nets that narrative provides for staging what's off, is not right, and should not make sense in the world. In his polemical teaching voice and inner voice, he casts the usual work of making sense as a weapon that uses judgment to support the ordinary violence of national, racial, and sexual supremacy and tries to sublimate desire into an erotics of propriety. Making sense normatively is a shortcut; it's what the unthinking do. Before Jim's death Falconer was satisfied with playing at making sense for others, assuming their lack of serious interest in unlearning the defenses against engagement that they put up against the world. Now his play seems more sadistic. The mourner does what he needs to do to get through the day. To look adequate, he has to appear to have an intention, to seem competent to obligations and plans: for him in the present, there is no coasting in the ordinary.

To start the novel's day he separates himself into consciousness and "chauffeur." The "it" here is his body: "More and more it appears to separate itself, to become a separate entity: an impassive anonymous chauffeur-figure with little will or individuality of its own, the very embodiment of muscular co-ordination, lack of anxiety, tactful silence, driving its master to work."[29] Identity is a thing for others, an interface; the contact of this interface with the multiplicity of others he encounters induces a space in which the subject accompanies itself and exchange is made possible by the bad or distracted modes of skimming that people use to get by in the ordinary. Many encounters in the novel are made possible by the flexibility of performative coherence that language and bodies can achieve. Falconer is relieved to be known only partially, and not just because it holds off other people. It is a relief to him to be mentally and affectively free, as long as the body is doing its personality thing. As is always the case, affects are exchanged in his transactions and create the reality-effect of realness, but the effects are deflections and seductions. As a man in mourning whose story is about whether he can bear to take in a substitute love object to reorganize his incoherent drives, he is also wary of the usual thing that passes for openness to the encounter, and he is comfortable scrolling through split-off selves to be, shall we say, episodic. The fact of these multiple movements is ordinary: what's special about A Single Man is the clarity with which internal separation allows for life to be lived through, sieved, reflected on, lied about, cared for, and thus enjoyed.

Yet while Falconer hates the incuriosity and phobias of the normative world, he refuses to substitute surface warmth for the inconvenience of intimacy. He says, "It's the enormous tragedy of everything nowadays: flirtation. Flirtation instead of fucking."[30] Why? To him, flirtation protects the fantasy and appearance that one is open to others when one is actually being defended, even averse; flirting is a form of defensive passivity passing off as an invitation to life. This is not just personal: Isherwood writes it as a judgment against his era's dissociated erotics, at least as they manifest in the university and gay cruising scenes through which Falconer moves. Saturated by the flashbacks that remind him of Jim's sustaining love and insecure about how to proceed through space and the present, his flirtation with the possibility of a world would feel like a pretense and a defeat of the psychological, social, and political project of being frank about desire.

What Falconer loves is "borrowed energy," which requires proximity, not understanding, not possession, just what animates being near difference, close to the enigma of the other that produces a lighting up.[31] He is interested, too, in how aggression and desire animate the smallest child, the teen, the prostitute, and the exhaustedly aged, all on the make for experience. This is the shape his inconvenience drive takes. He is miserable to see how showing up for the encounter is beaten out of people, who then look for conventions and signs to substitute for engagement. It *was* easier when Jim was alive. The couple buffered the world where the aversive sense of its inconvenience lived alongside the drive to be inconvenienced by desire. The shattering of sex, the bit of craziness that led him to stay close to love—to sit with it on the couch, to bump into it in the kitchen, to have at it sexually on an unlit beach—allowed for inhabiting the other spaces of life from many distances: the distances of neighborliness, collegiality, and the political. When he was happy this alienation seemed to be not just bearable but interesting, because love, even toxic love, has a way of cushioning things. Now, in a present carved out by mourning, the stark costs of the difference between the zero of sexual solitude and the one of the couple form have set him off as a speculator, a social theorist of the charade of intimacy that prevents real encounter. Now, dissociation spares him from despair. Throughout the novel and the film, he looks at the world through windows, across aisles, across the street, overhearing life, distancing it affectively when his body's too close for comfort, letting the world-impact flood him when his body is anonymous, and, when the world-impact is unavoidable, using the deflections of polemic and sarcasm to protect his optimism for life.

But if, in the novel, Falconer scrolls through scenes in a way both intensely present and curiously distant, the film figures this condition of being multiple by way of a differently split aesthetics. There are repeated flashes to the naked Falconer floating in a fish tank, his face turned away from the camera; while he floats we hear mournful music. This figure of beautiful dissociation makes it seem like a cross between floating and drowning. At the same time, he tenderly and satirically fixates on the world, judging the effects of its violent ordinariness and judging other people for the pleasure they might or might not provide.

But all of these images are folded into the tight script of a day in the life of a man who is planning to escape altogether from the genre of life—a suicidiation plot. From the still shown in figure 3.1, you get the picture of his meticulous preparation for a clean, cool ending: the white shirt and sheets that always encase him continue to compose him, and clearly he has had the thought that even after suicide he should like to be found wearing his glasses. The director directs the film just as the protagonist stages the final scene: as a conversion of disturbed life to the stilled life of a still life that can imagine itself only as beautiful, even after death.

What cannot be seen in the image, though, or in the tragic intent whose pressure builds throughout the film, is the comic setting that the film provides for this event once we reach it. As the plot moves toward death—the papers drawn up, the notes written—the tension rises. But in the final instance, and as Falconer readies the gun and himself, he keeps changing position and tries to get death right: his body shifts, wiggles, and grimaces, and before we know it the scene becomes slapstick, and the soundtrack has turned from operatic intensity to a sprightly, comic, sitcom-like air. Before, throughout, and after the event, the mood does not add up. The episodes turn out to be just one thing after another. Then the phone rings, and Falconer leaves the shot diagonally, ridiculously, to answer it: and that's the end of his attempt to end.

So much for planning definitive action. The event held in prospect merely dissolves, peters out. Falconer's comic departure from his ending makes the suicidal scene merely another prospect cut short, not building up into a story that makes final sense of his continuity. What are all the preparations for if we never achieve being the protagonist that we think we are? What *are* we living for if our idea of being a protagonist is all wrong, overinflated in order for us to protect ourselves from our ambivalence about needing the world we receive and our confusion about what to do with tenderness and vulnerability to formal and informal power?

Then, what does it mean to give up plotting for life? Is being on the make for life the same thing as being in life? Is the deflation of fantasies of heroic agency equivalent to a slow-death suicide?[32] Is it here the effect of being gay and therefore not counting in the fantasy of the good life for anyone who is outside gayness?[33] Can the freedom from a plot and a sitting with the modal multivalences of affect provide space not only for resting and thinking but also for loosening up into dissociation's alternative prospects? In A *Single Man* the comedic turn builds a temporary scaffold for an alt-world projection. It reframes the Final Event as a comic dissolve, where the elliptical becomes an ellipsis. In the film, after failing to not exist, Falconer returns to ambivalent action. He seeks out and picks up a student who believed the façade that Falconer has just failed to shed. The student therefore cannot know him. They talk past each other for a while and give up. The grooming plot dissolves too. But Falconer's return to using his imagination to reboot the relation of desire to action does not become illegitimate.

This suicidal moment, or whatever it is, is like much ordinary action, an incident that does not become event, a dot that might or might not be on a line, an impulse that does not quite achieve a concept.[34] Falconer dies at the end of the story anyway, of natural causes, it turns out, although one is directed heavy-handedly to consider the phrase *broken heart*. That the plot is structured by suicidiation and not suicide tells us something about how to read the mood and tone of this kind of moment. It's the kind of moment in which the subject, walking around the world doing ordinary things while living at a distance from what also saturates him, comes to sense that no drama of relief in others, in substances, in polemic, or in art can really repair the situation. He wants to be in life. But he is not able again to throw himself into being inconvenienced by the world.

III. On Dissociative Life

The structure of dissociative life has no organic relation to its representation. By *life* I mean something simple, like ongoing existence, but also something singular that is sensed affectively, a continuous process virtually apprehended, to which Deleuze points: "This is not some abstract, mystical notion of life but *a life*, a specific yet impersonal, indefinite life discovered in the real singularity of events and virtuality of moments. A life is subjectless, neutral, and preceding all individuation and stratification, is present in all things, and thus always immanent to itself. . . . A life is everywhere, in all the moments that a given living subject goes through and that are measured by given lived objects."[35] A life is sensed in the between of things; Tim Ingold describes it as a virtual continuity actualized in moments without being entirely constituted by their specificity.[36] By *dissociative life* I mean a life lived in intimate relation to life in a lifeworld that is also, and at the same time, apprehended ambivalently, from engaged distances, in an affective structure where inhabitants dwell in a detachment that does not signify an absence of feeling. In these cases, some of the displacement responds to the narrators' specific assemblage of biopolitical overdetermination: Isherwood's protagonist is a gay white man in no couple or family, who is aging with a diseased heart and softening belly during the high-water days of homophobic American Cold War militarism; Rankine's poetic memoir-figure is a Black woman living in America in a heterosexual family, friend, community, and national-imperial world who has their own dramas of mental and metastatic illness in the crosshairs of predictable white supremacy and George W. Bush's Iraq war.

In other words, these are historical works whose somatic events of disease and disturbance register the formal, gestural, and distributed life-attrition of lived inequality. Some of the dissociation they record, though, is temporized ordinary consciousness. Some of it is the singularity of individual perception. So, to call dissociation "structural" is to include diverse phenomena expressed in the world's predictable impact for different reasons, in different realist idioms, through institutions, the body, and sensoriums. To call out biopolitically induced dissociation is to see the interests of congealed power and privilege to use class, gender, sexuality, race, and national fantasy to create failed subjects.

Recalling our earlier taxonomies, in "Metropolis and Mental Life," Georg Simmel calls dissociation the ordinary state that socialization to modernity demands, an inside voice that performs affective pseudo-autonomy from the ongoing pressure of what Mark Seltzer calls "the official world."[37] On the other side of this model of dissociative structure is a view of the world's destructuration by catastrophe. Among models in which decomposition expresses itself in intense flailing at establishing patterns are the traumatic formations that Adorno styles as symptoms of "damaged life" and that Cathy Caruth would point to as evidence of unclaimed experience.[38] Here, too, "history is what hurts" and turns the sensorium into a survival zone that tries to defend against the damage of dissociation.[39]

For Caruth, any cure would involve converting dissociation into narrative, or whatever form of encounter would allow affective stuckness to get moved into a new pattern-form somewhere. It does not require a healing narrative that erases the symptom, but a virtually physical sense that the very movement of figuration is a movement of reconfiguration that can loosen the symptom into material for a better mode of existing. Adorno responds in a similar fashion to this imperative not to give trauma the last laugh, this time by reimagining lyric subjectivity. The lyric mode splits the subject into a symptom of the kinds of capitalist alienation that both provide an argument for work as a space of self-realization and allow for love of all sorts to perform a kind of freedom, whether in marriage or friendship. The time-boxing that constitutes the capitalist logic of the everyday forecloses the political resonance of life-reproductive action for reshaping the general world. A dissociated aesthetic, then, would be both evidence of damage and a pathway to an overcoming that does not neutralize being overwhelmed but makes room for affective creativity at the level of description and association, which in turn changes what the object is and can do.

So, what I'm describing is neither dissociation as an escape from the world that cannot be expelled nor any literal expression of the subject's alienation from juridical, political, and intimate normativity. Rather, dissociation happens because life emerges in the middle of a world. It is what happens after a sensual circuit breaker trips and dislodges confidence in anchoring, world-propping objects. The world becomes overclose and the defenses reorganize or merely throw themselves around. This allows the subject to maintain attachment to life without confidence about the object world's trustworthiness. The ordinary state of political injury and sensual incoherence becomes a psychic event of self-division that allows the subject or population to avoid becoming stuck in a drama of the intractable. The dissociative drama points more to a wandering like static electricity or dry lightning whose thunder never comes.

Dissociation is not an action, then, but a state of multiplicity that takes shape in existence. A psychoanalytically inclined reader like Daniel Stern would see a dissociative aesthetics as tracing the ordinary and inevitable displacement of affect from the concrete situation of its arousal. Dissociation appears in the discovery that there has been an affective event available only through delayed processing, a space and way of reencountering how one has been being in the world. As I argued in this chapter's first section, "delayed action" is structurally inevitable, a whiplash of self-displacement that forces reflexivity into being in life. That whiplash is the present and mostly a nonevent.

But affective catch-up usually emerges in the form of self-integration or symbolic binding, in which the encounter with the impinging world confirms the continuity of one's place in it. In a dissociative aesthetic, on the other hand, the affective event does not generate formal satisfaction in the sense of resolution. It's expansive. Think of the ordinary self-departures associated with the concept of mood. Christopher Bollas describes mood as the affective leftover of childhood anxiety triggered into animation by an encounter or scene in the present.[40] I prefer to think of mood more minimally as the experience of an affective noncontinuity between subjects and the atmospheres in which they're present. This is close to how Jonathan Flatley mobilizes the Heideggerian world-picture, but Flatley wants to convert detachment styles like melancholia into modes of optimism that sustain revolutionary imaginaries for the world.[41] In contrast, I see in this poetic something slower and more simple at first, more proximate to relief than repair, and that uses the meanwhile structure to generate a sense of the impasse and its potential transformation into next actions.

What if we called mood a structurally affective lag? To analyze a sense of failed attunement to the present might point to childhood, but it might just be what Shaka McGlotten calls a bleed, which is an affective disruption, whether from desire, the pressure of inequality in the ordinary, or just the impact of encounters.[42] That combination shapes both of these literary works. To study being in life without wanting the world is to dial back Flatley's optimism about association into a practice and discipline of dissociology, a zone of proximity crossing life and world where things do not add up but remain in range, shifting nearer and farther.[43] For structurally subordinated subjects such a frame can reroute the "rim of suspended being that makes bearable the uncertainty and pain of human relations" into a zone for a politicized affect theory.[44]

IV. Interlude: *Don't Let Me Be Lonely*

Claudia Rankine's lyric *Don't Let Me Be Lonely* is a post-9/11 work whose confidence in resilience and repair has been shaken so profoundly that each encounter with persons and the world before her seems to add to an archive of after pictures that document incidents without closing the case: because there is no simple before prior to the traumatic American event, the middle of life is an endless rhythm of incidents in the life. This episodic structure returns here, and in the succeeding members of Rankine's "American" set, *Citizen* and *Just Us*.[45] These episodes hit surprising limits: you never know when they're going to end because situations stop without achieving climax or closure, or anything we could recall as a shape whose causes are resolved in consequences. That is the brilliance of the genre of the encounter in Rankine's work: there are no beginnings, only scenes to be in the middle of. They are not shapeless, but defined by the rise and fall of the episodic, by the form of its movement and the reshaping of its emblematic moments, not by its delivery of closure, because there will be more, nor by the delivery of the comfort of a predictable unfolding or of wisdom statements that will set you free. The question is: How can we keep things, including selves, together whether they're at war or merely inconvenient to each other? Anthony Reed thinks of the lyrical subject of her "I" as not needing to be self-identical nor needing to be universal: local and on the move.[46] That seems right, but I think its episodic self-encounter serves a more extreme scavenging of history and the present too. A dissociative poetics emerges as a disturbed and searching historical consciousness.

Lonely opens with death as a life-defining beat: "There was a time I could say no one I knew well had died."[47] That "time" is unenumerated and takes place around a body that loves, overhears, makes jokes and wishes, and sits with the world, taking in its dings and being on the move through more. The episode form reminds you that there is always more to begin with: more racism, misogyny, heterosexuality, family, friendship, cancer, clinical and political depression. There are always more movies where dead stars still live, and more memories where poets remember the generativity of decomposition. There is a desire for radical hope. The structural continuity of these shifting scenes induces hypervigilance as a form both of focus and of distraction—of dissociation within the ordinary of crisis.

Soon the poem offers two stories of suicidiation. In these the present is so suffused with the ordinary of destruction that people who encounter even its potential rush to the end of the catastrophe, as if there's no slow time, no impasse, no testing, no wandering, no self-forgetting. It's Black life, it's the body's life, it's the intimate mediation called American life roiling from living through what is also not lived through. She cites Czesław Miłosz: "Whatever evil I had suffered, I forgot. . . . In my body I felt no pain."[48]

The protagonist girl lies flat on a roof with her feet hanging off the edge. We see her from above; we see her from below; we see the sky she's looking into. She's spraying poetry into that sky from memory, which is to say, as the time and evidence of her agency at producing objects that she wants to hold close. This is an affirmative sign of her dissociation: she's free from thinking of herself as an effect of the world and the street, geared toward using whatever is there to induce an endurance toward happiness, which isn't always ecstatic. The cost and benefit of dissociation is that it varies.

On the roof it's the happiness of space and of spacing out. Free dissociation emerges as a praxis of survival. Nonetheless, on the ground people read her hanging calves as steps toward a slow self-induced death. The street buzzes and the police are called: thus begins the narrator's book-long episodic and discontinuous encounter with a set of unanswerable questions: "Honey, what's your name? . . . Are you ok? . . . What the hell do you think you were doing? She loves him for asking."[49] The genre of the question peppers her first suicidiational move too: "Am I dead? . . . . I feel like I am already dead."[50] In this book questions generate other questions that sit with a complex of lonelinesses.

The lyric's suicidal imaginary opens up to a nonmorbid way of living with the broken bodies and subordination machines that generate the viscera of life and death, especially for anyone defined by their body as a weight: Black people living, dying, and dead, the cancerous, the reproductive, and the familial. Friends—and even more than that, strangers, that is, people whose weight remains to be felt—lighten things up. So if the collective that is the "American" is reanimated by the historical incident called "9/11," the book's manifest historical frame is not the narrator's primary trauma. As the lyric narrator tells it, already in youth she had subtracted parts of herself from a world poised against personal, bodily, Black, collective, hetero-feminine, and American thriving. It takes dissociation as a technology of citizenship. Throughout *Lonely* this congeries of subtraction takes on many literary forms. Laden with pictures and drawings of scraps and maps from the fecund space of catastrophe that constitutes the disruption called the American present, the book lays out a capitalist world where proximity to death by illness calls out the actuarial and the pharmaceutical; an ethno-supremacist world where the ever-present proximity of quick and slow death by racism produces mass exhaustion *and* not-caring; an elitist world, where extermination produces commentary more than prophetic resistance; barely any talk about money, yet so much activity of class domination in the form of supremacist strutting and bargaining with forms of insurance that don't ensure. George Bush, Colin Powell, James Byrd, pharmaceutical warnings on drugs whose side effects *might* destroy you, a cartoon map of America, too, as a failing bodily organ, and a *liver* because why resist puns when you are trying desperately to stay in life?[51] The narrative is about having no choice but to play close attention: but close attention is different from close reading. Taking in the world through a scanning focus is different from attempting to magnify specific details into profound exemplarity. If, in *A Single Man*, scanning used dissociation to betray the attachment that's made available during any encounter that merely flirts with life, in *Don't Let Me Be Lonely* it's an injury and vulnerability archive that also generates different, more livable patter and patterns than those housed in compartmentalization and affective suspension.

And so the lyric is full of puns. Puns break language; they're dissociative play. Aggression and fun, ungoverned. The text uses these kinds of whiplash to create cascades of almost-likeness in terms of pervasive blackness: "The years went by and people only died on television—if they weren't Black, they were wearing black or were terminally ill."[52] Drawing lines of association among what's been separated and deemed inconvenient builds a case for refiguring what passes as structure. Rankine's genres of the middle, her anecdotes, meanwhiles, and stagecraft, hold out for your consideration mourning, trying not to mourn, and outrage sitting together in the room of the page. This is less a book about what movement culture can do to amplify all that by joining voice and action: *Don't Let Me Be Lonely*'s everyday is from the local encounter with persons and the airwaves' atmospheres of the present.

The dissociative poetic also appears in the book's use of conversation, the overheard ones, the ones structured by unsaid things organized by captions and images, and the ones the narrator is actively in, whether directly or through overhearing. Here, listening models a pedagogy of receptivity, as though whatever happens makes a beat for the question, "What do I do with what you say?" The unsaid vastness between phrases provides relationality's infrastructure. The book contains a lot of one-sided dialogue, performing being in life without wanting the world. These nonconversations are shaped by internal monologue and apostrophe, two forms that hinge intimacy and absence: "What do we mean to each other? What does a life mean? Why are we here if not for each other?"[53] These questions are rhetorical, but no question is ontologically rhetorical. In the rhetorical question the speaker's aim is to induce dissociation: to disturb the interlocutor's confidence about what's transpiring, what to do, and what the shared knowledge actually is. What *can* go without saying? The question is ethical and political. Here the rhetorical question at once induces a scene of being tested and animates the ambition to be in the know. So in politicized contexts, a dissociative poetics is also a lesson in counterperformative splitting. It is taking the structural fact of being inconvenient and amplifying it to control the room. To convert a rhetorical question into an actual one is to engage in a political action about what gets taken for granted: to refuse, to out, what is left unsaid. To be left with a question instead of an answer is to live in the ellipsis. To squat and move around in the ellipsis denies norms their capacity to solidify the referent, to confront its uncanny substance as a gelatinous object of knowledge.[54]

Many of the poem's questions are also feeble, often dissociative defenses against more contact with what's overwhelming. The protagonist describes her mother's return from childbirth without a child. In response to the child's questions, the mother says nothing: the speaker asks, "Did she shrug? She was the kind of woman who liked to shrug; deep within her was an everlasting shrug."[55] The shrug is an ironic gesture that is defined, as a joke is, by its fatal brevity: in its own way the shrug is the body's rhetorical answer to a nonrhetorical question. Amid all this gesturing, her mother's voice floods the speaker, saying, "You don't remember because you don't care," as though memory itself were a sign of fidelity to witness and mourning. As the mother's critical, despairing, defensive, flat, and loving tones modulate, and as moods come and go, things remembered just string out and caring's holding power fades.

This style of variation within shattered yet continuous relations, in attachments that take place at an intimate distance, is expressed as well in the book's scroll-through media—television, poetry, blackboards, warning labels on medication, for example. Then, as critics like Cynthia Dobbs and Tana Jean Welch have documented, Rankine takes tone to be an agent of collective life; the same stories have different consequences according to tone's genres, such as melodrama, sarcasm, documentary recitation, ironic flatness, prose description, and stupefaction. The text loads image after image as though to induce in the reader confidence that there is always an alternative to dissociative rubbernecking at bodies that are marked for the next and the following catastrophe:[56] the tones of these episodes move from tragic and ironic to silly and to the painful beyond of comic, much like Falconer's do in A *Single Man*.

Likewise, *Don't Let Me Be Lonely* compels its readers to occupy the sociality of loneliness in America: to enter into a lyric transference with the intimacy within blocked relation, distributed attention, anxious unsaid things, and the scattered threat and optimism that are the everyday in which people imagine each other as allies, interference, or both. Often both. This mediated space of projection takes aesthetic form in a myriad of section breaks marked by the image of a staticky television (figure 3.2). The little monolith confirms that the transmission or communication has failed and is failing, and yet as a point of return it defines the present in which not only can "we" not see the whole story but must look elsewhere for a common of mediation, storytelling in another form.

Take the way the book documents its documentation. As orchestrator of the archive of suffering and form, *Lonely*'s zone of sense is so radically detached from the public world that the book's footnotes are unposted in the text and scattered at the back, to be tripped over only after the reader thinks that the reading event has been sealed off definitively. The footnotes are political, epidemiological, bibliographical, disjointed, and angrier than anything in the text in their very flatness. This is in contrast to the documentation performances of *Citizen* and *Just Us*: narrated context is the substance of *Citizen*, so its citations are flat citations, not demonstrations of historical depth; and in *Just Us*, the notes are continuous with the text's refusal to separate knowledges from each other, and so historical and personal sources and ruminations are all of a piece. It's as though keeping it all together and pres-

3.2 Television/noise of the world from Claudia Rankine, *Don't Let Me Be Lonely* (2004). Reprinted with permission from Claudia Rankine and Graywolf Press.

suring dissociation is a formally ethical and political obligation. In *Lonely*, though, this proliferation of unbound and attenuated notes leads to the comic diagnosis that the lyric speaker must have a personality disorder after all. Not quite a Fanonian shattering, it gets named "IMH, the Inability to Maintain Hope."[57] It is not that she is hopeless; it is that, being "too scared by hope to hope, too experienced to experience, too close to dead,"[58] she is, like Falconer, both intensely saturated by and at a distance from the world toward and away from which she is driven. But she's always in proximity: the world is inside, destroying life like a disease. This protagonist survives with the survivors in a penumbra defined not by story or its interruption but by a heap of gestures and tones and something else too: an acrid jokiness joined with genuine play, which always signals optimism about something. You can see some of this medium, genre, and affect-shifting in figure 3.3. The daughter is watching her mother, her Beckettian gaze delaminating her mother's lips and mouth from anything like a realist or historical body.[59]

My mother tells me I am just biding time. She means it as a push toward not biding time. She wants me to lead a readable life—one that can be read as worthwhile, and successful. My mother is not overly concerned with happiness, its fruitless pursuit or otherwise. As far as she can remember, there was only pain connected to the joy of childbirth. She remembers the pain and wants it to have been worthwhile, for a reasonable life.

As I watch my mother's mouth move, I ask myself: Am I often troubled by constipation? Have I ever vomited love or coughed up blame? Is anything wrong with my mind?

3.3 Transgenerational trauma style, from Claudia Rankine, *Don't Let Me Be Lonely* (2004), 40. Reprinted with permission from Claudia Rankine and Graywolf Press.

But it is not enough to call this splitting or shattering of the maternal image "violence." The cartoony mouth is sweet and simple, yet also a sour anchor and a failed refuge. The too-closeness of intimate relation induces dissociation as pleasure and necessity, love and prison, recognition and destruction. The mother aspires to reason while she speaks from pain, referencing joy sarcastically. The daughter responds to the emotional offering with her own admixture of intimacy and alterity: not only by ghosting her mother but also by staying with her noise; not only by writing solo but also by conversing; not only by becoming mouth but by becoming orifice in multiple ways, translating her mother's words into a clogging food that induces both constipation and vomiting.

It is as though the only way to remain engaged with the mother's dissociation without being attached or subjected to it is for the poet to assert a singularity in their own aesthetic style of being stuck, split, and expressive. Dissociative form is a twisting inheritance here, as it so often is. The cluster of familial gestures, powerful in their brevity and conventionality, converts to a scene that allows all of the knowledge involved in love's binding into the room of lyric consciousness and a practice that draws a membrane around desperation and love, without embracing their violence and demand as her own.[60] Indeed, one way to think of dissociation that originates in biopolitical pressures is to see its range of exhausted response and detachment as tragic pastoral vacation from affect's mimetic inclinations, while it nonetheless manifests a continued attachment to the genealogy of brokenness.

Emotions are always reflexive, context-spiraling, and belated to the incident that is becoming-event. Rankine's performance of them brings with it the affect of a profound dislocation across persons and generations that is, at the same time, the work of intimate assemblage. This style of dissociating resonates with what Patricia Williams calls the inheritance of a disinheritance that constitutes Black kinship.[61] Inheritance is here not a passive state, nor a belated one in which one adds up remainders and asks what kind of communication they are. Inheritance is active and a scene of intensive bargaining enacted in the intimacy of social pedagogy. It is another way to think about the unconscious components of the transgenerational tradition of trauma.

Williams's interest is in the pedagogies of care. The people who care for us, she argues, and especially mothers whose dreams have taken shape in proximity to the ordinary of historical violence, transmit patterns of attachment to those scenes. What's personal and impersonal about a life is, in all senses, affectively compelling, its mediating gestures and stories shaping the rhythms and weights of love while extending the pains and distortions of negating power. What's heartbreaking for Williams is that the reproduction of structural violence so often involves people recruiting each other to desire a common idiom—love what I love, dream what I dream, feel what overwhelms me, enjoy what I enjoy. This way they won't feel lonely and defeated by the wearing and threatening forces of life. The preservation of fidelity, the drive to stay in sync with another—which takes its own kind of courage—beats out the pursuit of justice and of happiness. This mix of false selves and toxic bargains in the face of protecting or maintaining love is one of the paradigmatic structures in which the inconvenience of other people induces anxious, genuinely ambivalent, attachment. Just as Williams brings to bear all the knowledge she has to loosen the tight knot of her mother's desire for defenses against what overwhelms and splinters her, so, too, Rankine's command and plea not to be lonely—it's both—places this chapter's archive in the annals of the affective phenomenology of structurally damaged life, whose exemplary figures—DuBois, Adorno, Fanon, and Williams, for example—also measure the disturbing psychic and physical effects of racialized subordination that they inherit and to which they themselves remain partially, unevenly, dissociatedly attached.[62] In this archive, "double consciousness" underdescribes the formally prolific work of ambivalence.

Peter Fonagy argues for this view of the politically archaic, anarchic, and hyperactive sensorium in his work on the transgenerational transmission of trauma.[63] Working with children and grandchildren of Holocaust survivors, Fonagy argues that history's disconcerting impact on intuitions involves much more than what ritual and memory convey. Phenomenological patterns indicating dissociation also pass on; future generations' physical and affective orientations to the world are fated to be out of joint. A child full of tics and rage, a grandchild of survivors, comes into his office: a story unfolds about the unsaid and blocked freedom habits that his mother took on from hers. History lingers in modes of coping and maladjusting. Subject to triggers in relation to disturbances that were telescoped decades and half centuries ago, these subjects of political dissociation could not know that their very bodily habits, styles of affective attunement, and gestures are anachronistic and out of tune too. In Rankine's adjudication of her mother's mouth, her friends' dementias and depressions, episodes of political violence, and transmedial events in the catastrophic ordinary, love involves allowing the rhetorical question of whether affective incoherence is bearable and where it comes from in order to remain overdetermined, rhetorical, and demanding, not suspended.

v. Proxemics

The event of dissociation is not defined by outcomes or dominant patterns or even feelings, but by attention to how life proceeds within the continuity of discontinuity. This requires rethinking the constitution of object and event, along with the forms relationality takes. By object, for example, I mean a scene of anchoring attachment, the site of disturbing or disruptive encounter in which one has discovered an attachment, an affective investment, or a sense of a shared real that holds up a part of the world about which one can feel both curious and ambivalent. Just as an object only exists once one has endowed interest in it, so, too, a scene is a situation laden with enigma and untapped potential. One can only be within it, responding to a sense of its contours, feeling them out and at the same time butting up against and through what turn out to be not laws but norms. A scene of structure, therefore, as Raymond Williams might say, is always a relation held in solution.[64] We might call the study of being in the middle of a relation without feeling integrated into it, as in a dissociative poetics, the study of proxemics.

As a field of study, proxemics was formulated by the anthropologist Edward T. Hall and was crucial for the development of the concept of "personal space" and other kinds of relational distance that could be taxonomized in degrees of intimacy, conventionally speaking. Unsurprisingly, I am interested more in proxemics as focalizing an affective sense of relational atmosphere along with being an orchestrated sense that produces and confirms norms of social ordering.[65] Liam Gillick uses this term to study the space of encounter, conversation, and world-extension that shapes the affective ambitions of the neoliberal ordinary, with its insistence on open cubicles and conversation, of being data for others and deprivatization; at the same time his writing and architectural art practice extend these practices to what he calls the "functional utopia."[66] A functional utopia is like a Foucauldian heterotopia insofar as it exists in the folds of the normative world; but what distinguishes Gillick's vitalization of proximity is the world held up by discourses of planning that make the next phase and the next after that real in language and form, even if they achieve the appearance of a static, normative impasse.

But to take the concept further, to see sociality as proximity can mean something quite separate from the normative measurement of belonging or being acknowledged or known. Proxemics is a fundamentally queer orientation to the atmosphere of affective impingement that I have been calling "inconvenience." I want to be near you, but what does that entail in terms of need, demand, obligation, the ephemeral, the enduring, the event, and the story of lives trying to make room for themselves in worlds? Comfort zones are also discomfort zones. About those, queerness presumes nothing and is foundationally skeptical of its own drawing of lines between the major and the minor, the liquid and the solid, seriousness and play, aggression and violence, proper and improper objects, and the deeply wrenching drives toward and away from identity. The world is continuously generating unincorporated spaces whose patina emerges from a collective imaginary's work and not just the projections onto it. In this understanding of political subjectivity as practice, affect, and resource, proxemics float the possibility that an aesthetics of proximity will find genres in dissociative life that will not feed back into normative worlding by direct or counter-worlding, or be recognizable elsewhere. The study of proxemics requires curiosity about what it means to be near, and whether the sense of it is commonly held in atmospheres and unsaid things, and in dramatic or ephemeral scenarios that never make their ways to plots of aggression and desire: proxemics allow us to think about the enigma of the adjacent other who still brings something to the sensed collective life that has not quite made a world.

Katie Stewart calls such inductive, conductive affect events "odd moments" within the ongoingness of things: the body jerks to life or the atmosphere shifts while at the same time there's a weight in the field of sense. "The uncanny sensation of a half-known influence" finds a resonance that marks a gap within the ordinary that just hangs there for projection.[67] It respects displacement and retains curiosity about a path that might not be narrative, but situational or episodic. In Stewart's work there's usually the gift of satisfaction in response to attending to the disturbance of a moment: seeing how things throw themselves together in a worlding allows affect to flow into phrases and signs in suspension, where moments in life appear as ekphrasis or tableau vivant. An intensified focus can push out some things and allow other things in *in a certain way*: dissociated consciousness provides a spacetime for occupying and navigating the inconveniences we want, don't want, or feel marked by but we're not sure how, and that we need to live with. This chapter's aesthetic cases suggest that survival depends on cultivating receptivity styles that can attend to the unequal price of vulnerability. The assessment of injury can add up so differently. The perspectives of dissociation, rather than being detached or nonchalant, allow for a flat, a gentle, and an outraged tone. Nuance and enigma clarify the pain of the dynamics of the present *and* the need to revise them from within the space of contact. Our proximity to each other is at once a thrill and irritating, but not always in the worst sense.

vi. Conclusion: Out, Damn Spots

Hannah Arendt writes that "The modern growth of worldlessness [is] the withering away of everything between us," including the failure of politics, of the optimism for forgiveness of what's irreversibly and intractably threatening in each other.[68] This chapter proposes a different way of seeing worldlessness: as a scene for life, but not for "a way of life" or "a good life." The difference between life in an ellipsis and these others is that their stress on being reliable against antagonism suppresses the inconvenient fantasies and the incoherence of practices that manifest the negativity or loose knottedness with which the subject and the world also move. Arendt would say that giving up the ambition to organize this material into an alternative general world is suicidal; Rankine's, Isherwood's, and Ford's work would suggest that this is barely, but importantly, a misrecognition. Life in the ellipsis of politicized dissociation is not identical to giving up; it's a condition of giving out that leads to feeling out, which is different from the heroics of assurance that accompanies most politically salient modalities of feeling otherwise. In ordinary diminishing proximity, people give out, figuring different subtractions from the unforgiving world. But while giving out, one remains in life. In querying attachment, one multiplies the approaches and forms that encounter can take. Here, in the historically precise social locations this chapter mobilizes, endemic pressures of structural and affective precarity, homelessness, migration, mourning—forms of displacement associated with property and the nation-state—both force the subject into exhausting dramas and open up new shoots defined by the many ways that incidents become event, including not at all.[69] This openness both to self and to world reorganization is the general situation that generates a dissociative poetic.

I have mainly described the tragic archive of this sensorium, but there is a comic one too. As Donna Goldstein and many other scholars of structural subordination have argued, dry camp tones and patterns of ironic dog-whistling also belong in this genealogy of life-affirming world-recession, although usually as rest stops between melodramatic flare-ups and flat acceptance.[70] These alternative frequencies live alongside other modes of perception and action, and put as much pressure on the present as do catastrophic events. In a politically dissociative consciousness, the distinction between openness and defense is unknowable, open to the inconvenient noise of the world's devastating realisms, resisting, shredding, but not dying from the encounter. Take, for a final example, Harryette Mullens's poem "Elliptical":

They just can't seem to . . . They should try harder to . . . They ought to be more . . . We all wish they weren't so . . . They never . . . They always . . . Sometimes they . . . Once in a while they . . . However it is obvious that they . . . Their overall tendency has been . . . The consequences of which have been . . . They don't appear to understand that . . . If only they would make an effort to . . . But we know how difficult it is for them to . . . Many of them remain unaware of . . . Some who should know better simply refuse to . . . Of course, their perspective has been limited by . . . On the other hand, they obviously feel entitled to . . . Certainly we can't forget that they . . . Nor can it be denied that they . . . We know that this has had an enormous impact on their . . . Nevertheless their behavior strikes us as . . . Our interactions unfortunately have been . . .[71]

What is the mood of this poem? What is the relation between its rage and its comedy? Where is it in relation to the world? Is it a court transcript or any conversation among elites about the humans they feel dragged down by, too proximate to? A writer has forced a cluster of sentences each to commit suicide on the page at the moment at which they would otherwise support their judgment. The evidence is suppressed that would explain supremacist reason in terms of the details that would, presumably, justify the power to generalize that their social standing would presume. Latour calls the units of this legitimacy fiction; this expertise drag, the "factish."[72]

But if all we know is of one population's affective assurance about some other people's collective inadequacy, the ellipsis releases other knowledge in the performative unsaid of a frictional sensus communis that cannot speak in the law's register. Neither player, not the judge-voice that speaks nor the editor-judge that cuts with an elliptical knife, speaks in tones of outrage; instead, the violence is in the antagonism among recessive gestures. The tragedy of reason when judgment is attached to power leaks out through the elliptical cut. The sentimentality of power toward itself for having to pass judgment on objects it deems inadequate also leaks out from the cut. The open secret that a writer and listener can always refuse to reproduce the privilege of what had been thought a performative utterance also plays itself out as a counter-power.

This staggering of tragic potentials also invokes the comic in the sense of allowing an imaginary of repair without erasing the situation of disrepair. The ellipsis slows things down, it makes the reader wait. But in accumulating a crowded series of interruptions, the poem also speeds things up, inducing an image of living with multiple kinds of negativity as "tragedy plus time," that classic definition of comedy. I venture that this is what suicidal ideation often does: act as a placeholder for the desire to stay in life but not in the world, an affect made unbearable by an incessantly pressuring structural continuity, an affect that taps into the comedic when the pressure produces the both/and right next to the neither/nor. In this chapter, that "incessantly pressuring structural continuity" is a mode of biopolitical negation, a force that mixes institutions of politicking and discipline with institutions of normativizing care. Agamben writes about the tragic as personhood violently shorn of its mask, reduced to its essential failure; the comic, in contrast, is that state in which the person is allowed the protection of living behind many masks, perhaps thin membranes away from system collapse but then available for life—which is to say, for expiation. The mask is the affordance of a structure of continuity and the comic is the affective atmosphere of an absurd but committed living-on.[73] In that sense, it is what Agamben would call a gesture, that movement in which "nothing is being produced or acted," but which releases from the image the energies it collects.[74]

There is something harsh and funny about the repetitions of power. There is something harsh and funny about the spectacle of the ironically self-pitying supremacist chorus taking pleasure at being "forced" into a performance of negative judgment against populations they love to feel superior to. The power Mullens takes is to cut off supremacist performativity at the pass, somewhat like the interruptive joy released by the phrase "reclaiming my time," when we follow its use as initiated by Representative Maxine Waters against bullshitters and liars. Mullens can't erase the brutality of white class supremacy but can model cutting off its sound and therefore its circulation and confirmation as a rational performance. Like refusing the rhetorical question, you can refuse the hegemon's self-authorization, merging the positions of audience and editor into a cutting and authorial counterpower: not just as an episode but in a collective practice. Here the critical, comic ellipsis wins the argument that it does not allow to get made and, in holding out for multiple moods and rhythms, releases the biopolitically defensive life from its worldly binding . . . into dissociation.

coda **MY DARK PLACES**

At a certain point in the writing of this coda, I stood up to get some air. When I returned, the page I'd left open next to the computer shot me the phrase, "Genital life gives way to bubbles, the notebook of a body's two eyes."[1] I didn't understand it, so I decided to read along to see whether I could create a context for it as I proceeded. I read until I realized that I'd actually seen the phrase hours ago and had run my eyes over the surface of it the way people run their mouths during conversations when they haven't quite found what they're trying to say: the phrase that can be returned to that allows for the making of fresh sense.

The book had flipped back. For a moment I was chagrined that I hadn't seen the phrase to remember it, and then I was doubly chagrined that I had expected myself to see everything, to know and place the parts in a whole in an instant and credible way, as though objects and genres are convenience machines that provide successful surrogates for thinking. But, as the last chapter argues, the way object/scenes come into form is always an outcome of scanning for repetitions: the form is at least an impasse, a semicolon, temporary housing, a transitional pattern on the move—a proposition for an infrastructure.

The blend-word *object/scene* is a performative reminder that a problem that captures analysis is really a convergence space of questions and interests that can be reorganized, walked around in, made incoherent, propositional, and part of a narrative, or not. Portmanteaus like this help me stay attentive to overdetermination, to give a living dimension to a problem. Object/scenes take shape in circulation, concepts, phrases, and descriptions. They change there, too, in the conversion space of analysis, where they get laid out in a context that changes what they can do.[2] Gayatri Chakravorty Spivak suggests something akin to this in defining the work of theoretical concepts with the words "descriptive/transformative."[3] It's not that a problem-object becomes a scene after a critical operation; it's that it already is one, a staging in a process whose activity, shape, and implication criticism takes up in the ways it tests out concepts.

I've argued throughout that writing this way makes not only transitional objects for reconfiguring specific attachments but also transformational environments that shift the structure of the world that the object/scene's presence draws together. Christopher Bollas writes that a transformational environment is an infrastructure that allows for substantive structural change without trauma, without suffering an experience of the world's absolute loss.[4] To achieve a transformational infrastructure is to loosen up at the moment when everything in me would prefer not to, would prefer for there to be a moving walkway between where I am and another place I can already see: a sidewalk embedded with concrete footprints that seem to have a destination in mind. "Genital life gives way to bubbles, the notebook of a body's two eyes." It turns out that my very experience of the changing discontinuous figure was what this concept was going on about.

This coda is about being and writing with unbearable objects—not by becoming hard like them or soft in empathic compensation, but by loosening them up and becoming loose with them, if not like them. Object looseness isn't captured by representation, because it is a moving condition. The writing in this book is meant to show some ways to transform the qualities of object/scenes by breaking them, testing out different potentials for the consequences they might produce, creating alternative-world workarounds subjectively and politically, and being able to be with the stress of ambivalence at the center of the inconvenience of sociality as such, whether in general or as a member of a population deemed to be inconvenient to the general supremacist happiness. The imprecise attachment manifested in the sense of the event of experiencing most inconvenience shows how badly we process the rise of this frictional intensity in its various situations, even when we want to be inconvenienced, receptive, or game for intimacy, solidarity, or other genres of identification. This chapter pushes at the wall of the ordinariness of this sensed experience to induce a different register for living with an object that seemingly can't be reassessed. It involves something like inducing a slackening in the unbearable object relation that shifts the situation but does not make it less unbearable.

If movement and motile aliveness are inevitably the case, what does it mean, then, to call something unbearable?[5] And why, in a book on the "inconvenient," am I turning to "the unbearable" in the end? After all, in this book I have undertaken to bracket the exceptional catastrophes, focusing instead on the problem of bearing nonsovereign life that circulates in the ordinary or as problems of violation, including rape and Black death—so pervasive that they often remain incidents rather than growing into transformational events. The thought experiments of the previous chapters focused on sex, the commons/democracy, and life as such, discovering from within a space of desirable relation a problem of ambivalent attachment that is not resolved by deciding to be good, right, simple, or withdrawn. If only decision could change a messed-up subjectivity or a screwed-up world.

In the introduction I suggested that these chapters follow Spivak and decades of decolonial thought in focusing on providing infrastructures for unlearning so many things, such as taken-for-granted privilege and perspectives, and, with Foucault, in using that loosening to induce heterotopic potentials for experimenting with a sociality not defined by its disasters.[6] To unlearn the objects that seem to be crucial to holding up the vastly inadequate world is to unlearn how one or a collective holds attachments, motives, and interests from within the lived space of an ongoingness that we want both to shred and maintain something of. This conceptual wedging and riffing are at the root of my turn to a critical infrastructuralism. What emerges are other ways to process inconvenience, the evidence that you were never sovereign—evidence the world forces you to face and a fact about which much genuine and confusing ambivalence ensues.

I have been describing throughout the inconvenience that the world poses to our will to stay attached to things in it and to it. The unbearable, though, is a different object/scene. The unbearable is a threat that feels like threat.

It leans toward the literal. It is best defined as any overwhelming affect that feels like it might cause system collapse but must be taken up, even as it may shatter its bearer. This relation is a technical one: the unbearable might be something we want or want to want unambivalently, like love; or it might be something we hate or a pure catastrophe that accompanies us without regard, regardless. The unbearable points to a pressure we feel that points to a system at its limit, a structure or a mind being tested until it appears to bend to the point of nearly giving out. Unlike suicidiation, which figures an end from which, usually, there is a retreat, the unbearable is the pure form of threat at its highest intensity. That is the paradox: to call a thing unbearable is to admit that it must be borne. It cannot be other than it is. It is defined by a forced relation to life that taps into insecure and depleted resources. It is a limit case of inconvenience to the reproduction of life.

So the analytic and political problem here is how to loosen the unbearable object without denying its undeniable pressure on life and on the attachment to life. Two strategies follow, and this coda is a third. The unbearable object/ scene is never fully faced, if by "faced" we mean incorporated, understood, mastered. As a limit it is only sensed and backed off from but never entirely averted. By the time it's sensed, it's already inside—as a frack, not a fact, of life. The focus here is on writing about limit-case encounters from a position of active life-threat that this book has not yet entertained. The topic is rape/ murder: an ordinary thing.

The texts are James Ellroy's *My Dark Places* (1996) and Bhanu Kapil's *Ban en Banlieue* (2015). If previous chapters looked at the pressure that relationality places on bearing and bearing with what we want, these writers decide to take on *what they do not want* to accommodate or adjust to. They take on facts of rape/murder to break a reproductive structure whose violence is extensive and pervasive. They accept the dissociated nature of their actions as lifesaving attempts to stay in relation. The unfinished business of catastrophe becomes one more thing that shapes the ordinary. Unlike other outsiders who also partly benefit from membership in protected classes, they do not take it on, in Rosalind Morris's terms, to provide "an ideal (the ideal, in this case) encounter with alterity, or an instrument for learning to imagine the place of another. . . ."[7] The object is already in them as a structuring fact of life, but they can't bear to live with it the way they know how.

Their aim is not to get to the root of relation or to dominate knowledge but to affect the infrastructure in which relation forms. A relation that explicitly reminds them constantly that it is ever also a nonrelation. One can't do this alone: infrastructures are social, and so both works play with address and are performative toward their internal and external interlocutors. Kapil and Ellroy choose to make a project of interrupting the way they/we usually live with rape/murder in order to set it loose in multiple modes of visceral experience, writing, and demonstration. Their formalism allows for disturbed epistemes: their aesthetic infrastructuralism allows for different tropes, topoi, worldings. They make new contexts to change their objects: they're deliberate, but not scientific, associologists.[8] One of them, Kapil, casts infrastructural art as political, occupying and disturbing from the outside of what is also within the narratives that bind shame to the realism of empire, racism, and misogyny. Ellroy incorporates the structural violence of the world into a radically private story-loop anchor and amplifies them both many which-ways. Both texts are all bound up with the police. Their first point is that a cold case is just an abandoned one, suspended and preserved for potential life. Their books are a return to the scene of the ordinary crime.

A woman's rape/murder provides a central ellipsis in these books: an act whose informational and causal gaps the authors cannot skip over or fill in. The works are primers in how to configure and desire being in the unbearable space of ordinary life-snuffing without leaping to resolve it wholly like some fetishist, savior, or suicide. Ordinary seems to stand in for women here but that's not always the case: any death that's a surprise but not a shock will no doubt tap into a biosocial pattern. They execute this attitude through writing that foregrounds the object/scene's very inconvenience to the analyst: as W. R. Bion says, such inconvenience generates the frustration where ideation begins. The material ground of worldmaking splinters and genre fails their books.[9] Extremely noisy in the house of form as a consequence, the pieces both resort to italics and ellipses. They do it so frequently that one cannot read unaware that they are using even unfinished, unsatisfying thoughts to shake up the object that represents the relation. In chapter 3 of this book, the ellipsis stands for the intersection between what goes without saying and what cannot be said or known; for Rankine and Isherwood, it stood as a placeholder for a life that keeps going at the limit of life. In Ellroy's and Kapil's books, the weight of the ellipsis opens the door to riffing, mystical knowledge and ritual to infuse the unbearable with resonances that confirm that where the unbearable is, the beyond of realism is realism. It produces generative destructions of hastily built scenes and the many meanwhiles of the internal monologue. Sometimes being with oneself is unbearable. Without muffling what's irreparable in the story they tell, these writers use that pressure to transform the implication of the cases.

In these memoir/histories live and dead people are broken and continue to break, but the adaptive rewriting keeps them signifying, animated. Pointing to the object/scene's active penumbra, they work with speculation and reverie, with sweat, stain, and smudge. They want to, but cannot entirely, return bare life to a sacred life because it is not up to individual will to shift what's collectively impinged. So both books fold life at the limit into the ordinary world: there's conversation, tea, sleeping on people's couches, being neighbors, distraction, desire, arranging furniture, love, and neglect. Both writers are mystics, too, using the "somatic experiencing" of their bodies to change the event through the way their figural flights fall into the puddle of gesture.[10] They use their animating incidents to induce migraines in the world, expanding what's in the region of a dead body.

Ellroy: "Storytelling was my only true voice. Narrative was my moral language . . . I wrote my novel and sold it. It was all about L.A. crime and me. [But] I was afraid to stalk the redhead and give her secrets up." "I wanted to write a novel but instead I wrote this," writes Kapil. These are historicist documents of delayed witness that cannot execute the genres they originally sought to use: the novel, the historical novel, the case. They reinvent the procedural by pressing hard on procedure. Their attempts at the novel, historical fiction, and palimpsest seem sad, like relatives waving goodbye from the shore. Their phrases about structural inequality as the origin of pervasive predation say something true that seems to hang on a wall far away; as is so often the case, the origin story doesn't disturb a problem's intelligibility or reproduction. It often doesn't relieve the pressure of the ongoing life of the unbearable. When forces fall on persons, a capsulizing analysis seems plausible. But the works refuse to be satisfied by the logic of the structure in the symptom that brings it to mind. Too much is happening.

This is not just because the animating incident is a death, but because the incidents involve rape/deaths *for which available genres make too much sense.* Contextualization can make a tableau, a repetitive scenario exemplifying historical or normative form. These authors want to see what else can be done in the wake of sensational, not sensationalist, exposition. They want to loosen the situation despite its easy banalization. Both reenact crime in order to redistort and make worlds on shakier foundations than the ones that routinely maim and kill women, people of color, and ordinary proletarians. Both reclaim the performativity of the object/scene, writing wild internal monologue in the first, second, and third person. In both works file cabinets and notebooks provide technical control, both hoarding and allowing for the reordering of details. So in both of these works affect and decision are not enemies. Affectivity gives the rational a purpose.

One more thing before we move into the weeds of Ellroy's and Kapil's singular modes of transforming the effects of the unbearable. Tonally, the works radically diverge. Their ways of going about it, their styles of handling the unruly material of predictable structural injury, are also strongly differentially gendered. Ellroy adapts hard noir style to house his intense receptivity to details and his compulsion to speculate. Kapil recalls the intensities of écriture féminine to spread affective events in the descriptive living color of the indefinite sentence, controlling its affirmative swells by admitting what's unbearable about them in many serial forms. Style gives resilience a structure; if ordinary resilience is an inevitable feature of ordinary inconvenience, in the scene of the unbearable, style is a way of talking about what happens when the trauma kills someone but doesn't kill you.

Overwhelmed with surplus life, they each approach the places of their raped and dead objects to play out a logic of exposure to the unbearable as a source of knowledge that is better not to be managed properly. They treasure the inconvenience of the alterity of proximity and redraw the world around it. For both, speculative ritual substitutes for aspirational assurance in the mode of magical causality and punctured atmospheres. This way the dead are barred from interment in the genre of the cold case. If the unbearable remains irreparable, a reanimation of the scene is the point of their pressured writing. There is no leaving things behind. There's displacement and dilution. There's revisiting out of respect. There's addition, too, living on in the wake of not dying with the dead, as Christina Sharpe writes.[11] There's the hole in the world made by an undefeated will, as Sara Ahmed writes.[12] There's the work of continuing to not be defeated in depletion, despite everything. There's the ongoingness of invention alongside both compelled and chosen repetition. There's the constant ideational pressure of figuring out obligation. All of these shape the inconvenience drive here that slackens the sovereign fantasy of the engaged writer.

James Ellroy's My Dark Places

My Dark Places is the story of a child's longing for his mother, who was maybe raped and surely murdered when he was ten. Before and after her marriage her name was Geneva Hilliker. Children found Geneva Hilliker's body in a field where they'd gone to play baseball through the Babe Ruth League.

Ellroy includes on the book's first page a picture of his mother's remains at the scene of the crime, a photograph taken by a cop as evidence on June 22, 1958. She was left face down in the grass in an unzipped flower-print party dress, her naked back covered by dirt and leaves, her strangulated neck still bound by the nylon stocking ligatures that took her life. It's unclear where consent was in the sex: "the redhead" had been seen drunk on a date with a "swarthy man" multiple times the previous evening, lively and flirty until she wasn't. A tampon was jammed way up in her: but that could mean a lot of things.

Ellroy shows the photo and describes it at length, returning to it to acknowledge something both real and mystical because it was both of those things: a thing that happened and an unfinished paranormal puzzle he needs help figuring, figuring out, and bearing. Out of love and desperation, he even jams himself into likeness with it, calling the Bildungsroman segment of his memoir "The Boy in the Picture" and including the photograph the cops took of him, too, the same day she was found. Ellroy casts both bodies as crime scenes preliminary to the kind of autopsy only he remains to provide.

"My mother's last night alive defied strict interpretation."[13] The absence of her face, because she is face down, makes it easier to make her generic, which is what police need to do to solve a crime should the evidence not collect into an easy story that closes a case fast. This incident barely made the news. The case was never closed. In an unclosed case, the victim becomes a datum in a pattern that absorbs and is absorbed into the patterns of the world. Explicating this process as a feature of criminal modernity has been Mark Seltzer's crowning achievement.[14] But if scholars of serial killers know that they seek to be as general as their victims, this memoir is a study of the serial killed, a category overfull with silenced women that generates website fetishes and vibrant decadent character types but resists theorizing as a kind of subjectivity, as they are defined by the strangely random inevitability of their stuckness in the elliptical cut.[15] In life they may have played with and aspired to become all kinds of pattern. The way they're forced to be general in death is not within their control.

Ellroy's book is one that can break you with the sheer number of rape/murders of women it catalogs, the heavy ordinariness of it. This literary method, which is also police procedure, involves pornotroping, as Hortense Spillers would say.[16] Ellroy huffs, puffs, repeats, gets aroused by and intensely heteropathetic in the face of both sexual difference and his mother's event, acting at once regressed and aspirationally entitled. But, also, to solve a cold case without "persons of interest" who can be tested, interrogated, and tracked, it is necessary for the forensic mind to return to the scene of many crimes to determine whether yet-unspecified perpetrators will shake out into the pattern that completes the form of the unresolved case. If a murder isn't solved in the first forty-eight hours, he learns, it's not likely to be.

It becomes clear that the rape/murder isn't the origin of his particular brokenness. For him, the brokenness had already happened in his parents' cruelty toward and manipulation of him during their marriage and their divorce. It was overwhelming, and he went into himself. So for Ellroy, *My Dark Places* is an optimistic book about transforming crimes and consequences through the power of brainstorming for life: "You had a killer and a victim. You had an unidentified woman. You had three female witnesses and a drunken male witness. You had a seven-hour time span and a geographically localized series of prosaic events that resulted in murder. You could extrapolate off the established facts and interpret the prelude in an infinite number of ways."[17] Ellroy writes that he uses his mother-longing as fuel in all of his novels as well as in this memoir and a later book, *The Hilliker Curse: My Pursuit of Women*. If the latter book is more a pornoautobiography in the tradition of the anonymously written *My Secret Life*, then *My Dark Places* is the story of what's left when the judicial apparatus fails to tell a story that can use judgment to imitate closure, releasing the surviving intimates from the waiting room. Getting the story right as an act of love allows for a higher justice in the face of the law's inadequacy. That's standard for the true crime memoir, as is the regret at its inevitable failure to put loss on rewind. What's especially paradigmatic here are Ellroy's strategies of preserving and making new futures for the unbearable object by redisturbing it, making it into a scene, telling its stories from multiple scales and perspectives, and being near it without pretending to possess it.

Brainstorming is what Ellroy can do to stay with his object and honor its incendiary eternal openness. In a brainstorm the object is never exhausted; only the thinkers are. In this mode Ellroy exemplifies a desire for our invested objects to be known and yet available for unlimited adaptation and adumbration. Using speculation to churn out potential facts, he follows out similar solved and cold cases, fantasy cases, and scandalous ones like the "Black Dahlia," from which he'd made his own noirish fictions. He also borrows other noncelebrity stories of murdered women, imagining the slaughter in "prosaic" detail and deriving satisfaction through the poetic justice of laying out how to hunt down the responsible sociopaths called ordinary men. He sickens himself and the reader with pressure of the unbearable with the effect that the process of his own education in unlearning his triggers of love and hate generates an almost airless atmosphere, full of pressured speech, storytelling, desire, and wandering, destroying assurance with not much else on the other side.

My Dark Places is split into three sections that pursue from different angles the timeline of the incident and its transformation into event: the crime from the time of the body's discovery until the leads ran out; the crime as the reboot of his own life story, told from childhood on; the crime as an effect of capitalist geography in the industrial development of the San Gabriel Valley in southern California. Throughout there's the crime in the present of the writing, where Ellroy learns how to use the pattern-trained eyes of police procedure to open up a frustrating past to the relief of an extended present. Between the chapters are lyrical epistolary passages in italics, letters to the mother that promise to pursue her, never to abandon her. The book is autopoietic, autoethnographic: it approaches its object the way a good ethnography does, with fidelity to paying attention but no pretense to definitive capture.

Ellroy travels to the field, tracking his mother's migration, circulation, history, and fantasy. She was a nurse at a weapons factory in the decades after World War II: that matters. She was an alcoholic, which matters also. He includes anything that contributes to conveying the historical atmosphere in which her tendencies developed. The San Gabriel Valley and Los Angeles had their own way of absorbing limit-case incidents into the ordinary. He intensifies and amplifies that ordinary to refuse its default sense of scale, banality of pattern, and distribution of anonymity.

He documents first the childhood he had with the murder, which was shaped by his alcoholic, misogynist, pathetic, and neglectful father, Armand, who solicited James to stalking and mother-hatred from the moment of their divorce. The son moves in with the father after her murder and develops his own grandiose adolescent loneliness, homophobia, and addiction, and becomes involved in Nazism and petty crime. He documents stalking all kinds of girls and women, especially ones who are like his mother: divorcees with an edge. He wants, and occasionally hooks up seriously with, women who appreciate the intensity of his drives and the loquaciousness of his stories.

Ellroy's story of his patterns tells not just of compulsions; they induce method too. He returns to the simple and literal details that are or might be related to her so that there's something to hold on to, a pattern if not a person, to anchor reverie and projection and aggressive play. Putting x next to y, and getting into it, might reveal new likeness, and a new likeness is a new path. Throughout this book I've used the word *play* to describe this kind of flailing, pointing to a testing out of what can be done in order to slacken a knot. He adapts everything to this register of intensified play, even the Watts riots: "The riot . . . reconflagrated in my head and ruled my thoughts for weeks. I ran stories from diverse perspectives. I became both riot cop and riot provocateur. I lived lives fucked over by history."[18] Near-psychotic riffing and historicism combine in *My Dark Places* to create heterotopic folds in the lived real that might, through sheer vividness if nothing else, break the deadness of what he knows too well into something living.

Section 2 of the memoir is indeed a brilliant historical novel: the San Gabriel Valley emerges live from the shadows. Its history of immigration, industrial development, and class formation and its spatial, racial, and industrial proximity to L.A. and Watts become vibrant resources for aesthetic and criminal activity. All provide atmospheres of violence with different opportunities for pleasure and hiding. Ellroy wants to bring everything to float the atmosphere in which his mother, before she evaporated, participated in historical life as one more tiny dent. But her details, too, go nowhere in terms of plot: without plot we have tableaux, the horror of stuckness in a scene whose intensities rise and fall tenderly, revealing the banality of pattern and life attrition.

In section 3 Ellroy describes collaborating with Bill Stoner, a detective who protects himself from becoming broken with his objects by becoming a theorist of motive, just to hold on to the possibility that pattern indicates a principle of a reasonable world. If you can say phrases, you're not one of them—the killer or his dead; if you can say phrases, you have somewhere to store the cases. If you can repeat yourself, you have a line on life. Ellroy spends a lot of time using free indirect discourse to capture the intensity of the affect of crime-related thinking, whether the thinker is a criminal, a victim, or a cop. Stoner is said to have learned that

> Men killed women for capitulation. . . . Men did not kill women because they were systematically abused by the female gender. Women killed men because men fucked them over just that rigorously and persistently. . . . He learned that men killed women out of boredom. . . . Stoner learned that men killed women for lawn mowers and crockpots. . . . Men killed women and got gooey over women in a heartbeat. . . . Stoner learned that men killed women by proxy. . . . Stoner learned that men killed women because the world ignored and condoned it.[19]

The violence of the book's initializing murder amplifies in series like this one. Like Ellroy, Stoner uses analogy and pattern to fill up the holes in any particular story by moving to another register, of the becoming generic and close to dead that hovers around women in what usually passes as normal heterointimacy. Every section's relentless listing of the rape/murders that might be part of the fact set of Ellroy's mother's murder are, in any case, part of the story she bears. What makes her generic—and there are so many things—is part of what holds together the story she bears too.

Ellroy imitates Stoner, learning forensic psychology and criminal profiling from him. But most of all, he learns composure from his mentor, which is to say, he unlearns the manic sensorium that had kept his appetite for appetites alive. What does it mean to remake the scene of women's ordinary sexual injury from a searing film loop into a space of composure? Stoner is the kind of cop who has learned to do things other than redistribute his chaos when he's overwhelmed. Before meeting the detective, Ellroy was severely lacking this quality. Stoner teaches Ellroy to interview murderers of women and potential witnesses by holding back so they can spill the beans or at least give an affectively rich account of how they live so perilously close to evaporation. He teaches Ellroy how to pierce the grandiose defenses of heteromasculinity.

Then, together, in segments of reality TV, they adapt Ellroy's New Journalism techniques of self-amplifying macho vulnerability in order to reenact the scenarios his brain reenacts nightly as autonomic ideations about his mother. He writes long-form journalistic pieces about her death and life, and Stoner sets up phone banks should people remember what might become clues. They get nowhere with the case reenactments: people use what he stages just to air grievances about heterosexuality that they carry around and that haven't yet found their crime or a public. This, too, is part of the wound the book holds: if you listen to the straight world, you'll hear that people are unhappy with the normative sexuality played out from sexual difference, thanks to those bastards and bitches who weren't worthy of open-hearted trust. Not everything is a crime, but the toggle between injury and crime becomes cast here as continuity rather than leap.

In short, the inconvenient object of the dead beloved mother becomes animated by her son's aggressive play.[20] At first, at age ten, he feels liberated by her death, free to hate and desire her, but then he spends the rest of his life aggressing and loving his cluster of substitutes without moral or affective limit. As Juliet Mitchell argues for critical consciousness in general in the essay "Theory as Object," Ellroy learns to use the space between himself and the unbearable objects that scenify his world.

One might think that a dead object is the biggest victim, as it can't resist postmortal projections onto it; and once the figurative barnacles are there, they stick, not definitively but as associations that can bury the object in statements. From this angle, any object needn't be inconvenient at all, but just a body waiting for a coffin, figurative or otherwise. But *My Dark Places* shows that dead objects of desire are at the same time the most Teflon things of all, forcing you to speculate and return to yourself without end, mocking you with an inconvenient refusal to respond adaptively, providing an enjoyment akin to tickle torture, with equal emphasis on both terms.

The dead body's very convenience to speculation is thus inconvenient to the person or world that has a vested interest in using knowledge about it to do justice to something. It allows for pedantic grandiosity. But it is also a tool for composing the subject in incomplete spaces, allowing creativity to make things into other things by changing their resonance. The artist of the unbearable is stuck with what Ellroy calls "life in ellipsis,"[21] but at the same time generates heterotopian path potentials from within that life. From this work, the ordinary of straight sexual injury becomes something other than the dark side of being sentenced to life. What looks like crazy ideating and genre flailing gets a reprieve from the thin surface of facts, showing that facts are not fates. Thought never does justice. Nothing does, if justice means closing the case.

I noted earlier Bion's argument that the encounter with frustrating objects is the origin of what we later call "thinking." It's not only especially disappointing objects that induce thought, though, as Lacan writes, because the object of sustaining attachment is always averted, elliptical, inevitably not there for you but near you, filtering the space dynamically made with the frustrations of nonsovereignty.[22] This produces a constant encounter with ambivalence about the ups and downs that come from wanting to be near something, to bear it but in a different way. Ellroy collects stories, paper, photographs, and memories of arousal in the curved set-space called sexuality that includes erotophilia. "Frustrating" indicates ongoing desire, a wearing out that also fuels a not-giving-up that one is not entirely controlling either. It measures the space of dispossession in a field of intense proximity: it's personal, it's social, it's in the world. For Ellroy, and potentially the rest of us, frustration forces ideation that seeks neither rescue nor repair but the life-saving gift of an attentive proximity that feels at once like a holding pattern and a wild, serious thought-experiment involving alternative futures for the objects who appear falsely to be without futures. To stay in the room with the live problem of exemplarity produces a meanwhile, an entanglement or enmeshment, and the task of forging a form, or composure, for staying in ambivalent life.

Bhanu Kapil's *Ban en Banlieue*

As for Kapil, *Ban en Banlieue* emerges from the dark places of speculative writing that are uncannily similar to those forged by Ellroy. There is another crime of rape/murder. This time the tableau is a gang rape of a stranger: at age twenty-three, Jyota Singh Pandey was raped and vaginally immolated by a pipe wielded by strangers on a taxi bus in South Delhi, India, on December 16, 2012. They threw her from the bus when they were finished. Her intestines spilled onto the sidewalk. She lived her last minutes as a spreading stain, dying into becoming "a desiccating form," "a blob of meat."[23]

For Kapil, to call Pandey Ban draws together many forces, ideas, and histories. Pandey has been banned from the set of humans whose existence deserves to be protected. Kapil also uses *Ban* like a pun, a resonance machine. For one, it references herself, Banu, cut off from even the sound of the pronoun. The book also explicitly names Ban from Giorgio Agamben's "bare life," the members of which set are banned, collectively untreasured and unrecognized as the kinds of beings who are worthy of political existence. Deemed faux-ontologically outside of sacred life, the function of the banned is entirely political, therefore. The law seems to determine what's sacred. The law likes to reduce things to the merely physical so it can destroy them without conscience. Deemed already dead or close to it, like the impaired, injured, and death-proximate Americans of Rankine's *Don't Let Me Be Lonely*, the banned for Kapil are always being rediscovered, reprocessed, charged with and for their combination of inevitability and inconvenience. Kapil uses the mythical and sacred space of the widow who's been burnt but refuses to die as a path for the rape victim, the racism victim, the girl whose life is shaped for unfreedom, tapping into the Hindu tradition to ride the wave of pink lightning and mermaids and storytelling of lives after, which is to say with, life. She makes a sensual presence both in time and out of time for the mortally injured kept alive in the stories the event generates. The book's aesthetic refuses unimaginative erasures and negations of power and has to create a new ongoingness to secure forms of life *as historical* without having to be limited by the shape and resonance of injury. Injury is a thing that happened; so is figuration that takes up and rides the spirit.

The Ban concept in Kapil's book is a membrane that gathers up those kinds who seem to be incapable of achieving the likeness that implies belonging to the comfortable Common. It is an outside that eats away the bone of the inside. It confirms the infrastructures and hierarchies that hold up specific worlds but does not allow them to define the real. Despite public demonstrations against rape/murder as structurally tolerated injury, the rape victim Pandey's stain remains a seeping thing. Kapil keeps it seeping. Kapil figures the rape as a thing the privileged and some of the vulnerable want to step over or around because it is just a fact in the set of predictable violences that wear out the world—rape happens, racial violence, too, so unsurprising that it's hard to choose which instance of them to make an event out of. Whole swatches of the social put those incidents over there, in the pile of the unlucky or as an exemplary member of the ordinary set whose predictability keeps the freshly injured from being processed as a sacrifice. Like Ellroy, Kapil can't bracket or forget it and models a way to be committed to redrawing and staying with the trail of the entrails, the scene of them.

Just as his mother's rape/murder is not Ellroy's first traumatic loss, however, Pandey's 2012 rape/murder isn't the event that brings the book's writer-protagonist, "Ban," into the political space of ordinary violence: the rape/murder is an aftershock of many causes, another one more thing. A race riot occurs on April 24, 1979, in Southall, Middlesex, England: she is ten years old. Race riot here means a rampage by white people, but not just all or any white people. There is a National Front meeting in the town hall. A multitude of antiracists were peacefully protesting the meeting, but the explosion did not originate in the enemy camps. The race riot's protagonists were the Metropolitan Police. This story is an old one, which is one way an incident becomes amplified, general, an event.

A white antiracist activist named Blair Peach was killed during this riot by an illegal police weapon that was wielded by a member of that protected class. Peach's picture is in Kapil's book, but Kapil does not dwell on it. It looks like a scan from the daily newspaper obituaries. In contrast to Ellroy's narrative captioning of his mother's "after" picture, there is no before and after pictures of Peach. There is no picture of Pandey either: not from her obituary, a random surviving college pose, nor of her ruptured body spread out on the sidewalk.

The author's naked body holds open the vitality of their place. It shines on the cover and appears in the book. On the intense color cover she reclines nude on the dirt between a green forest and a few thick, leafless branches, turned away from us like a bass viol on its side. Her black hair and bare back, ass, and legs face the lens, unevenly brightened by the camera's flash. Kapil's face, like Ellroy's mother's, is not visible: in facing the forest and showing her back she becomes specific yet also anonymous, general.

On the back cover of *Ban en Banlieue*, her back and black hair return bare and beautiful, still stained by the flash, but now her legs are cut off by one side of the book. The angle is also slightly different. Here she lies next to a high fence of green bush on one side and, on the other, high, vertical, yet tangled branches that mark the outer margin of the space she inhabits in the image and in the book: the stick wall covers the book's spine. "Ban is a spine."[24] Perhaps these woven and stacked sticks point to the rape/murder victim's intestines, spilled out on the sidewalk. Perhaps both walls represent the figural omnipresence of the security state and its almost magical capacity to turn anything beautiful into a weapon against life. Perhaps the fence refers to the Christian thorns of sacred sacrifice: how could they not hover here as a referent, redistributed to the predictably defeated and unavenged? Perhaps the fence that keeps people and worlds inside and out at the same time points out the thin fantasy of the thing called sovereignty and the other thing called privacy: Everything here is in relation. Everything here is exposed. The branches may also mark the space of proximity and spectatorial composure that Kapil is asking the reader/viewer to take up with her: a life stripped down and apprehensible but not available to hold close or personalize entirely. When we look, we look from distances. It is important to remember, once you've opened the book, that she *wants* to be there physically; it is already in her psychically. It is her choice and desire to sacralize the space against its own obscenity. She transforms the event by showing up to the scene and by bringing stories of violent death that generate afterlives merging "dead and living things—all the creatures of the sea are breathing with me and for me, their mouths on my chin, my lips," until the next life begins, and she is "almost but never quite dead."[25]

Later we piece together that the image returns us to Kapil's childhood, too, to a subjective nakedness forced on her at ten years old by the genocidal postcolonial world of ordinary Englishness, a world she carries with her: the cover exposes uncoverable and unrecoverable harms, but it is not nihilistic. A book is an optimistic act. Beauty and the stain hook arms.

So, although *Ban en Banlieue* is dedicated to Blair Peach, who's been murdered by the state's police, the story in the book's air is not entirely about him. The story is that the protagonist Ban felt done for in advance of, to one side of, and after the race riot. Peach died, but what does it mean to say that Ban "lived"? If you live so close to death, are you alive in the ways that people mean it, head capable of tilting toward an elsewhere? Kapil's somatic poetic, her reception of the world, perceives the race riot the way animals feel earthquakes coming, and as she feels it approach she lies down in the forest, expecting to be snuffed by it too. The cover echoes that too. But she is its survivor.

All of this is in service of her failed attempt to make a novel of the "race riot."[26] Here the white "race riot" is the event that needs a novel or film to document both who did what and the inside feeling of it. A race riot is what white people do in that book when the inconvenience of the difference they have created becomes unbearable to them; when they cannot bear not to represent the general substance of the world. Suddenly they feel the unbearable weight of being just a kind of thing, a general-specific, a convention.

Police riots are ordinary. They happen frequently. It was the police's rage for order and white-power sympathies in defense of a population's privilege that leaked out all over the sidewalks and onto, or should I say into, the resistant bodies. A race riot novel might explain what the people do who are sick of the world. It would narrate what Joshua Clover casts as the "instrumental irrationality" of world-destructive self-defense.[27] It might capture what Kapil calls the "low levels" of nonverbal racism and misogyny that are just humdrum noises in people's heads and their mild, almost instantly forgotten, disgust, the substance of shame they'd be ashamed of if they were caught in the ideational act that they could always disavow as what was "in the air" or just where their mind went.[28]

If it were a novel, Ban en Banlieue would begin in childhood's ordinary spaces, where Ban plays with friends and gender and explores the world before she gets caught up and reeled in, made proper, or at least scared. As a Brown migrant to a white empire that is revved up by the fear of the decline of imperial prestige and control that has already happened, she senses that she already has no future and an impaired present, with little space to enjoy random, enigmatic pleasures or politically organized ones. As it is 1970s England, it is England in the wake of Enoch Powell's racist-populist "rivers of blood" speech, with its tenderness for the subjective pain of white citizens, the same England Steve McQueen recently returned to in Mangrove.[29] It's not that white power has been diminished, because there's still plenty of that, but, Powell argues, damage has been done to white confidence, and that must not be stood for.[30] Whites no longer can be sure that they're the referent for the citizen, the human, the person, and they're flailing with sharp objects. In the speech, Powell describes white constituents stage-whispering to him their rage at becoming merely one of many. They're shaking with the fear of experiencing the a priori disrespect they had gotten to casually enjoy being the source of, not the object of: "They found their wives unable to obtain hospital beds in childbirth, their children unable to obtain school places, their homes and neighbourhoods changed beyond recognition, their plans and prospects for the future defeated; at work they found that employers hesitated to apply to the immigrant worker the standards of discipline and competence required of the native-born worker; they began to hear, as time went by, more and more voices which told them that they were now the unwanted."[31] *Ban en Banlieue* never reaches the race novel that plays out the story and backstories accompanying it.[32] It reaches historical narrative without achieving form. It refuses the difference machine's insistence on margins that clarify intelligibility and allow for ranking of the importance of incidents of violence, as they are all ultimately exemplary. It refuses Powell's claim that immigrant struggles are individual problems because the general populace struggles too. *Ban en Banlieue*'s practice of proxemics, of associative object-disturbance, is not exactly flat, but a topology: things happen, and other things, and people and other objects are coordinated, and some encounters light things up. The world is not only human movement but an atmosphere both encountered and, when possible, overheard. And what is overhearing the world? Is the disturbance an incident that might become a transformative event, the soundtrack to ordinary movement, or both? What happens to events without narrative membranes to ease their transit across the cuts between this disturbance and that? "Genital life gives way to bubbles, the notebook of a body's two eyes" was an attempt to teach how to stay with what you can never get inside of.[33] *Ban en Banlieue* documents incidents of the white British difference machine's murderousness of the emblems of difference it creates to hate, by which I mean persons and also genres of people.

In the book, life after the white police race riot involves a series of episodes in which action catches up to affect, which is to say that it always is incensed, delayed, and distorted. One word that Kapil uses for the convergence of gesture and episode is *errors*, as in the chapter called "[13 Errors for Ban]"; the brackets there and throughout the book signify material without a genre's confidence about sequencing and events. An "error" is the trace of indecisive and greedy writing that marks the impulse to tell a story that builds too much sense into sense—an impulse she keeps fighting. From the beginning there's "write [re-write]," "mouth [jaw]," "brush [touch]," "violet [orange]"; there's "is [was]," "gold [rose] [blue]," "section [incarnate]," "contorted [leaped]," "sacrificial [bridal]." Later on there's "Memorial ritual [street puja]," "a brown [black] girl," and so on up to "energy [light]," "die off [become]," "externalize [read them.]," and "precedes [follows] it."[34] For Kapil, an error is the inevitable error forced by aspirational documentation, the turning of a thing into what it isn't on the way to transmitting a sense of what it is. All of this toggling adds up to an ethics that's beyond the book's other wish for structuralist satisfaction, which locates the ongoingness of life in bargains of substitutability. Here, in the end, the energy of her rich, creative indecision builds a new sense universe from the ellipsis that can't predetermine value, which includes letting into the room the history of conventions about what to do with "kinds of people" as potential fire starters. "One thing next to another thing doesn't mean they touch."[35] But the inconvenient pressure of affective proximity is the situation you cannot avoid.

It is hard, and takes will, to wedge things open just a crack. Supremacists are everywhere in Ban's world, feeling defensive-aggressive about the world they have made, and the crisis of lost white importance in capitalist, social, and citizenship terms closes things up. In the banlieue, the margin-outskirts of the city, all kinds of people—Black, Brown, and white—are closing their blinds and hunkering down. Banlieues are slums and warehouses for the socially devalued, but they are also scenes of life that bear the struggle to survive that disallows coasting and forces conniving for life, in contrast to the domestic reenactment of the everyday where the neighborhood people on the couch at night wait for the sirens to fade so that one more day of the ordinary can be said to have been survived and sealed.

At the same time, supremacy binds the world of vertical hierarchy into a thing that feels like it's serving one single interest. Angry whites harass Brown neighbors and prank them, too, pissing in their milk just to have a bit of what they call fun; they're meanwhile organizing political parties and fostering loose-cannon agents who exercise their "freedom" to judge, to humiliate, and to injure Brown people. But the supremacists in Ban's life are not always white and English. They are also the native and migrant men who are isolating and beating their wives. The supremacists are also her own parents, whose difference machine refuses Sikhs while embracing Hindus. This shatters Ban's first love and breaks gender-queerness for her too. This wall of harshness leaves behind a preference for figuration, which can't be stopped, over sex and heritage, which have made their negative mark but whose effects can only be diluted or redistorted, not erased. She lives on, attached to the dead and to life, not inside or outside of them but on permanent verges. "I made a verge or hill or rim out of everything. I made a woodland out of my life. I lay down beneath the trees in my life."[36] Later she takes a lover to a verge and reenacts letting the world in active-passively: it shames her, does not reclaim her. In this book you never know whether something works, if *work* means contain and repair. But you have to show up to try something memorial, nonreproductive, and forward moving. "Do these bright colors have their own autonomy or generative power? I don't know."[37]

Life here begins with the literal. As the race riot is registered in the impending air, she lies down "on a verge," waiting to be killed; when she survives, she drags the shadow of the incident's absolute vulnerability with her. To Ban, all of it feels sexualized in the bad sense, in that it exhausts her with intensity she wants to want. But the inconvenience of the world she wants to trust becomes spread out among friends, lovers, audiences, collaborators: the people who move in and out. Performance, shamanic transference, and the help of other artists and friends extend heterotopic gestures into momentarily livable spaces, which helps develop the historical present as a scene teetering between violence and cleanup.

This is one purpose of her style of reenactment, a pedagogy. Just as a riot will damage its own lifeworld context, the poet refuses to install rich inner or alter-lives in the spaces of damage that the nation form, capital, and the rain are constantly washing clean. Years later the dissociation remains as a form of life to be acknowledged as a nonfoundational foundation, and also to be returned to. Memory is an inconvenience that cannot be controlled for optimism. Things don't have to add up in this model, they just have to be reanimated so that they can remain partners in consciousness and life.

> Are you sick and tired of running away?
> Then lie down.
> Invert yourself above a ditch or stream beneath a bright blue sky.
> Then pull yourself up from your knees to clean.
> Clean the street until all that's left is a ring of oily foam, the formal
>   barrier of a bad snow.[38]

"Life" becomes defined not by citizenship, class ascension, embodied genealogy, or optimism but by a richness of circulating impacts that bruise and spark into reverie. She sets things off but then things change, the way a house that's been vacated even for a bit becomes different anyway on its own, somehow seeming thinner and dustier, the spiders having done some work, a crack in the window having let in moisture that maybe it wouldn't have let in if one had stayed home.[39]

Indeed, as the book closes, Ban names names, thanking people who made a space with her but not a totality. She is, therefore, not just documenting the incidents whose becoming-event is an indefinite set, but demonstrating the friend's gift of willingness to be there just in case the gristle moves and the tender flesh dissolves. As Catherine Malabou argues in *The New Wounded*, if we want to belong to other people and the world, then it's up to us to submit to the scene of life whose terms are opaque to us even if it seems like destroyed life. Kapil seeks this through statements. One's capacity to read, to take a statement in and to see what it changes, what memory and forgetting and redistortion induce, is also training in the inconvenient. "Ban is not an immigrant; she is a shape or bodily outline that's familiar: yet inaccurate: to what the thing is. How to look good on Skype. A vaginal opening. By 2011, she's a blob of meat on the sidewalk. . . . This is the first problem of the project; an interest in duration as the force by which—something: might become."[40] In the face of this mess of self- and worldmaking, Kapil dirties genre: Why should it be spared? The "notebook" is the infrastructure for this action, a material means without a narrative genre. The book ends with selections from her notebooks. They record the world like a Foucauldian genealogy, a cluster of impacts that intend a body. They record episodes she makes, wishes she had made, reenacted successfully or not; and they record gestures of destruction of this book that, because they are recorded, remain something in the trace.

Traces are literalized in the substance of writing itself. Kapil uses charcoal to write and to represent the contact of the world because that's what humans are made of. Charcoal in this book is like what many people mean when they say we are all made of stars. "Charcoal . . . The life food or emblem of Ban herself."[41] But charcoal, what writing and bones come from, what smears and burns and pollutes and creates infrastructure, is what's animal in the world: it's "there, there."[42] But it is also everywhere, like rape/murder. The inconvenient object is already partially incorporated; the inconvenient object has to be countenanced. She screams colors because they are never fully represented by the artifacts that remind us of them.[43] The piece lays out rituals that allow for return to be a return not to the incursions of the world of the Real, but to a breathable space of figuration that refuses the supremacist act's aspirational sovereignty over the concrete encounter. It is realism for the nonsovereign. It thus scenifies to make the immediacy of the event of another rape/murder, another patriarchal/police/imperial action; it showcases that people can use the inconvenience of their bodies to make a new prospective, affective sense of things. An act of realism is not the same as representing what really happened.

Conclusion: On the Inconvenience of Other People

The unbearable is the limit case of the inconvenience of other people, where *people* stands in for any object that one needs for the world to proceed, and where *inconvenience* stands for the fact that attachment is never easy and always, in the end, as John Steiner writes, a threat to one's grandiosity, one's own organization of reception and defense.[44] Politics is one place we work out the inconvenience of other people; intimacy another; walking along the street another: and in any space of competition for the feeling of a superior freedom, the stuff of national-capitalist, biopolitical, and animal wars of position.[45] What's left after self-help often points to openness as what's healthy and defense as what clots, stultifies, creates impasses in the social. Blockage is deemed to be a bad thing; flow, a good thing. But this insistence on x and its other has done tremendous damage to our conception of ourselves and the social, presuming that we know flow and ease when we feel them, solidarity when we proclaim it, care when it's an intention, and who the embodied brutal enemy is, even though it is completely ordinary to be surprised that our affect was all wrong and a bad representation of our wish. Was the wish a bad idea, once our judgment about it was revealed to be only an expression of loneliness and drive? Or can we think differently about the encounter with the inconvenience of other people: that we might desire not only them or any objects but also the inconvenience?

This desire for inconvenience is central to the force of ambivalence that I have laid out as the scene for this book's investigation of the complexities of staying attached to life and life's good hard things. It is also what I have implied throughout the book when I have used the language of "brokenness." Here's an inventory of that concept. Each chapter has involved an infrastructural interruption to the reproduction of a relational mode that links persons to an object that is partly threatening because it's in the neighborhood of desire. One wants to want love, one wants to want sex, one wants not to hate strangers or the world, which is to say that one wants to be hooked into by some things one doesn't control. The brokenness of the world that thrives on the exploited labor of workers and lovers of the family form; the brokenness that comes from the friction of wanting to be protected from and by imperial war; the brokenness of the subject who is subject to racism, misogyny, and intimates who are bad at intimacy: these positions, manifestly subject to the wish for and against sovereignty, often run out of gas in exhaustion and longing and resort to bitter projections.

And yet. In each chapter our protagonists figure out ways to make an otherwise, a heterotopia, without losing entirely access to the world's holding capacities. They try to figure out how to move better with their objects and therefore to change the atmosphere of the world for which those objects themselves provide infrastructures. Christina Sharpe describes something of the same movement in Dionne Brand's "wake work," her mode of writing as "keeping watch with the dead."[46] In this book, the disturbing erotics of the joke, the commons concept as such, posttraumatic stress disorder from ordinary racialization and nonnormative sexualization all describe the scene of difference as a source for subjectivity that is always subjectivity-in-brokenness, if *brokenness* means a subjectivity that is not just shaped but constituted by the external world's force. One takes form in brokenness, but the brokenness is not an absolute obstacle to living, enjoying, having ambition, or longing. They accompany each other, enabling forgetting and negative projections of revenge but also holding and attaching, *if we're lucky*. That luck is not in the positive but the proximity, the cohabitation, of the impossibility and the positivity.

So there's negating, diminishing brokenness in the ordinary. There's what Kathleen Stewart describes, in the Heideggerian tradition, of the world throwing itself together, like a self-repairing zipper.[47] Then there's affirmative brokenness. This is what chiropractors do when they crack your neck. This is what it means not to fight a preoccupation but to treat it like a crush, like the placeholder it is, like a magnet for a questioning attention. What does this magnetizing knot stand for? When the object breaks into you there's no erasing it, which is what I've been long arguing about trauma. Instead there's relating to it, using it, genre flailing around it, making it do things apart from the force of its first effects. There's staying in proximity and thinking about what else the atmosphere can do. When I say a book breaks me, this is what I mean: I am changed by it, startled and thrilled that something has become unbound in me. I become the loosened object, in proximity to an uncomfortable enigma but not a fate.

All of this returns us to why I took the time to show you how Ellroy's maximalism and Kapil's minimalism work toward the same things: an infinitude of context-making, the necessity of multiplied topoi, the ethics of reference, and the "queer art of failure" that animates the generativity of any infrastructure.[48] This enables them to maintain their fidelity to trying to stay attached to their object without possessing it, while shaking up what counts as the relevant frames and atmospheres for it; add refusing easy models of affective and historical knowledge and intersubjectivity. They wanted to be near the object in a new way and to change what it can do.

Their respect for the insistence of the personal, the historical, and ritual provides a context of infinitely animated movement.[49] But also there is a lot of napping. Both books indeed contain a shocking number of scenes of napping, of being in a dark place with the eyes closed against a field of intensified aliveness. Reclining, ideation, dissipation, a new chapter. Kapil calls it "lying on the floor of England," "lying on the floor of the world": not failing to be a person but stopping to let the rush of the world continue its velocity into times and spaces unforeclosed by the weight of Events.[50] They create spaces for thought experiments to follow their own logics into the universe, where rational extension and wild causality are impossible to distinguish. Weirdly, napping is akin to having sex, a hyperintensive mode of self-loosening that often reaches a limit. Napping involves fading, spreading and receding. What the books have left to do is to make spaces for the unfinished business of being with the object that is already in them. What they have left to do is to acknowledge the other writers who come with them to make a new case for warming a cold case out of love for the people whose taken-for-granted injury lives otherwise in the noise. What they have left us are displays of what to do with the power to keep, let's just say, showing up.

c.1 Eric Thayer, "Sorry for the Inconvenience We Are Trying to Change the World," November 2, 2011.

acknowledgments

My love and gratitude go to Courtney Berger at Duke University Press for cultivating this book and for our sustaining friendship during troubled times. Ken Wissoker and Cathy Davidson were immensely generous with their enthusiasm and curiosity. I give immense ongoing gratitude to Robyn Taylor-Nu and Rivky Mondal for their beyond-the-job-description editing of the chapters, by which I mean disentangling text and fierce critical engagement and conversation. For reading and commenting on the whole thing, I thank so much Rivky Mondal, Roger Rouse, Jonathan Flatley, and the Duke readers—and, at whatever scale of engagement, you, in advance. It means a lot to be read. For great engaged intellectual and loving friendship, I thank Lorelei Sontag. For listening to me think aloud, reading outside of their comfort zone, and being just the greatest imaginable partner in life, my love goes to Ian Horswill. There are enough words—too many, in fact—but what's there can't keep up with a life that keeps being surprising.

Darby English, Zachary Loeffler, and Kris Cohen were deft readers of the introduction. Joe Fischel, Dana Pollan, and Sianne Ngai were very helpful with chapter 1, as were critically active audiences at the Duke Annual Feminist Theory Workshop and the University of Iowa. Discussants in workshops at UC Santa Cruz and Stanford, especially Eric Stanley, Chris Chitty, and Vaughn Rasberry, plus interlocutors at Cornell, the American Anthropology Association, Claudia Rankine and the engaged colleagues at Pomona, the Modernist Studies Association, and the International and Interdisciplinary Conference on Emotional Geographies were crucial for "Being in Life without Wanting the World." Deborah Cowen, her students, and the incisive interlocutors at the American Association of Geographers, along with some extremely grouchy and enlivening audience members at Cornell, were profoundly helpful in shaping chapter 2. A different version of chapter 2 was published as "The Commons: Infrastructures for Troubling Times," *Environment and Planning D: Society and Space* 34, no. 3 (2016): 393–419. Anahid Nersessian was helpful with the coda. Please forgive me if I've neglected to affirm your labor: I always paid attention. The book was written over many years.

I was lucky to have been pushed by some amazing books and essays, mostly written by people I don't know, during this phase of thought development. Some were directly on topic, such as anything by my dear friends Max Cavitch, Jonathan Flatley, and Julietta Singh, and others whom I don't know—John Steiner and Kiese Laymon. Works such as *Speculate This, American Sonnets for My Past and Future Assassin,* and everything written and edited by Rankine, Sean Bonney, Joshua Clover, Juliana Spahr, Fred Moten, Renee Gladman, Dean Spade, and Angela Davis, plus what I could take in by John Keene, Alexis Pauline Gumbs, Kim Tall Bear, Beth Povinelli, Barbara Browning, Ronaldo Wilson, the Feel Tank Chicago and Covid Silver Linings writing groups, all reshape my brain and make me feel so lucky, even when I haven't been. Finally, and of course, the inspiring work of my dear friends, interlocutors, and coeditors—Saidiya Hartman, Erica Rand, and Katie Stewart—has held me in the world. Writing Matters! How it matters, how it interferes—it's up to us to take up and do something with what hooks us.

Thanks very much to Stephanie Brooks for allowing me to reproduce and write with "Lovely/Caution"; to Thomas Hawk for the intensity of his Creative Commons framing of the Detroit library disaster; to Bryan Snyder of Reuters for his shot of the die-in on the Boston Commons. Gratitude also to Liza Johnson, director of *In the Air,* the cast of which includes Daphaney Bauer, Lee Brown, and April Hobbes; to Bhanu Kapil for permission to include excerpts from *Ban en Banlieue* (2015); to Claudia Rankine and Graywolf Press for allowing me to think with and to reprint parts of *Don't Let Me Be Lonely: An American Lyric* (2004); and to Juliana Spahr for permission to include excerpts from *This Connection of Everyone with Lungs: Poems* (2005), *Well Then There Now* (2011), and *The Transformation* (2007). This recitation may not convey the warmth and depth of my gratitude to these works and writers: I'm still heated up by learning from them.

notes

Preface

1 See Rabin, "U.S. Suicides Declined Over All in 2020 but May Have Risen among People of Color." *The New York Times*, April 15, 2021, accessed April 18, 2021, https://www.nytimes.com/2021/04/15/health/coronavirus-suicide-cdc.html.

Introduction

1 On comedy as a scene for revealing personality as a mechanical stuckness, see the tradition of humanistic comedy theory from Bergson, *Laughter*, to Zupančič, *The Odd One In*, and Dolar, "Comic Mimesis," 570–89.
2 J. Butler, *Frames of War*.
3 "Being affected" is how the Spinozan tradition of affect theory introduces the dynamics of affect that animate the human from a nonhuman space. See,

for example, Deleuze, *Spinoza*. Entanglement is a central concept both for Fred Moten and Elizabeth Povinelli in describing the a priori form of social relations. I find it only moderately useful, insofar as it presumes an intensity and an ethical scene that I think only sometimes applies. But when it does, it's a powerful concept and logic. See Moten, *Black and Blur*; and Povinelli, *Geontologies*.

4 See Byrd, *Transit of Empire*; Cattelino, *High Stakes*. See also the extremely rich reconsiderations of sovereignty throughout Nohelani Teves, Smith, and Raheja, eds., *Native Studies Keywords*, and the "curated section" titled "Sovereignty" in the *Journal of Cultural Anthropology*, https://journal.culanth.org/index.php/ca/catalog/category/sovereignty.

5 The phrase *other people* carries weight in many films and books. It usually designates ground zero of social irritation from the pressure to adapt or submit to other people's stuckness, will, and desire—or other cats' mere existence. In *The Book of Other People*, Zadie Smith translates this tendency into character study. I learned to notice this phrase from Klausner, "Cat News." A later instance includes Shields, *Other People*.

6 Critical theory of "the neighbor" has developed ways of thinking about the projected pressures of proximity, adding to classic political accounts of paranoia. See Copjec, "Sartorial Superego," 65–116; Hofstadter, "Paranoid Style in American Politics," 3–40; and Santner, Žižek, and Reinhard, *The Neighbor*.

7 Harris, "Whiteness as Property," 1707. As for women walking alone at night, it's worth noting here that sexual violence to women and girls happens mainly in a situation with an intimate partner or at home, which means the image of the abandoned street is itself what we might call, after Freud's "screen memory," a "screen trope," a fantasia that blocks out how predictably the threat of violence in the lure of intimacy escalates from the intimacy drive to unbearable, and sometimes unliveable, situations. Chapter 1 and the coda in this book return to this scene of the torque. Most sexual violence happens among intimates in proximity to the domestic: the inconvenient there is more about the sense that women's performance of autonomy is a structural threat to the couple's or family's happiness. The literature of powerful testimonies to the predictable crash of love into violence is vast; recent rich resources include González-López, *Family Secrets*; and Snyder, *No Visible Bruises*.

8 For scholars new to the concept of the liebenswelt, or "life world," introduced by Edmund Husserl and Alfred Schutz and first made known to me through Jürgen Habermas, see Harrington, "Lifeworld," 341–43. In this chapter the term *lifeworld* is interchangeable with "the ordinary," but it brackets the separation between material or structural and subjective conditions that conventionally accompany the term. In this book the structural is not outside of anything but expresses itself in institutions, subjectivities, and other processes through which it becomes reproduced. See the section and chapters on infrastructure and mediation.

9 Joshua Chambers-Letson points out that the logistics that established the very architecture of global commerce also produced the means of production of both slavery and racism. So while this chapter looks at infrastructure building as a heterotopic tool, its emancipatory potential is released and releasing only if its users want it. Chambers-Letson, *After the Party*, 179–89. See also the analysis of the Cold War's long-term infrastructural effects in the clarifying, materialist, and affectively attuned work of Joseph Masco in *Theater of Operations*.

10 Harney and Moten, "Michael Brown"; Mbembe, "Necropolitics"; Puar, *Right to Maim*.

11 On supremacist love and resentment as entitled affects, see Ahmed, "In the Name of Love."

12 I learned to think about propinquity and contiguity from conversations with Joan Copjec. See Copjec and Sorkin, eds., *Giving Ground*.

13 In drawing out the enigmatic and designified signifier, and the concept of the psychic enclave or retreat, Jean Laplanche and John Steiner offer important resources for my thinking with the sensed but often partly acknowledged registers of affective exchange; I draw on these throughout the book. Laplanche, *New Foundations for Psychoanalysis*; Laplanche, *Essays on Otherness*; Steiner, *Psychic Retreats*; and Steiner, *Seeing and Being Seen*.

14 Cavell's large corpus of work on comedies of remarriage as figures of the philosophical skepticism he advances makes this claim about love being the scene to which we show up abundantly without having to be good at it. See, for example, his classic *Pursuits of Happiness*.

15 Tsing, *Friction*. Tsing's conceptualization of friction is usually far more engaged and conscious than this book's proposition about the frictions of inconvenience, but its rigor and exemplary storytelling have accompanied me throughout this process.

16 As a description of the singular encounter that draws someone into an image, or what I think of as a scene, Roland Barthes's concept of the punctum serves as a resource to think with in detailing what Freud calls the "economic problem" of the rise and fall of intensities in response to the world. Barthes, *Camera Lucida*.

17 I refer here both to the vernacular and psychoanalytic negativity of "ambivalence." The vernacular sense of "mixed feelings" is weighted heavily toward the negative, as though positive attachments would at best and realistically feel unmixed. Most famously, the psychoanalytic version of the concept is associated with Melanie Klein. Her construction of ambivalence was at first in extremis along axes of love and hate of world-sustaining objects like the breast and the mother. The descriptive development of the complex dynamics of love and hate in terms of fear, envy, and gratitude and reparative *positions* extended through her career. She criticized Freud for being too binaristic with respect to love and hate, so my resistance to her dramatization of psychic dramas feels somewhat tu quoque. Klein's classic essays are "A Contribution

to the Psychogenesis of Manic-Depressive States," "Mourning and Its Relation to Manic-Depressive States," and "Some Theoretical Conclusions Regarding the Emotional Life of the Infant."

18 The literature on projective identification following Melanie Klein's introduction of the concept tends to find its clearer and more stable home in T. Ogden, "On Projective Identification." Theorists and clinicians continue to debate the question of whether use of the other to make bearable the subject's intensely difficult internal states is an extraordinary aggression or ordinary propping. Some useful summaries include W. Goldstein, "Clarification of Projective Identification"; and Mendelsohn, "Projective Identifications of Everyday Life." Joshua Chambers-Letson has usefully turned this concept toward rethinking the dynamics of aggressive racialization in a time of heightened white-racist negativity and antiterrorism in the United States. See Chambers-Letson, "Homegrown Terror."

19 On Wilhelm Reich's question to Freud, "Where does the misery come from?" see Rose, "Where Does the Misery Come From?"

20 Goffman, "Footing."

21 I address the aspiration of critical thought toward at once establishing, disturbing, and transforming objects of engagement, including questions, in Berlant, "Genre Flailing."

22 Many queer, Indigenous, and disability theorists richly conceptualize the specificity of time emerging from the lived perspective of an overdetermined, specific, yet collective body. A wide range of queer work that is engaged with these problematics and archives can be found in the recent cutting-edge collection edited by Siobhan Somerville, The Cambridge Companion to Queer Studies. My particular focus on living through the present also draws me to care modes as marking durational urgencies: see Fink, Forget Burial; and of course Dean Spade's mighty work in the "right now" of Mutual Aid: Building Solidarity during This Crisis (and the Next). See also Goodley, "Dis/Entangling Critical Disability Studies"; Kafer, Feminist, Queer, Crip; and Samuels, "Six Ways of Looking at Crip Time." Mark Rifkin amply engages with the question of Indigenous survival as more than a reckoning with pasts throughout the oeuvre, but notably in Beyond Settler Time. See also P. Smith, Everything You Know about Indians Is Wrong.

23 Hardt, "Affective Labor"; and Hardt and Negri, Multitude. See also Negri, "Labor of the Multitude"; Diaconu, "Patina-Atmosphere-Aroma"; Dawdy, Patina; Moten, Stolen Life; Sharpe, In the Wake; and Warren, Ontological Terror. See also important critiques of strong theory by Eve Sedgwick and Sylvia Yanagisako, which claim an aversion to rigid figurations of process. See Sedgwick, "Paranoid Reading"; and Yanagaisako, "Immaterial and Industrial Labor." I see strongly figurative works as more dynamic than that, because they are more figurative, involving methods of testing out rather than bearing down. But that might be more about what we read for and against than about what's on the page.

24 In this sense these writers of the present-in-transition fulfill the image bequeathed by Juliet Mitchell in "Theory as an Object."

25 Eve Sedgwick quips at one point that, unlike Elizabeth Bishop, she's not trying to lose her objects but to loosen the space her collection of them can inhabit in an ensemble of no particular order. Sedgwick, *Touching Feeling*, 8. My use of *loose* is not to increase spaciousness but to make different ones available from within the scene of attachment.

26 Berlant and Edelman, *Sex, or the Unbearable*, 5.

27 This perspective resonates with the model of movement as a productive entangling of conceptual and lifeworld materiality. See Harney and Moten, "Michael Brown"; and A. K. Thompson, *Premonitions*.

28 Foucault, "Of Other Spaces," 22.

29 Although not uncontroversial, the strongest materialist and theoretical writing on Foucauldian heterotopias includes Teyssot, "Heterotopias and the History of Spaces."

30 On lifeworlds, see note 8 above.

31 The concept of the "cultural dominant" is Fredric Jameson's, in and after *Postmodernism*. Sometimes he invokes the achievement of such a dominant as the other to "sheer heterogeneity" (6) and sometimes as a synonym of *hegemony*, an organizing force that tries to organize diverse domains of the social (158). I'm pushing at the second definition, which professional and lay theorists often misperceive as "the Real."

32 Clover, "Genres of the Dialectic."

33 Jameson, *Political Unconscious*, 81.

34 On the concept/context toggle, producing a dynamic representation of history, see Bosteels, *Actuality of Communism*.

35 Kapil, *Ban en Banlieue*, 30.

36 Foucault, "Of Other Spaces." Delaney, *Times Square Red*; Jagoda, *Network Aesthetics*.

37 I came on my own to proxemics, framing it as a dialed-back preliminary concept of "belonging," but I discovered during early revisions of chapter 3 two scenes of related thought and art to move with: Edward T. Hall's ethnographic work on proximity as a social, mathematical, and neuropsychological emanation, and the social space work of Liam Gillick. See further discussion in chapter 3, note 65. This concept resonates with Ben Anderson's great work on atmosphere as well in *Encountering Affect*.

38 The strongest statements about queerness as an ethics have shaped my sense of the relation of the personal and the impersonal obligation among intimates, whether strangers or mutually known. That kind of toggle is central to this book's discussion of the infrastructures of inconvenience. Amin, *Disturbing Attachments*; Chen, *Animacies*; Dean, *Unlimited Intimacy*.

39 I learned to think about overdetermination by studying Louis Althusser, Étienne Balibar, Jacques Rancière, Roger Establet, and Pierre Macherey in

Reading Capital, and of course Althusser, "Ideology and Ideological State Apparatuses," and Jameson, *Political Unconscious*. In this tradition, clear and concrete figurations of a process are deemed to be defenses against facing its multiple causes of situations, scenes, antagonisms, and events and therefore holding tight to a simplified model of "solution." In the decades after these interventions into how to think about structure and structure-related subjectivity, overdetermination has been made structuralist again by Slavoj Žižek and his formidable allies. I prefer this other tradition's general framing of the event, the scene, and the social formation of the ideologeme as at once the distillation, amplification, and transformative extension of an overdetermined problem. See also Pignarre and Stengers, *Capitalist Sorcery*.

40 On breaking with the reproduction of an intimate public, see Best, *None Like Us*.

41 Adorno, *Aesthetic Theory*.

42 Brennan, *Transmission of Affect*.

43 Not only are there many theoretical arguments about how the contemporary object works, but consensus is abundant that the World Bank, the European Union, and authoritarian states are allied sources of the contemporary world that accept fully and are committed to spreading the neoliberal model of constantly adjusting market-prejudiced policy and the individual responsibility to self-exploit, with progressively less and less support from state infrastructures for those who are unable to find traction in the world of whack-a-mole opportunism. The centrality of social and economic chaos to contemporary capitalism has become an affective fact for many, leading to radical political animation and also mass resignation. The centrality of counter-logics in the form of alternative economic and social infrastructures for creating a counter-chaos is also central to much vitalizing contemporary thought. Such a bibliography is too enormous to contain here; for exemplary condensations, see Harvey, *Enigma of Capital*; Postone, "Thinking the Global Crisis"; Gibson-Graham, *Postcapitalist Politics*; Clover, *Riot. Strike. Riot*; and Bear et al., "Gens."

44 The forms of life induced by processes of structuration have been addressed quite differently by various materialist analyses of the structure/infrastructure relation. In one—the more economistic and structuralist one—a great distance is maintained between the scramble of everyday life's reproductive activity and the institutions managing the capitalist control of value. In the other, the contemporary literature on infrastructure, subjectivity, and wealth are seen as more fully and productively bound up with each other. This infrastructure literature is more extensively cited in my investigation of the commons concept in chapter 2. My main teachers from this perspective have been McCormack, "Elemental Infrastructures for Atmospheric Media"; and Sahlins, "Infrastructuralism."

45 R. Williams, "Structures of Feeling." For a witty and effective synthesis of the feminist and queer traditions that established infrastructure as a measure of

the material and affective dynamics of relation, see Wilson, "Infrastructure of Intimacy."

46 Here I refer to many literatures imagining a transformation of the social and economic infrastructures based on forms and temporalities of value other than property, sovereignty, and wealth. Three particular traditions have shaped this analysis. The feminist and queer literature on "social reproduction" is too vast to lay out here, but my foundations go from Silvia Federici's entire oeuvre to Gibson-Graham's *A Postcapitalist Politics* to Katz, Marston, and Mitchell, eds., *Life's Work*. A clear recent review essay points accurately to developments in the discourse; see Norton and Katz, "Social Reproduction." See also Arruzza, Bhattacharya, and Fraser, *Feminism for the 99%*; and Cooper, *Feeling Like a State*.

47 I learned to focus on crafting terms for thinking the overdetermination of the always developing historical present through Foucault's "Nietzsche, Genealogy, History," which argues for seeing the body as a constantly but discontinuously mutating effect of the world's impacts. I use *infrastructure* here to point to such a potentializing process that animates spaces of social convergence, in alliance with the anarchist tradition that turns to infrastructuring as a means by which to reimagine the transformation of living in concrete social relations and material relations. Recent anarchist thought that's been sustaining, clarifying, and powerful for me include A. Thompson, *Premonitions*; and Klausen and Martel, eds., *How Not to Be Governed*.

48 Sahlins, "Infrastructrualism."

49 Cowen et al., "Elemental Infrastructures for Atmospheric Media." See note 44. In addition to the citations in note 44, see Rubenstein, *Public Works*; and Rubenstein, Robbins, and Beal, "Infrastructuralism." The latter essay argues that "the alignment of infrastructure with the concept of the public good or the commons is essential to our definition" (577), whereas this introduction argues against the vague implication of such "alignment." That essay's interest in infrastructural complexity and contradiction, though, is in line with this chapter's resistance to the pastoral, reparative simplicity that the commons concept also wields.

50 Deborah Cowen, "Disrupting Distribution: Subversion, the Social Factory, and the 'State' of Supply Chains."

51 Warner, *Publics and Counterpublics*; Muñoz, *Cruising Utopia*; Rodríguez, *Sexual Futures, Queer Gestures*. In 2017 at the University of California, Berkeley, Warner gave a Tanner Lecture on infrastructure titled "Environmental Care and the Infrastructure of Indifference." In it his logics are intelligible in proximity to the concept of the counterpublic but are not manifestly affiliated with queer thought. A video of the lecture is available online: "Tanner Lectures: 2017–2018 Lecture Series," University of California, Berkeley, March 20–22, 2018, https://tannerlectures.berkeley.edu/2017-2018-lecture-series/.

52 Tsing, *Friction*; and Tsing, *Mushroom*.

53 Taylor, "Double-Blind."

54 Fanon, *Black Skin, White Masks*, 124.

55 Jameson, *Political Unconscious*; Deleuze and Guattari, *A Thousand Plateaus*.

56 See note 21.

57 Roitman, *Anti-Crisis*; Koselleck, *Critique and Crisis*.

58 Gilbert, *Common Ground*, 107–18.

59 Ngai, *Ugly Feelings*, 28.

60 Phillips, "Close-Ups."

61 Laplanche and Pontalis, "Fantasy and the Origins of Sexuality."

62 Relevant essays where Spivak asserts the need for, elaborates, and transforms what she means by unlearning include "Criticism, Feminism, and the Institution," "Can the Subaltern Speak? Speculations on Widow-Sacrifice," and "Politics of Translation." Spivak is continuously modifying her concept: see Danius, Jonsson, and Spivak, "Interview with Gayatri Chakravorty Spivak."

63 See Tlostanova and Mignolo, eds., *Learning to Unlearn*. See also Jimmy Casas Klausen's recent critique of the binarist programmatic practice expressed in much decolonial work in his review of *On Decoloniality*, by Walter D. Mignolo and Catherine E. Walsh, and *The End of Cognitive Empire*.

64 There's always the lure of the footnote . . .

ONE / SEX *Sex in the Event of Happiness*

1 For a popular essayistic encounter with this question of countering erotophobia in proximity to assault, see Friedman and Valenti, *Yes Means Yes*. Another inspiring piece on this topic is Delaney, *Times Square Red*.

2 For more on the difficulty of thinking sex with and without world-building optimism, see the chapter "Sex Without Optimism" in Berlant and Edelman, *Sex, or the Unbearable*, 1–34.

3 The title of this subheading gestures toward that of Jacqueline Rose's essay "Where Does the Misery Come From?" (1989), which extends Wilhelm Reich's "Sexual Misery of the Masses" to see the implantation of sexual difference as the scene of sexual unhappiness. This chapter suggests not sexual difference but erotophobia as that scene, the association of sex with all threats to sovereignty, which often drowns out the desire for threats to sovereignty for which sex, and other intimacies, also stand. See Rose's "Feminism and the Psychic" in *Sexuality in the Field of Vision*, 1–25.

4 *Body genre* comes from L. Williams, "Film Bodies."

5 Freud, *Jokes*, 25, 195–97.

6 Freud, *Jokes*, 185.

7 For my other constantly evolving discussions of genre, see Berlant, *Female Complaint* and *Cruel Optimism*.

8 See Freud, *Jokes*; Žižek, *Žižek's Jokes*; Limon, *Stand-up Comedy in Theory*.

9 Foucault, *History of Sexuality*, vol. 1.

10 Freud, *Jokes*, 101 and throughout.

11 Cohen, *Jokes*.

12 Bergson, *Laughter*; Gunning, "Crazy Machines; Trahair, *Comedy of Philosophy*; Zupančič, *Odd One In*.

13 *Continuous presentness* is Stanley Cavell's term for the ambition of skeptical consciousness as an experience of acknowledging the world. See Cavell, *Must We Mean What We Say?*, 300, 344. The classic book-long discussion of comedic conversation figured in the couple form as an expression of free being is Cavell, *Pursuits of Happiness*. Cavell pursues investigations of the failure and defeat of conversation he associates with melodrama and irony in *Cities of Words* and *Contesting Tears*.

14 On soured comedic sensibility and its association with Jewishness, see Litvak, *The Un-Americans*.

15 In *Jokes*, Freud distinguishes between the "comic" and the "joke" to differentiate modes of aggression within humor, but I see no need for that in these broad terms, except to point out that *comedy* implies a relation of the set-piece and narrative expectation, although those expectations change over time. What matters in the comedic is the pleasure in the work of staying in sync along with the pleasure of disturbance, whereas the joke focuses more on the disturbance as its own punctum of nonsovereign experience and self-suspension, even for a flash. The happy punctum is what it is: a thrill, a momentary thrall.

16 I'm not sure it's worth saying this, but the argument I'm making rubs strongly against the conclusions Bergson reaches in *Laughter* insofar as he claims that the purpose of laughter (and implicitly of comedy) is to humiliate people in order to advance social normativity. Bergson, *Laughter*, 67, 96.

17 I am referring to Euro-cosmopolitan modernity insofar as it's shaped by the acquisitiveness of capitalist appetites that shape intimacies at once as above markets and as markets. See Illouz, *Why Love Hurts*.

18 I learned to think about ongoingness as a feature of the comedic from Cavell (see those works cited in note 13) and Critchley, "Comedy and Finitude."

19 Winnicott, "Use of an Object."

20 The temporality of the sexual encounter before, during, and beyond the bodily performance of the event is what makes Janet Halley's argument about the problem of adjudicating sex so powerful in *Split Decisions*.

21 The fact that all of the films in this chapter involve intergenerational sex as a figure both of social reproduction *and* crises of relation involving many kinds of consent was made apparent to me while reading Fischel, *Sex and Harm*.

22 Steiner, *Psychic Retreats* and *Seeing and Being Seen*.

23 Deleuze's comments on the irreconcilable, and the incoherent, conflict between his model of desire and Foucault's model of pleasure are completely relevant here. See Deleuze, "Desire and Pleasure," 189–90.

24 Hocquenghem, *Homosexual Desire*; Delaney, *Times Square Red*; Bersani, *Homos*; Dean, *Unlimited Intimacy*; McGlotten, *Virtual Intimacies*. Many more works could be listed here, clearly.

25 See also Rodríguez, *Sexual Futures*, *Queer Gestures*; Nguyen, *View from the Bottom*; and, from a different but proximate perspective, all of Stockton's work, from *Beautiful Bottom, Beautiful Shame* to "Reading as Kissing." Marlon Riggs stands here as testimony to much work in the 1990s and beyond by gay and trans men of color that demonstrated and theorized the varieties of attachment and being known in the space made by the forces of impersonality, equality, and recognition in erotic politics. See Riggs, *Black Is, Black Ain't* (1994). Robert Reid-Pharr's *Black Gay Man* does the same. This note could be longer than this chapter, but my ambition here is to begin listing queer work traditions that allow for the mutual extension of the ambivalence and insecurity of excitement in desire's resonances, both negative and affirmative.

26 The work of Susanna Paasonen is exemplary in this light: its sex and sexuality are at once conceptual and descriptively rich. See, for example, Paasonen, *Many Splendored Things*.

27 Foucault, "Friendship as a Way of Life," 309.

28 Duggan, "Beyond Marriage"; Povinelli, *Economies of Abandonment*; Manalansan, "Servicing the World." See also Cornell and Seeley, "There's Nothing Revolutionary."

29 As Annamarie Jagose has argued, affect theory has also a tendency to dematerialize the "thing" into orientations toward trauma or longing. See Jagose, *Orgasmology*.

30 I am looking back toward Arendt, *Origins of Totalitarianism*, to her near antagonist, Jacques Rancière, from *Disagreement* and *Hatred of Democracy* to *Dissensus*; Hardt and Negri, *Multitude* (2004); and Honig, *Antigone, Interrupted*.

31 Phillips, *Equals*. See also J. Butler, *Precarious Life*; J. Butler, *Frames of War*; and Rodríguez, *Sexual Futures*.

32 Berardi has reiterated this argument in many subsequent books, but I discovered it first in his *Precarious Rhapsody*, 85–104.

33 Kael, "The Current Cinema: *Tango*"; L. Williams, *Screening Sex*, 112–33.

34 The character's manifestation of resistance to the fear of freedom is what locates him within the idiom of existentialism.

35 Bollas, *Shadow of the Object*.

36 Laplanche, "Theory of Seduction."

37 Ross, *May '68*; Foucault, *History of Sexuality*, vol. I.

38 Cavell's work on conversation and love throughout *Pursuits of Happiness*, *supra*, is especially relevant here.

39 Salecl, *Choice*; Power, *One Dimensional Woman*; McRobbie, "Notes on the Perfect."

40 Ross, *Fast Cars, Clean Bodies*.

41 In saying this, with its air of blithe unrisky solidarity, Jeanne refers to the auto worker strikes that paralyzed Paris in '68.

42 For an extensive and thoughtful elaboration of what androgyny has meant and can mean, see Stacey, "Crossing over with Tilda Swinton." For a straight history, see encyclopedia entries like Mary Ellen Snodgrass's "Androgyny and Feminist Literature," 20–22; and Hargreaves, *Androgyny in Modern Literature*.

43 Gilles Deleuze provides the main exception to this pattern of casting the event as a potentially ruptural intensity operating according to a merely extensive internal logic. In *The Logic of Sense*, *The Fold*, and elsewhere the extension and intensity of an actualization or occasion are joined by the generativity of associations in movement, the singularity of the actualization, and the incompossible internal dynamics among the same that signals how the event both produces the new and speaks from a virtual register that is accessible, but never in totality, through its mediations. There's so much more to say than this, apart from that my analysis of the event as a becoming that never becomes but resonates and reconfigures its prehensible elements derives its productive/destructive energy from thinking with Deleuze's work. Many synthetic essays and encyclopedia entries on the Deleuzian event exist. Two works to which I constantly return are Wellbery, "Theory of Events"; and Patton, "World Seen from Within."

44 *Events* of love in Alain Badiou's work *In Praise of Love* and *episodes* of sex in mine have a complicated relation, as his events begin with episodes to which he attaches an obligation to fidelity. In Badiou's work the arc from sex to love, from the encounter to love, takes on a burden of affective self-evidence that, for analytic and political reasons, I reject. At the same time, he is not insensitive to the ambivalence of inconvenience on which I focus: that which accompanies fidelity to any revolutionary structural break. As I am focusing on the modes of continuity from which new forms of life emerge, even if they claim a revolutionary break *as their ambition*, and as I believe that the event is not always or even usually featured by immediacy, and as I venture that "breaks" are at best heuristic overdescriptions to organize attention within a field of processes, I cannot accede to the confidence in affective self-transparency on which his thought relies. But as with all of my interlocutors in this book, Badiou's care to follow his nose helps me refine my own inclinations.

45 D. Thompson, *Last Tango in Paris*.

46 Badiou, *In Praise of Love*, esp. chapter 4, "The Truth of Love" (38–52).

47 Bertolucci and Arcalli, *Bernardo Bertolucci's Last Tango*, 34, 180.

48 Augé, *Non-Places*.

49 David Bowie, "Changes," on *Hunky Dory*, RCA Records, 1971.

50 Bertolucci and Arcalli, *Bernardo Bertolucci's Last Tango*, 110–16.

51 The view of film as a museum of historically embedded gestures is boldly enunciated in Agamben, "Notes on Gesture."

52 See note 18.

53 "Get the Butter" lives on the internet in numerous humorous websites, for
    example: "Keep Calm and Go Get the Butter," http://www.keepcalm-o-matic
    .co.uk/p/keep-calm-and-go-get-the-butter/; "Brokeback Mountain II: Go
    Get the Butter," http://uncyclopedia.wikia.com/wiki/Brokeback_Mountain
    _II:_Go_Get_the_Butter; and "List Inconsequential: Get Da Buttah: Recipes
    Inspired by Our Favorite Sex Scenes in Film, Spectrum Culture, April 29, 2009,
    https://spectrumculture.com/2009/04/29/get-da-buttah-recipes-inspired-by
    -our-favorite-sex-scenes-in-film/. The phrase is usually cited as a trigger for
    violence: for example, in the "go get the butter" meme, QuickMeme, http://
    www.quickmeme.com/meme/3q1av7. For a narrative of its backstory, see
    Stone, *Everything Is Personal*; Riley-Smith, "Was It for Real?"; Sophie Taylor,
    "Last Tango in Paris Star Maria Schneider Dies at 58," BBC.com, February 3,
    2011, accessed December 11, 2020, https://www.bbc.com/news/entertainment
    -arts-12355496#:~:text=French%20actress%20Maria%20Schneider%2C%20
    best,Bernardo% 20Bertolucci's%20controversial% 201972%20film; Lina Das,
    "I Felt Raped by Brando," *Daily Mail*, July 19, 2007, accessed December 11,
    2020, http://www.dailymail.co.uk/tvshowbiz/article-469646/I-felt-raped
    -Brando.html; Emily Yoffe, "Go Get the Butter," *Slate Magazine*, February 4,
    2011, accessed December 11, 2020, http://www.slate.com/blogs/xx_factor/2011
    /02/04/maria_schneider_dies_at_58.html. Stone emphasizes that the rape *was*
    in the script, not the butter. Also, the *Daily Mail* article represents the rape
    in Schneider's biographical context more complexly than the headline does,
    quoting her as saying that both she and Brando felt "a little raped." For a typi-
    cally tonally aggressive but historically accurate rendition of the ongoing de-
    bate about the real and the represented sex in the film, see Michael McCaffrey,
    "Raping Truth: Brando, Butter and *Last Tango in Paris*," Memories, Dreams,
    Reflections (blog), December 5, 2016, http://mpmacting.com/blog/2016/12/5
    /raping-the-truth-brando-butter-and-last-tango-in-paris.

54 For Bataille on sovereignty, see *The Accursed Share*.

55 Sedgwick, *Epistemology of the Closet*, 22–24.

56 Thanks to Don Reneau for wondering aloud about the gum.

57 Cavell, *Pursuits of Happiness*.

58 Forrester, "On Kuhn's Case."

59 I've discussed this at greater length as "the enabling cliché" in Berlant, *Female
    Complaint*, 202–4.

60 During the final encounter between the pedophilic/pederastic father and his
    son—on the DVD the scene is called "Heart to Heart"—Billy asks whether it's
    true that his father is a "serial rapist and a pervert" who harmed the child's
    friends. The father is quiet and gently honest about it, confirming the rumors.
    Solondz writes the father's honesty as a process of staying true to his son, who
    asks for refinements that force the elder Maplewood to emerge from behind

saying that he "touched," "fondled," and made love to them to admitting
that he "fucked" them and that it was "great." The son then asks whether the
father would "fuck" him, and the father (whom thus far we have seen loving
the son from a respectful distance) says, "No. I'd jerk off instead." Both characters cry throughout this exchange, which makes their broken conditions
simultaneous but neither reciprocal nor equal.

61 In the February 1957 issue of *Cosmopolitan*, actor Steve Allen remarked, "I guess
you can make a mathematical formula out of it. Tragedy plus time equals
comedy." "Steve Allen's Almanac," *Cosmopolitan* 142 (February 1957): 12. But
this has been variously attributed also to Mark Twain, Mel Brooks, Woody
Allen, and Carol Burnett.

62 Think, then, about Louis Althusser's famous use of the knock-knock joke of
ideological interpellation in "Ideology and Ideological State Apparatuses."

63 Foucault, "Friendship," 310.

TWO / DEMOCRACY *The Commons*

Epigraph: Bonney, *The Commons II*, 26.

1 I learned to think this way about the limits of any figural logic of transfor-
mation from Spivak, "More on Power/Knowledge." This model segues with
Žižek's introduction, "The Spectre of Ideology," and his chapter "How Did
Marx Invent the Symptom?" in *Mapping Ideology*.

2 Hall, "The Problem of Ideology."

3 On "affirmative speculation" as opposed to the foreclosing style of capitalist-
reproductive "firmative speculation," see uncertain commons, *Speculate This!*

4 Bonney, *The Commons*; Bonney, *The Commons II*. I'm also describing here the
process of "governmentality," an anchor for Foucault's description of how
state power distributes, obliges, and deputizes the mass to scan and surveil
itself and to tattle. As many scholars of "un-governmentality" have argued, to
become ungovernable and to generate infrastructures for living in a thriving
relation require unlearning the state's moral and juridical imperative. Foucault, "Governmentality."

5 You will note that I fluctuate between using *the common* and *the commons* in this
chapter. I tend to use one or the other for reasons that make local sense, with
the former tending to be a concept; the latter, a space.

6 This argument persists throughout Federici's oeuvre. See, for example, Federici, "Women, Land Struggles." The political theory bibliography on equality
as a real-time negotiated process is vast. For a thought piece, see Phillips,
Equals. For literature reviews, see Power, "Which Equality?" For the foundation of my own thinking about the groundlessness of equality, see the work of
Jacques Rancière, starting with *The Ignorant Schoolmaster* and *Disagreement*. See
also Davide Panagia's terrific *Rancière's Sentiments*.

7 See Žižek, "How to Begin."

8 Linebaugh, *Magna Carta Manifesto*, 278.

9 I refer here to the vast corpus of Michael Hardt and Antonio Negri, but especially *Commonwealth*.

10 See Barthes, "Myth Today"; Stoler, "Epistemic Politics."

11 See R. Williams, "Ideology"; and R. Williams, *Keywords*, 204–7, 210–12.

12 See Kant, *Critique of Judgement*; Arendt, *Lectures on Kant's Political Philosophy*.

13 John Brenkman argues that the Kantian paradigm opens intersubjectivity to the *necessary* mediation of the liberal public sphere, where taste and aesthetic judgment form aspirational worlds. This is debatable, but see his beautifully argued and demonstrated "*This Is Beautiful*."

14 See Shaviro, "Beauty Lies in the Eye." For this perspective see also Brodsky, "'Judgment' and the Genesis"; Cornell, *Just Cause*; R. Johnson, "An Accord in/on Kantian Aesthetics"; Zerilli, "Toward a Feminist Theory."

15 Žižek, "How to Begin," 53.

16 Hardt and Negri, *Commonwealth*.

17 See Virno, *Grammar of the Multitude*.

18 The statements *We're all in this together* and *We're all in it together* accounted for more than 10 million hits on Google during the first four-and-a-half months of 2019. News outlets, corporations, restaurants, cities, churches, TikTok performers, storefronts, and countless individuals embraced, performed, and insisted on the "we."

19 Harney and Moten, *The Undercommons*.

20 Harney and Moten, "The University: Last Words." This manuscript was circulated by the organization FYPU (Fuck You. Pay Us.), which at the time of this writing was a weekly online symposium organized by rent-burdened graduate students at the University of California, Irvine. It took shape starting in April 2020, mainly as a way to support and publicize the broader Cost of Living Adjustment Movement (COLA) that started at the University of California at Santa Cruz in September 2019 during the transition to online teaching that was brought about by COVID-19. See "Campaign Timeline," Pay Us More UCSC, https://payusmoreucsc.com/campaign-timeline/.

21 Muñoz, *Cruising Utopia*.

22 Muñoz, "'Gimme Gimme This,'" 97.

23 Cavell, *Emerson's Transcendental Etudes*, 64.

24 See Cavell, *In Quest of the Ordinary*, 32.

25 Terada, *Looking Away*, 3.

26 This thought about overpresence was derived from reading about the production of historical distance in the face of the traumatic and ordinary too-closeness of the world in Phillips, "Close-Ups."

27 The publication history of "For the Union Dead" is complicated. It first appeared in *The Atlantic* in 1960; its performance at the Boston Arts Festival

in 1963 was its own inaugural antiracist political event. Its official publication date is 1964, in *Life Studies*. Cited passages are from Lowell, *Life Studies*, unless otherwise cited.

28 Lowell, "For the Union Dead," 63.

29 See, for example, Axelrod, "Colonel Shaw in American Poetry"; and LeMahieu, "Robert Lowell, Perpetual War."

30 Lowell, "For the Union Dead," 64.

31 As of this writing there are yearly ritual commemorations in the United States of the US destruction of Hiroshima and Nagasaki in 1945 but no monument to it. During the late 1980s the state proposed enshrining the plane from which was dropped the nuclear bomb, the Enola Gay. Protests prevented it. Protests continue: see "Controversy over the Enola Gay Exhibition," *Atomic Heritage Foundation*, October 17, 2016, accessed July 3, 2020, https://www.atomicheritage .org/history/controversy-over-enola-gay-exhibition.

32 Lowell, "For the Union Dead," 64.

33 See Rowe, *At Emerson's Tomb*. Rowe's nuanced reading of Emerson's politics is exemplary in Emerson studies, locating him on the progressive side of race issues early on and mainly on an antisocialist side of class struggle—socialism is always yet to come. He fights for no economy, just against the false consciousness that saturates human ideas and practice. As many Emerson critics write, Rowe argues that Emerson accommodated capitalism as the realist mechanic of his moment. His critiques, especially in the 1850s, were more focused on modeling how to get out of the collective mentality to save the soul. Again, my reading here on the utility of the commons concept is not making a general claim about Emerson in any phase of his liberalism but to build on how he uses the commons to break with reproducing the normative world as such, in an antisocial way that's antithetical to what we see in Lowell.

34 At least since John Dewey's 1903 essay on Emerson, scholarship has recognized the imprint of Spinoza's thought on Emerson's own sense of how to use the singular soul toward a transcendence of, say, ideology or historical being. Many dissertations have been written on this topic, but of recent published work I point to Greenham, *Emerson's Transatlantic Romanticism*.

35 Buell, *Emerson*.

36 Emerson, *Nature and Selected Essays*, 81.

37 Emerson, *Nature and Selected Essays*, 37.

38 Adorno, "Resignation," 291.

39 Buell, *Emerson*, 65.

40 Folsom and Price, *Re-Scripting Walt Whitman*, 71. Richardson, *Emerson*.

41 Marx, *Economic and Philosophic Manuscripts*.

42 Emerson, *Journals and Miscellaneous Notebooks*, vol. VII, 1838–1842, 349.

43 Emerson, *Nature and Selected Essays*, 55. See also Cavell, *Emerson's Transcendental Etudes*.

44 Emerson, *Nature and Selected Essays*, 35.

45 Arsić, "Brain Walks," 89.

46 Emerson, *Nature and Selected Essays*, 38.

47 Spahr, *Well Then There Now*, 61.

48 I learned to think about "linkage" as the apriority of attachment from Bion, *Second Thoughts*.

49 Emerson, *Nature and Selected Essays*, 60.

50 See Star, "The Ethnography of Infrastructure"; Star, "Infrastructure and Ethnographic Practice"; Bowker and Star, *Sorting Things Out*; Star and Strauss, "Layers of Silence."

51 For one of many examples, see Harvey, "Neoliberalism as Creative Destruction."

52 Hardt and Negri, and Negri himself, write extensively on the importance of institutional development, whether they call it the state or no. See Cesare Casarino and Antonio Negri, *In Praise of the Common*; Hardt and Negri, *Assembly*.

53 See, for example, Gordon, "Why Historical Analogy Matters." Thanks to Rivky Mondal for the citation.

54 Hardt and Negri, *Declaration*; Edelman, *No Future*; Bersani, *Is the Rectum a Grave?*

55 Spahr, *The Transformation*, 206.

56 More recently, Spahr reprised the project of playing out the plural in entangled sexual and political narratives of building belonging. See Spahr and Buuck, *An Army of Lovers*.

57 Spahr, *The Transformation*, 207.

58 I learned to think about the pressures and cadences of contact improvisation from conversations with and the writing of Michele Beaulieux. See Beaulieux, "Starting by Believing Maria"; Beaulieux, "Shift from Rape Culture"; Beaulieux, "How the First Rule"; and Beaulieux, "Can't We Just Dance?"

59 See Spahr and Retallack, *Poetry and Pedagogy*; the journal *Chain* edited by Jena Osman and Juliana Spahr and published from 1994 to 2005 (a reissue can be accessed online at https://jacket2.org/reissues/chain); Spahr and Young, *A Megaphone*.

60 Spahr, *The Transformation*, 207.

61 Spahr, *This Connection of Everyone*, 3–8.

62 Spahr, *This Connection of Everyone*, 9.

63 Spahr, *This Connection of Everyone*, 63.

64 Spahr, *This Connection of Everyone*, 74–75.

65 See Adorno, "On Lyric Poetry and Society," 37–54; Eliot, *The Waste Land*.

66 Spahr, *Well Then There Now*, 61.

67 Spahr, *Well Then There Now*, 71.

68 Sarlin, "Vulnerable Accumulation."

69 Spahr, *Well Then There Now*, 71.

70 Spahr, *Well Then There Now*, 56–58.

71 Schumacher, *Aristotle on the Nature*, 20.

72 Gentner, "Structure-Mapping"; Gentner et al., "Metaphor Is Like Analogy."

73 Virno, *Grammar of the Multitude*; Pittman, "The Reserve Army of Affectivity."

74 P. Williams, *Alchemy of Race*, 217.

75 Cirque d'Art's philosophy of pedagogy and ongoing training apparatus can be found at "Cirque d'Art," Southern Ohio Museum, accessed June 8, 2020, http://www.somacc.com/cirque-dart/.

76 Virno, *Grammar of the Multitude*, 29–30.

77 On "footing" see Goffman, "Footing."

78 de Certeau, *Practice of Everyday Life*, 117.

79 Thanks to Luis-Manuel Garcia Mispireta for sending me evidence from the commentary class of this song's credibility as an anthem for solidarity, one that that calls not on full subjective or affective convergence but on concerted practical activity that manifests attentiveness, tenderness, respect, and pleasure. See the WhoSampled App, http://www.whosampled.com/sample/view/1427/Wiz%20Khalifa-Say%20Yeah_Alice%20Deejay-Better%20Off%20Alone/.

80 Berlant, *The Female Complaint*, 9.

81 The literature on postwork relations to labor begins with the autonomists. For compilations of some of the strongest contemporary arguments, see D. Ford, "Abolish Work!"; D. Ford, *Dispatches from the Ruins*; and Weeks, *The Problem with Work*.

82 Sianne Ngai writes, "The gimmick is thus an aesthetic judgment uniquely reflecting on the genre's capacity for absorbing and transcoding nonaesthetic judgments." This description is a good way to talk about the internal dynamics of social form and normativity that organize the conventional world. See Ngai, *Theory of the Gimmick*, 36.

83 Contemporary thought about being plural often neglects French feminist work on the multiplicity of being both in self- and social relation. I'm referring here to Luce Irigaray's classic *This Sex Which Is Not One*. So, too, does it neglect the non-European traditions that begin with nonsovereign being. My education first came from reading work on ancestral coexistence: McGarry, *Ghosts of Futures Past*; R. Morris, *In the Place of Origins*; and more recently Fuhrmann, *Ghostly Desires*.

84 Antonio Negri names the problem of the organization-to-come-after in the face of a deconstituted civil society. See Negri, "N for Negri."

85 On charismatic authority, first see Weber, *On Charisma*. Much varied use of the concept churns within the literature, especially on narcissistic leadership and contemporary media. See, for example, Gustafsson and Weinryb, "Populist Allure"; Bello, "A Dangerous Liaison?"; Grewal, "Authoritarian Patriarchy"; and Turner, "Charisma Reconsidered."

86 Regarding reoccupation of public space, in addition to the work of Hardt and Negri, including *Assembly*, it is worth reading slowly and seriously on

constituent power in Casarino and Negri, *In Praise of the Common*, especially but not limited to the chapter "Vicissitudes of Constituent Thought" (134–90). On the copresence of action in the ordinary, see Butler and Athanasiou, *Performative in the Political*; and J. Butler, *Notes Toward a Performative Theory*.

87 Flatley, "Refreshments of Revolutionary Mood." On the difficulty of maintaining such a mood, see also Gould, *Moving Politics*.

88 Woodward and Bruzzone, "Touching Like a State."

89 Schneider, "Breaking up with Occupy."

90 Kim, "How the Floyd Protests."

91 Gonzales-Day, *Lynching in the West*. See also his antiracist photography collection: Gonzales-Day, *Profiled*.

92 Fausset, "What We Know About."

93 I would have used the word *sentimentality* rather than *feeling-with* if *sentimentality* wasn't such a trigger, evoking emotional excesses and forced equivalences across difference with which many don't want to identify. I define *sentimentality* as the presumption that shared feeling about something in the domain of desire or threat creates bonds that presume, or hope for, more general likeness across distances of time and lifeworld experience. As an ideologeme, sentimentality links people who don't otherwise share a lifeworld in ways that can fuel worldbuilding and social change from the ground of shared critique, shared outrage, and shared refusal. At the same time, though, those very points of convergence can produce infelicitous expectations that the same critique presumes a profound likeness in the world that people want to bring into being. You can't have mass politics without sentimentality, but it does not provide much skill for working through the antagonism or differences among potential comrades. See Berlant, *Female Complaint*.

94 For a precise summary of this general and contemporary ordinariness of crisis during the pandemic, see Amster, "History's Crystal Ball."

95 Linebaugh, *Magna Carta Manifesto*, 279. See also the elaboration of this view in Linebaugh, *Stop, Thief!*

96 de Angelis, *The Beginning of History*.

97 Green, *The Fabric of Affect*, 211. This set of linked observations about bound and unbound affects appears throughout Green's work. See, for example, Green, *Key Ideas for a Contemporary Psychoanalysis*, 81, 131.

98 Bogost, "Blogging Stops Unplanned Pregnancy."

THREE / LIFE *On Being in Life without Wanting the World*

Epigraph: Arendt, *Essays in Understanding*, 16.

1 Hoagland's "Fear of Narrative" throws out twenty different proposals for what a dissociative poetics suggests about an attitude toward language. See also Burt, "The Elliptical Poets."

2 For thinking about the "lateral pressures" of the present and the ongoing temporalities of dissociating being or dissociated "self-states" in the present, this chapter is especially indebted to the work of Daniel Stern and Philip M. Bromberg, along with a few anthologies that contextualize their innovations. Stern, *Present Moment in Psychotherapy*; Bromberg, *Standing in the Spaces*. Bromberg also focuses clinically on affirmative dissociation. Their work is anthologized and contextualized in Dell and O'Neill, *Dissociation and the Dissociative Disorders*. I am currently enraptured by the analysis and writing of Richard A. Chefetz in *Intensive Psychotherapy*. Add to these analyses the dissociative effects of being riven by race, sexuality, ethnonational identity, and capitalist models of self-overcoming laid out in Eng and Han, *Racial Melancholia, Racial Dissociation*; Max Cavitch's tour de force essays on dissociation and on the queer child, "'Do You Love Me?'"; and Cavitch, "Dissociative Reading." Psychoanalysis is just beginning to think of the impersonality of history on persons on the bottom of so many social hierarchies, mostly in terms of the posttraumatic stress disorder of identity. See also the material throughout the chapter.

The sexual and racialized relation among multiple valences of intimacy, dissociation, and suicidality is this chapter's case-based focus. The aesthetic expression of this concentrated scene of convergence forces us to think about genres as infrastructures for processing life wherever it appears: it's all mediated. See the Coda for more on this.

3 John Steiner figures one version of dissociation as a "psychic retreat," a much simpler phrase than the internal dynamic of defense, displacement, and psychodynamic historical inheritance it anchors analytically. Like all effective armoring, the dissociation style of the psychic retreat allows subjects to move through the world without being destroyed by its impacts. The extra protective layers of defense, however, and the mess of cause-and-effect disturbance associated with this kind of affective processing express themselves in personality in wildly masked and distorting styles of defense that might well appear to the subject as reason, not symptom. Symptoms work as defense until they don't. The two cases this chapter amplifies only begin to tap into the expression of internal division and defense that this structure of processing points to. See something of the range of exceptional self-knotting in the ordinary in Steiner, *Psychic Retreats* and *Seeing and Being Seen*. See also note 63 for Peter Fonagy's work on how historical context shapes some of these structures and their expressive styles across generations.

4 Foucault, *History of Sexuality*, vol. 1, and *The Birth of Biopolitics*.

5 Fanon, "The Fact of Blackness." Fred Moten points out that this title is a mistranslation—it ought to be "The Experience of Blackness." See Moten, "The Case of Blackness." In *Black Skin, White Masks*, see also the chapters "The So-Called Dependency Complex of Colonized Peoples" (83–108) and "The Negro and Psychopathology" (141–209).

6 The literature on academia and broken mental health expands daily; it is never intersectional enough but is working to fold what Tressie McMillan Cottom calls "the education gospel" into disability studies and critical-therapeutic attention to racial and economic hardship. Cottom, *Lower Ed*. *See also* the extremely interesting work of Dolmage, *Academic Ableism*; Peake and Mullings, "Critical Reflections"; Price, *Mad at School*; Taub and Thompson, "College Student Suicide"; and Thompson and Neville, "Racism, Mental Health."

7 See Celani, *The Illusion of Love*; Fairbairn, *Psychoanalytic Studies of the Personality*; and Fairbairn, "Theoretical and Experimental Aspects."

8 The concept of the supertext, a work that stretches across adaptations and series, was introduced in Berlant, *The Female Complaint*.

9 Adorno, *Minima Moralia*.

10 Shange, *For Colored Girls*, 6, 64.

11 On the "meanwhile" that allows self-division to produce a prospect for individual and collective worldmaking, see Berlant, "The Traumic."

12 Newton and Blake, *Revolutionary Suicide*.

13 I learned to think about finitude as an ontological aesthetic of any concept of life from Critchley, "Comedy and Finitude." Fanon and many who succeed him refuse any model of a Black ontology, as it has been denied by European concepts of being; they would situate the death-proximity of being in life for Black people as an on-the-ground habitation of the palette of a sensible nothingness created by white negation. What I am describing here can overlap with, but is not identical to, Afropessimism. See, for an extended meditation, Warren, *Ontological Terror*; Moten, "The Case of Blackness"; Moten, *Stolen Life*, throughout; and the fantastic exchange between Saidiya Hartman and Frank Wilderson that thinks through taking up the unfinished business of Black being without suffusing it with Black optimism for the overcoming of history: Hartman and Wilderson II, "Position of the Unthought."

14 The "suicide epidemic" is global and deeply connected to economic downturns. But most of the rich work on this phenomenon tends toward its emergence in the ordinary of localized crises. For an instance of good contemporary data-gathering in support of the meme of the suicide epidemic, see Koons, "Latest Suicide Data." See also Tavernise, "U.S. Suicide Rate Surges." On linking India to the global suicide pandemic, see Vikram Patel's work generally, including summary essays such as Patel and Gonsalves, "Suicide Prevention"; and Patel, "Burden Is Even Greater." The suicide epidemic became a trope notable in Japan during late twentieth-century economic crises: see, for example, Thomas, Chang, and Gunnell, "Suicide Epidemics." This epidemiological pattern became an event reported almost daily in the United States and Europe during and since 2008, when men in economic failure began self-cancelling, sometimes taking down others, in serious num-

bers. Some other key conceptual texts include Davis, "'We've Toiled without End'"; Stevenson, *Life Beside Itself*. See also notes 244, 263.

15 So much work exists on biopolitical death-proximity as a register of racialized, sexual, laboring existence and consciousness, some notable instances of which are distributed throughout this chapter. Most people would probably begin with Patterson, *Slavery and Social Death*; and Gilmore, *Golden Gulag*. Also see Cheref et al., "Suicidal Ideation"; Morrison and Downey, "Racial Differences in Self-Disclosure"; and O'Keefe et al., "Seemingly Harmless Racial Communications."

16 See, for example, "Global Economic Crisis"; Mills, "'Dead People Don't Claim'"; Rodríguez Andrés, "Income Inequality, Unemployment."

17 The clinical literature on suicidal ideation reviewed from the 1960s to the present controls for a lot, but only recently has it genuinely begun to investigate the wasting effects of biopolitical subjectivization on the distinction between life and death, where suicide might preserve a commitment to a better but unrealized life, and living might be resignation and not affirmative dissociation. The distribution of death-inclined thoughts among subordinated populations focuses particularly on LGBTQ+ youth and ethnic/racial minorities, with military personnel as contrast. The earlier literature claims that self-identified "whites" were more inclined toward suicidal ideation, but that is not the current view; age variation, ethnic/racial location, and the duration of stress in life are seen as more intensively shaping the scene of suicidiation and now include a more searching focus on the action of diminishing effects in ordinary life. The most widely cited text on suicidal ideation is Bolger et al., "Onset of Suicidal Ideation."

18 For suicide and suicidiation as measures of the nightmare of biopolitics for all populations arranged by its status hierarchies and protocols, see Kalish and Kimmel, "Suicide by Mass Murder"; "Suicide: Facts at a Glance," National Center for Injury Prevention and Control, Centers for Disease Control and Prevention, 2010, accessed August 4, 2017, https://www.cdc.gov /violenceprevention/pdf/suicide-datasheet-a.pdf; Laymon, "How to Slowly Kill Yourself"; and Laymon's revised *How to Slowly Kill Yourself and Others in America*. See also Moore, "Premeditated Manslaughter"; and Moore, "Reflections." [ed: See also Berlant and Stewart, "Suicidiation," in *The Hundreds*, 61.]

19 Lacan, *Ethics of Psychoanalysis*, 120–23.

20 The dissociation literature is enormous, of course. This note contains a skim across the top of my reading that's tilted toward generalized concepts of dissociation in the Freudian/Winnicottian traditions that have recently expanded in range both toward the neurosciences and toward cultural structuration alongside early childhood structuration (the focus of much of the psychological and psychoanalytic literature). A resource for pursuing diverse powerful orientations to this object/topic is Dell and O'Neill, *Dissociation and the Dissociative*

Disorders. See also Abram, *Donald Winnicott Today*; L. Butler, "Editorial"; Crawford, "If 'The Body Keeps the Score'"; Kaplan and Laub, "Affect Regulation in Extreme Traumatization"; Main and Solomon, "Discovery of an Insecure-Disorganized"; T. Ogden, "Some Theoretical Comments"; P. Ogden, Minton, and Pain, *Trauma and the Body*; Schore, *Affect Dysregulation and Disorders*; Schore, *Affect Regulation*; Stern, *Interpersonal World of the Infant*; van der Kolk, *Body Keeps the Score*; and van der Kolk and Fisler, "Dissociation and the Fragmentary Nature."

21   In some ways this lateral configuration of discontinuous but ongoing attachment/attention can be read in conversation with Foucault's discussion of Nietzschean genealogy in "Nietzsche, Genealogy, History."

22   Deleuze, "Pure Immanence," 28, 29, 31, 25–34.

23   Derrida, *Writing and Difference*, 371.

24   Nancy, "Elliptical Sense."

25   On the satirical and suicidiation, see Daniel, "Joy of the Worm" (unpublished manuscript). On the centrality of an indestructible substance in being to the joy of comedic disturbance, see Zupančič, *The Odd One In*, 11–60.

26   R. Williams, "Structures of Feeling."

27   Isherwood, *A Single Man*, 31.

28   Isherwood, *A Single Man*, 3.

29   Isherwood, *A Single Man*, 14.

30   Isherwood, *A Single Man*, 176.

31   Isherwood, *A Single Man*, 50.

32   See Berlant, "Slow Death."

33   On LGBTQ+ suicidiation in particular, see the groundbreaking reparative critical aesthetic work of Kate Bornstein in *Hello Cruel World* and "Hello, Cruel World Lite"; and of Rob Cover in *Queer Youth Suicide*, "Suicides of the Marginalised," and "Conditions of Living"; and the astonishing queer, indigenous, theoretical, visceral searching memoir-poetics of Billy-Ray Belcourt in *History of My Brief Body*.

34   Whether or not it induces an act that completes the idea in death, the suicidal idea inevitably opens up a cluster of unknowns about why some people give out in the scene of attrition-from-adjustment that building a life also demands. Sometimes the act is a communication and a judgment about the world, and it is sometimes literally the end of the road for someone who is no longer able to imagine a way out or even entertain the possibility of an otherwise. I first learned to think about this appearance of suicide as a political problem of speculation and scholarly inquiry in the suicidal anchor story of Spivak's "Can the Subaltern Speak?" and throughout her engagement with Mahasveta Devi in *Imaginary Maps* and "'Draupadi' by Mahasveta Devi."

35   Deleuze, "Pure Immanence," 28.

36 Ingold's entire oeuvre works toward an account of what maintains the self-continuity of life. See the essays in Ingold, *Being Alive*, for crisp formulations.

37 Seltzer, "The Official World."

38 Adorno, *Minima Moralia*; Caruth, *Unclaimed Experience*.

39 Jameson, *The Political Unconscious*, 102.

40 Bollas, "Moods and the Conservative Process," 102.

41 Flatley, *Affective Mapping*.

42 McGlotten, "Ordinary Intersections."

43 Flatley, *Affective Mapping*; Latour, *Reassembling the Social*.

44 T. Ogden, "Some Theoretical Comments," 387. On further "word and thought magic" that enables the functionally disturbed to maintain affective form, see Fonagy et al., *Affect Regulation*, 331; Fonagy and Target, "Dissociation and Trauma."

45 Note that the first two members of the set, *Lonely* and *Citizen*, are marketed as American lyrics; and the third, as a *conversation*. Rankine has commented that "An American Lyric" was a marketing device suggested by publishers before it became a project. See Jenny Buchner et al., "Interview: Claudia Rankine," cited in Dobbs, "Diagnosis Race," 178.

46 Reed, *Freedom Time*, 99–103. I was also aided in thinking about Rankine's place in using the experimental form of Black being by Shockley, *Renegade Poetics*.

47 Rankine, *Don't Let Me Be Lonely*, 5.

48 Rankine, *Don't Let Me Be Lonely*, 35; Milosz, "Gift," 53.

49 Rankine, *Don't Let Me Be Lonely*, 36.

50 Rankine, *Don't Let Me Be Lonely*, 7.

51 Rankine, *Don't Let Me Be Lonely*, 54.

52 Rankine, *Don't Let Me Be Lonely*, 5.

53 Rankine, *Don't Let Me Be Lonely*, 62.

54 On the gelatinous as a form of disturbance with world-making potential, see Tompkins, "On the Gelatinous."

55 Rankine, *Don't Let Me Be Lonely*, 5.

56 See Dobbs, "Diagnosis Race." This terrific essay covers some of the trans-media ground that follows, plus it provides a deep dive into John Henryism; see also Welch, "*Don't Let Me Be Lonely*." Both essays focus on media-induced subjectivity crisis and the ordinary trauma of structural subordination that makes Black attachment to life in Rankine's work saturated by the neighborliness of ordinary and violent death. Both understand subjectivity formation to be a medical and a political issue. See also Warner, "The Mass Public."

57 Rankine, *Don't Let Me Be Lonely*, 23.

58 Rankine, *Don't Let Me Be Lonely*, 23.

59 I refer here to Samuel Beckett's play *Not I*, most famously enacted by Billie Whitelaw in 1975: "[1973] 'Not I' (Samuel Beckett)," YouTube, October 17, 2020,

accessed December 6, 2020, https://www.youtube.com/watch?v=M4LDwfKxr-M. See Beckett, "Not I."

60 Miller, *Jane Austen*.

61 P. Williams, *Alchemy of Race and Rights*.

62 See Gilroy, *Postcolonial Melancholia*; Du Bois, *Souls of Black Folk*; Adorno, *Minima Moralia*; Fanon, *Black Skin, White Masks*; Fanon, *Wretched of the Earth*; P. Williams, *Alchemy of Race and Rights*. The idea of this archive of damaged life was introduced in Berlant, "She's Having an Episode." See also Rei Terada's brilliant engagement with DeQuincey's weird thanatovitalism in "Living a Ruined Life."

63 See Fonagy, "Transgenerational Transmission of Holocaust Trauma."

64 R. Williams, "Structures of Feeling."

65 In the early 1960s E. T. Hall developed this concept as part of an everyday life theory of behavioral psychology focused on distancing mechanisms in intimate (including urban) spaces. The other version, which I love but which insists on a scenic or architectural base for thinking proximity, is to be found in Liam Gillick's conceptual aesthetics. What I'm proposing here with respect to the affective spacing of social relation resonates some with both projects but is less bound by architectural and institutional referents. See Gillick, *Proxemics*. For Hall, see Ickinger, *Proxemics Research*. A recent special issue of *Anthropological Quarterly* on proximity resonates with the current project and with earlier work on queer intimacy as a scene of not necessarily wanting the object but wanting to be near it: the problem of managing, being managed by, or wondering about attachment that is here characterized by the affective sense of "inconvenience." See the special issue: Obadia, ed., Anthropological Quarterly 93, no. 1 (2020).

66 Gillick, *Proxemics*.

67 Stewart, *Ordinary Affects*.

68 Arendt, *Promise of Politics*, 201.

69 On existential contemporary homelessness, see Virno, *Grammar of the Multitude*.

70 D. Goldstein, *Laughter Out of Place*.

71 Mullen, "Elliptical," 23.

72 Latour, *On the Modern Cult*, 1–66.

73 Agamben, *End of the Poem*, 18–21.

74 Agamben, "Notes on Gesture," 56.

Coda: My Dark Places

1 Kapil, *Ban en Banlieue*, 28.

2 For an elaboration of this sentence, see Berlant, "Genre Flailing."

3 Spivak, "Subaltern Studies," 205.

4 Bollas, "The Transformational Object."

5 See the introduction for ruminations on the concept of the unbearable: a synonym for the incursion of the Real, an intensely felt pressure that threatens a person's or a community's capacity to proceed, a proclamation indicating a loss of faith that one or a community can go on.

6 Danius, Jonsson, and Spivak, "An Interview with Gayatri Chakravorty Spivak"; B. Johnson, A World of Difference; Mignolo and Walsh, On Decoloniality; Dunne and O'Rourke, "A Pedagogics of Unlearning."

7 Morris, "Conflicts and Crisis," 601.

8 Latour, Reassembling the Social. The difference between Latour and Kapil/ Ellroy, as I go on to demonstrate, is that Latour's notebooks are imaginably successful organizational tools for transforming the object at hand, whereas Ellroy and Kapil record failures to find form apart from a circuit of return to the scene of what at once cannot become otherwise and cannot but become something else if the subject/world that deems itself responsible to the injury makes a new world or layout for it. Like their object/scene, the artists become different by the failure of their tools to generate even the factish, the densely heuristic fact. The transformational infrastructure relies on being *on the verge* created by continuous proximity to that frustration.

9 Bion, Learning from Experience, 28–29 and throughout.

10 [ed.: The manuscript had "(93)" after "'somatic experiencing,'" presumably referring to a text about that form of treatment for PTSD.]

11 Sharpe, In the Wake.

12 Ahmed, Willful Subjects.

13 Ellroy, My Dark Places, 293.

14 Seltzer, Serial Killers.

15 The *serial killed* are barred from self-witness except if they were stalked and talked about it. I'll address this in my forthcoming On Humorlessness. Meanwhile, in his essay "Stalked by Love," Timothy Melley argues that the narrative function of heterosexual stalking novels is to establish the realist utility of feminist paranoia and to create an atmosphere of hetero-realism from that perspective.

16 Spillers, "'Mama's Baby, Papa's Maybe,'" 206.

17 Ellroy, My Dark Places, 295.

18 Ellroy, My Dark Places, 153. This sublation of external violence into aesthetic method involved identification with a criminality that straddled both the law and its transgression in the guise of an intense amount of teenage identification with Nazis and white supremacists, coupled with stalky misogyny. Alcoholics Anonymous transferred the thug life of drug life to sex appetites. His pattern of sociopathic rage and manic, searching internal storytelling lasts throughout much of his life, even after he stops drinking: "I lived out most of my dope-fueled sex dreams sober. The real world eclipsed my fantasy world. My one persistent fantasy was that story I knew was a novel" (186).

19 Ellroy, *My Dark Places*, 203, 206–7, 211, 212, 216.

20 On the string as a figure for the subject's lifelong testing of the world, see Mavor, *Reading Boyishly*; and Winnicott, *Playing and Reality*.

21 Ellroy, *My Dark Places*, 415.

22 Lacan, "Dialectic of Frustration."

23 Kapil, *Ban en Banlieue*, 21, 20.

24 Kapil, *Ban en Banlieue*, 74.

25 Kapil, *Ban en Banlieue*, 82.

26 Kapil, *Ban en Banlieue*, 41.

27 Clover, *Riot. Strike. Riot.*

28 Kapil, *Ban en Banlieue*, 48.

29 *Mangrove*, directed by McQueen, is episode 1 of *Small Axe*, which streamed on the BBC One/Amazon Prime platforms. This film returns to the case of the Mangrove Nine, who were prosecuted by the English state for "riot and affray" *caused by the police* in response to the West Indian Notting Hill community's public demonstration in self-defense. At the same time, in 2020, film director Aaron Sorkin launched *The Trial of the Chicago 7* on Netflix. Sorkin's film about the lust of the Chicago police state to beat up protestors against the Vietnam War tells much of the same story about the law's rage for deference to the white state. But in *The Trial of the Chicago 7*, the state's enemy is a class of white educated elites who are resented and targeted. So the US police were in what was at once a class war and an ideological one, in contrast to the class-internal and racially fractious story of *Mangrove*. It is as though in 2020 the mainstream media reignited the 1970s to school the present on the necessity of forceful resistance by any means to the violent persistence of the modern state apparatus that has turned its weapons, along with its usual colonial appetites, onto citizens and denizens. In both films, the Black Panthers are the heroes and the leaders.

30 "Enoch Powell 'Rivers of Blood.'"

31 "Enoch Powell 'Rivers of Blood.'"

32 Kapil, *Ban en Banlieue*, 20. In the afterword Kapil distinguishes fiction from specific form so that the generativity of the monster can keep the form living beyond norms (96).

33 Kapil, *Ban en Banlieue*, 28.

34 Kapil, *Ban en Banlieue*, 7, 10, 18, 20, 88, 101, 108.

35 Kapil, *Ban en Banlieue*, 13.

36 Kapil, *Ban en Banlieue*, 102–3.

37 Kapil, *Ban en Banlieue*, 48.

38 Kapil, *Ban en Banlieue*, 28.

39 Kapil, *Ban en Banlieue*, 96.

40 Kapil, *Ban en Banlieue*, 20–21.

41 Kapil, *Ban en Banlieue*, 20.

42 Kapil, *Ban en Banlieue*, 19.

43 Kapil, *Ban en Banlieue*, 23.

44 Steiner, *Psychic Retreats*.

45 Gramsci, *Selections from the Prison Notebooks*.

46 Sharpe, *In the Wake*, 17.

47 Stewart, *Ordinary Affects*.

48 I learned to think about maximalism this way from Dango, "Contemporary Styles."

49 Halberstam, *Queer Art of Failure*.

50 Kapil, *Ban en Banlieue*, 66, 24.

bibliography

Abram, Jan, ed. *Donald Winnicott Today*. New York: Routledge, 2013.

Adorno, Theodor. *Ästhetische Theorie (Aesthetic Theory)*. Translated and edited by Gretel Adorno and Rolf Tiedemann. Frankfurt am Main: Suhrkamp Verlag, 1970. Reprinted as a new translation by Robert Hullot-Kentor. New York: Bloomsbury Continuum, 1997.

Adorno, Theodor. *Minima Moralia: Reflections on a Damaged Life*. Translated by E. F. N. Jephcott. 1951. London: Verso, 1974.

Adorno, Theodor. "On Lyric Poetry and Society." In *Notes to Literature*, vol. 1, edited by Rolf Tiedeman and translated by Shierry Weber Nicholson, 37–54. New York: Columbia University Press, 1991.

Adorno, Theodor. "Resignation." In *Critical Models: Interventions and Catchwords*, translated by Henry W. Pickford, 289–93. New York: Columbia University Press, 1998.

"Afrofuturism." Special issue, *Science Fiction Studies* 34, no. 2 (July 2007).

"Afrofuturism." Special issue, *Social Text* 20, no. 2 (Summer 2002).

Agamben, Giorgio. *The End of the Poem: Studies in Poetics.* Translated by Daniel Heller-Roazen. Stanford, CA: Stanford University Press, 1999.

Agamben, Giorgio. "Notes on Gesture." In *Means without End-Notes on Politics,* translated by Cesare Casarino and Vincenzo Binetti, 49–61. 1996. Minneapolis: University of Minnesota Press, 2000.

Ahmed, Sara. "In the Name of Love." *Borderlands* 2, no. 3 (2003). Republished in *The Cultural Politics of Emotion,* 2nd ed., 122–43. New York: Routledge, 2014.

Ahmed, Sara. *The Promise of Happiness.* Durham, NC: Duke University Press, 2010.

Ahmed, Sara. *Willful Subjects.* Durham, NC: Duke University Press, 2014.

Althusser, Louis. "Ideology and Ideological State Apparatuses." In *Lenin and Philosophy and Other Essays,* translated by Ben Brewster, with an introduction by Fredric Jameson, 121–76. New York: New York University Press, 2001.

Althusser, Louis, Étienne Balibar, Roger Establet, Pierre Macherey, and Jacques Rancière. *Reading Capital: The Complete Edition.* London: Verso, 2016.

Amin, Kadji. *Disturbing Attachments: Genet, Modern Pederasty, and Queer History.* Durham, NC: Duke University Press, 2017.

Amster, Ellen J. "History's Crystal Ball: What the Past Can Tell Us about COVID-19 and Our Future." *The Conversation,* June 28, 2020. Accessed June 28, 2020. https://theconversation.com/historys-crystal-ball-what-the-past-can-tell -us-about-covid-19-and-our-future-140512?fbclid=IwAR1sJ9TLlGx8hPG-GdP2r8B_KJM7-nqAummmHdCFBBqK3AG8ZoNgjpjiIL7c.

Anderson, Ben. *Encountering Affect: Capacities, Apparatuses, Conditions.* New York: Routledge, 2017.

Anker, Libby. *Orgies of Feeling: Melodrama and the Politics of Freedom.* Durham, NC: Duke University Press, 2014.

Anonymous. *My Secret Life: An Erotic Diary of Victorian London.* Edited by James Kincaid, introduction by Paul Sawyer. 1900. New York: Signet, 2007.

Arendt, Hannah. *Essays in Understanding, 1930–1954: Formation, Exile, and Totalitarianism.* Edited by Jerome Kohn. New York: Harcourt, Brace, 1994.

Arendt, Hannah. *Lectures on Kant's Political Philosophy.* Chicago: University of Chicago Press, 1992.

Arendt, Hannah. *The Origins of Totalitarianism.* New York: Harcourt, Brace, 1951.

Arendt, Hannah. *The Promise of Politics.* Edited by Jerome Kohn. New York: Schocken, 2007.

Arruzza, Cinzia, Tithi Bhattacharya, and Nancy Fraser. *Feminism for the 99%: A Manifesto.* New York: Penguin, 2019.

Arsić, Branka. "Brain Walks: Emerson on Thinking." In *The Other Emerson,* edited by Branka Arsić and Cary Wolfe, 59–97. Minneapolis: University of Minnesota Press, 2010.

Augé, Marc. *Non-Places: Introduction to an Anthropology of Supermodernity*. Translated by John Howe. London: Verso, 2009.

Axelrod, Steven. "Colonel Shaw in American Poetry: 'For the Union Dead' and Its Precursors." *American Quarterly* 24, no. 4 (October 1972): 523–37.

Badiou, Alain, with Nicholas Truong. *In Praise of Love*. Translated by Peter Bush. 2009. New York: New Press, 2012.

Barthes, Roland. *Camera Lucida: Reflections on Photography*. Translated by Richard Howard. New York: Hill and Wang, 1981.

Barthes, Roland. "Myth Today." In *Mythologies*, translated by Annette Lavers, 109–59. New York: Hill and Wang, 1972.

Bataille, Georges. *The Accursed Share*. Vol. 2 and 3, *The History of Eroticism and Sovereignty*. Translated by Robert Hurley. Cambridge, MA: Zone, 1993.

Bear, Laura, Karen Ho, Anna Lowenhaupt Tsing, and Sylvia Yanagisako. "Gens: A Feminist Manifesto for the Study of Capitalism." Generating Capitalism series. *Fieldsights: Society for Cultural Anthropology*. March 30, 2015. Accessed December 6, 2020. https://culanth.org/fieldsights/gens-a-feminist-manifesto -for-the-study-of-capitalism.

Beaulieux, Michele. "Can't We Just Dance? Not If We Want to Create Safer Brave Contact Improvisation Spaces." *CQ: Contact Improvisation Newsletter* 45, no. 1 (Winter/Spring 2020). Accessed July 3, 2020. https://contactquarterly.com /contact-improvisation/newsletter/view/cant-we-just-dance#$.

Beaulieux, Michele. "How the First Rule Brought #MeToo to Contact Improvisation." *Contact Quarterly* 44, no. 1 (Winter/Spring 2019): 46–50.

Beaulieux, Michele. "The Shift from Rape Culture to Consent Culture." *Reservoir of Hope* (blog). October 2, 2019. https//reservoirofhope.home.blog/2019/10/02 /the-stages-of-safer-brave-contact-improvisation-spaces/.

Beaulieux, Michele. "Starting by Believing Maria: Responding to Sexual Violence in Safer Brave Contact Improvisation Spaces." *CQ: Contact Improvisation Newsletter* 44, no. 2 (Summer/Fall 2019). Accessed July 3, 2020. https:// contactquarterly.com/contact-improvisation/newsletter/#view=starting-by -believing-maria.

Beckett, Samuel. "Not I" (1973). In *First Love and Other Shorts*, 11–32. New York: Grove Press, 1974.

Belcourt, Billy-Ray. *A History of My Brief Body: A Memoir*. Columbus, OH: Two Dollar Radio, 2020.

Bello, Walden Flores. "A Dangerous Liaison? Harnessing Weber to Illuminate the Relationship of Democracy and Charisma in the Philippines and India." *International Sociology* 35, no. 6 (September 2020): 691–709. Accessed July 3, 2020. https://doi.org/10.1177/0268580920942721.

Berardi, Franco "Bifo." *Precarious Rhapsody: Semiocapitalism and the Pathologies of Post-Alpha Generation*. London: Minor Compositions/Autonomedia, 2009.

Bergson, Henri. *Laughter: An Essay on the Meaning of the Comic.* Translated by Cloudesley Brereton and Fred Rothwell. New York: Macmillan, 1911.

Berlant, Lauren. *Cruel Optimism.* Durham, NC: Duke University Press, 2011.

Berlant, Lauren. *The Female Complaint: The Unfinished Business of Sentimentality in American Culture.* Durham, NC: Duke University Press, 2008.

Berlant, Lauren. "Genre Flailing." *Capacious: Journal for Emerging Affect Inquiry* 1, no. 2 (2018). Accessed October 22, 2019. http://capaciousjournal.com/cms/wp -content/uploads/2018/06/capacious-berlant-genre-flailing.pdf.

Berlant, Lauren. "She's Having an Episode: Patricia Williams and the Writing of Damaged Life." *Columbia Journal of Gender and Law* 27, no. 1 (2013): 19–36.

Berlant, Lauren. "Slow Death (Sovereignty, Obesity, Lateral Agency)." In *Cruel Optimism,* 95–120. Durham, NC: Duke University Press, 2011.

Berlant, Lauren. "The Traumic: On Bojack Horseman's 'Good Damage.'" *Post45,* November 22, 2020. Accessed December 15, 2020. http://post45.org/2020/11 /the-traumic-on-bojack-horsemans-good-damage/.

Berlant, Lauren, and Lee Edelman. *Sex, or the Unbearable.* Durham, NC: Duke University Press, 2013.

Berlant, Lauren, and Kathleen Stewart. *The Hundreds.* Durham, NC: Duke University Press, 2019.

Bersani, Leo. *Homos.* Cambridge, MA: Harvard University Press, 1996.

Bersani, Leo. *Is the Rectum a Grave? And Other Essays.* Chicago: University of Chicago Press, 2009.

Bertolucci, Bernardo, and Franco Arcalli. *Bernardo Bertolucci's Last Tango in Paris: The Screenplay, with Critical Essays by Pauline Kael and Norman Mailer.* 1972. New York: Delta, 1973.

Best, Stephen. *None Like Us: Blackness, Belonging, Aesthetic Life.* Durham, NC: Duke University Press, 2018.

Bion, Wilfred R. *Learning from Experience.* 1962. London: Karnac, 1984.

Bion, Wilfred R. *Second Thoughts: Selected Papers on Psychoanalysis.* Northvale, NJ: Jason Aronson, 1993. First published by Heinemann in 1967.

Blogost, Ian. "Blogging Stops Unplanned Pregnancy: The Joy of the Bad Analogy." *Ian Bogost* (blog), June 18, 2009. Accessed June 25, 2020. http://bogost.com /writing/blog/blogging_stops_unplanned_pregn/.

Bolger, Niall, Geraldine Downey, Elaine Walker, and Pam Steininger. "The Onset of Suicidal Ideation in Childhood and Adolescence." *Journal of Youth and Adolescence* 18, no. 2 (April 1989): 175–90.

Bollas, Christopher. "Moods and the Conservative Process." In *The Shadow of the Object: Psychoanalysis and the Unthought Known,* 99–116. New York: Columbia University Press, 1987.

Bollas, Christopher. *The Shadow of the Object: Psychoanalysis of the Unthought Known.* New York: Columbia University Press, 1987.

Bollas, Christopher. "The Transformational Object." In *The Christopher Bollas Reader*, introduction by Arne Jemstedt and foreword by Adam Phillips, 1–12. New York: Routledge, 2011.

Bonney, Sean. *The Commons*. London: Openned Press, 2011.

Bonney, Sean. *The Commons II*. London: Openned Press, 2009.

Bornstein, Kate. *Hello Cruel World: 101 Alternatives to Suicide for Teens, Freaks and Other Outlaws*. New York: Seven Stories, 2011.

Bornstein, Kate. "Hello, Cruel World Lite: Beta 1.0.1: An Outlaw's Mini Guide to Survival Basics in the 21st Century." *Kate Bornstein* (blog). Accessed August 4, 2017. http://katebornstein.typepad.com/files/hcw_lite_101.pdf.

Bosteels, Bruno. *The Actuality of Communism*. London: Verso, 2014.

Bowker, Geoffrey C., and Susan Leigh Star. *Sorting Things Out: Classification and Its Consequences*. Cambridge, MA: MIT Press, 1999.

Brenkman, John. "The Concrete Utopia of Poetry." In *Culture and Domination*, 102–38. Ithaca, NY: Cornell University Press, 1987.

Brenkman, John. "This Is Beautiful, or, The Urge to Persuade." In *Mood and Trope: The Rhetoric and Poetics of Affect*, 137–81. Chicago: University of Chicago Press, 2020.

Brennan, Teresa. *The Transmission of Affect*. Ithaca, NY: Cornell University Press, 2004.

Brodsky, Claudia. "'Judgment' and the Genesis of What We Lack: 'Schema,' 'Poetry,' and the 'Monogram of the Imagination' in Kant." *The Eighteenth Century* 51, no. 3 (Fall 2010): 317–40.

Bromberg, Philip M. *Standing in the Spaces: Essays on Clinical Process, Trauma, and Dissociation*. New York: Psychology Press, 1998.

Buchner, Jenny, et al. "Interview: Claudia Rankine." *South Loop Review. Creative Nonfiction and Art* (2012): 63–67.

Buell, Lawrence. *Emerson*. Cambridge, MA: Harvard University Press, 2004.

Burt, Stephen. "The Elliptical Poets." In *Close Calls with Nonsense: Reading New Poetry*, 345–56. Saint Paul, MN: Graywolf, 2009.

Butler, Judith. *Frames of War: When Is Life Grievable?* London: Verso, 2009.

Butler, Judith. *Notes toward a Performative Theory of Assembly*. Cambridge, MA: Harvard University Press, 2018.

Butler, Judith. *Precarious Life: The Powers of Mourning and Violence*. London: Verso, 2004.

Butler, Judith, and Athena Athanasiou. *The Performative in the Political: Conversations with Athena Athanasiou*. Malden, MA: Polity, 2013.

Butler, Lisa. "Editorial: The Dissociations of Everyday Life." In "Dissociation in Culture," edited by Lisa Butler. Special issue, *Journal of Trauma and Dissociation* 5, no. 2 (2004): 1–11.

Byrd, Jodi A. *The Transit of Empire: Indigenous Critiques of Colonialism*. Minneapolis: University of Minneapolis Press, 2011.

Caruth, Cathy. *Unclaimed Experience: Trauma, Narrative, and History*. Baltimore: Johns Hopkins University Press, 1996.

Casarino, Cesare, and Antonio Negri. *In Praise of the Common: A Conversation on Philosophy and Politics.* Minneapolis: University of Minnesota Press, 2008.

Cattelino, Jessica R. *High Stakes: Florida Seminole Gaming and Sovereignty.* Durham, NC: Duke University Press, 2008.

Cavell, Stanley. *Cities of Words: Pedagogical Letters on a Register of the Moral Life.* Cambridge, MA: Belknap, 2005.

Cavell, Stanley. *Contesting Tears: The Hollywood Melodrama of the Unknown Woman.* Chicago: University of Chicago Press, 1996.

Cavell, Stanley. *Emerson's Transcendental Etudes.* Edited by David Justin Hodge. Stanford, CA: Stanford University Press, 2003.

Cavell, Stanley. *In Quest of the Ordinary: Lines of Skepticism and Romanticism.* Chicago: University of Chicago Press, 1994.

Cavell, Stanley. *Must We Mean What We Say?* 1969. Cambridge: Cambridge University Press, 2002.

Cavell, Stanley. *Pursuits of Happiness: The Hollywood Comedy of Remarriage.* Cambridge, MA: Harvard University Press, 1984.

Cavitch, Max. "Dissociative Reading—Philip Bromberg and Emily Dickinson: A Review of *Awakening the Dreamer: Clinical Journeys* by Philip M. Bromberg." *Contemporary Psychoanalysis* 43, no. 4 (Fall 2007): 681–88.

Cavitch, Max. "'Do You Love Me?' The Question of the Queer Child of Psychoanalysis." *Psychoanalysis, Culture and Society* 21, no. 3 (Sept. 2016): 256–74.

Celani, David P. *The Illusion of Love: Why the Battered Woman Returns to Her Abuser.* New York: Columbia University Press, 1994.

Chambers-Letson, Joshua. *After the Party: A Manifesto for Queer of Color Life.* New York: New York University Press, 2018.

Chambers-Letson, Joshua. "Homegrown Terror: Projective Identification and Waafa Bilal's Domestic Tension." *Journal of Asian-American Studies* 19, no. 2 (June 2016): 169–92.

Chefetz, Richard A. *Intensive Psychotherapy for Persistent Dissociative Process: The Fear of Feeling Real.* New York: W. W. Norton, 2015.

Chen, Mel Y. *Animacies.* Durham, NC: Duke University Press, 2012.

Cheref, Soumia, Robert Lane, Lillian Polanco-Roman, Erin Gadol, and Regina Miranda. "Suicidal Ideation among Racial/Ethnic Minorities: Moderating Effects of Rumination and Depressive Symptoms." *Cultural Diversity and Ethnic Minority Psychology* 21, no. 1 (Jan. 2015): 31–40.

Clover, Joshua. "Genres of the Dialectic." *Critical Inquiry* 43, no. 2 (Winter 2017): 431–50.

Clover, Joshua. *Riot. Strike. Riot.* London: Verso, 2016.

Cohen, Ted. *Jokes: Philosophical Thoughts on Joking Matters.* Chicago: University of Chicago Press, 1999.

Cooper, Davina. *Feeling Like a State: Desire, Denial, and the Recasting of Authority.* Durham, NC: Duke University Press, 2019.

Copjec, Joan. "The Sartorial Superego." In *Read My Desire: Lacan against the Historicists*, 65–116. Cambridge, MA: MIT Press, 1994.

Copjec, Joan, and Michael Sorkin, eds. *Giving Ground: The Politics of Propinquity*. London: Verso, 1999.

Cornell, Drucilla. *Just Cause: Freedom, Identity, and Rights*. London: Rowman and Littlefield, 2000.

Cornell, Drucilla, and Steven D. Seeley. "There's Nothing Revolutionary about a Blowjob." *Social Text* 32, no. 2 (Summer 2014): 1–23.

Cottom, Tressie McMillan. *Lower Ed: The Troubling Rise of For-Profit Colleges in the New Economy*. New York: New Press, 2017.

Cover, Rob. "Conditions of Living: Queer Youth Suicide, Homonormative Tolerance, and Relative Misery." *Journal of LGBT Youth* 10, no. 4 (2013): 328–50.

Cover, Rob. *Queer Youth Suicide, Culture and Identity: Unliveable Lives?* Burlington, VT: Ashgate, 2012.

Cover, Rob. "Suicides of the Marginalised: Cultural Approaches to Suicide, Minorities and Relationality." *Cultural Studies Review* 22, no. 2 (Sept. 2016): 90–113.

Cowen, Deborah. "Disrupting Distribution: Subversion, the Social Factory, and the 'State' of Supply Chains." *Viewpoint*, Issue 4. October 2014. https://www.viewpointmag.com/2014/10/29/disrupting-distribution-subversion-the-social-factory-and-the-state-of-supply-chains/, accessed October 28, 2014.

Crawford, Allison. "If 'The Body Keeps the Score': Mapping the Dissociated Body in Trauma Narrative, Intervention, and Theory." *University of Toronto Quarterly* 79, no. 2 (Spring 2010): 702–19.

Critchley, Simon. "Comedy and Finitude: Displacing the Tragic-Heroic Paradigm in Philosophy and Psychoanalysis." *Constellations* 6, no. 1 (1999): 108–22.

Cvetkovich, Ann. *An Archive of Feelings*. Durham, NC: Duke University Press, 2003.

Dango, Michael T. "Contemporary Styles: A Taxonomy of Novel Actions." PhD diss., University of Chicago, 2017.

Daniel, Drew. "Joy of the Worm: Suicidal Slapstick in Antony and Cleopatra." Unpublished manuscript. 2017. PDF.

Danius, Sara, Stefan Jonsson, and Gayatri Chakravorty Spivak. "An Interview with Gayatri Chakravorty Spivak." *Boundary 2* 20, no. 2 (Summer 1993): 24–50.

Davis, Elizabeth. "'We've Toiled without End': Publicity, Crisis, and the Suicide 'Epidemic' in Greece." *Comparative Studies in Society and History* 57, no. 4 (Oct. 2015): 1007–36.

Dawdy, Shannon Lee. *Patina: A Profane Archaeology*. Chicago: University of Chicago Press, 2016.

Dean, Tim. *Unlimited Intimacy: Reflections on the Subculture of Barebacking*. Chicago: University of Chicago Press, 2009.

de Angelis, Massimo. *The Beginning of History: Value Struggles and Global Capital*. London: Pluto, 2007.

de Certeau, Michel. *The Practice of Everyday Life*. Translated by Steven Rendall. Berkeley: University of California Press, 1984.

Delaney, Samuel R. *Times Square Red, Times Square Blue*. New York: New York University Press, 1999.

Deleuze, Gilles. "Desire and Pleasure." In *Foucault and His Interlocutors*, edited by Arnold I. Davidson, 183–92. Chicago: University of Chicago Press, 1998.

Deleuze, Gilles. *The Fold: Leibniz and the Baroque*. Translated by Tom Conley. 1988. Minneapolis: University of Minnesota Press, 1993.

Deleuze, Gilles. *The Logic of Sense*. Edited by Constantin V. Boundas, translated by Mark Lester and Charles Stivale. 1969. New York: Columbia University Press, 1990.

Deleuze, Gilles. "Pure Immanence" (1965). In *Pure Immanence: Essays on a Life*, edited and translated by John Rajchman, 25–34. New York: Zone, 2001.

Deleuze, Gilles. *Spinoza: Practical Philosophy*. Translated by Robert Hurley. 1988. San Francisco, CA: City Lights Publishers, 2001.

Deleuze, Gilles, and Félix Guattari. *A Thousand Plateaus: Capitalism and Schizophrenia*. Translated and with foreword by Brian Massumi. Minneapolis: University of Minnesota Press, 2004.

Dell, Paul F., and John A. O'Neill, eds. *Dissociation and the Dissociative Disorders: DSM-V and Beyond*. New York: Routledge, 2009.

Derrida, Jacques. *Writing and Difference*. Translated and with an introduction by Alan Bass. 1967. New York and London: Routledge, 1978.

Devi, Mahasveta. *Imaginary Maps*. Translated by Gayatri Chakravorty Spivak. London: Routledge, 1993.

Diaconu, Mădălina. "Patina-Atmosphere-Aroma: Towards an Aesthetics of Fine Differences." In *Analecta Husserliana: The Yearbook of Phenomenological Research*, edited by Anna-Teresa Tymieniecka, vol. 92, 131–48. Hanover, NH: World Phenomenology Institute, 2006.

Dobbs, Cynthia. "Diagnosis Race: Troubling Etiologies in Claudia Rankine's *American Lyrics*." *Literature and Medicine* 38, no. 1 (Spring 2020): 168–88.

Dolar, Mladen. "The Comic Mimesis." *Critical Inquiry* 43, no. 2 (Winter 2017): 570–89.

Dolmage, Jay Timothy. *Academic Ableism: Disability and Higher Education*. Ann Arbor: University of Michigan Press, 2017.

Du Bois, W. E. B. *The Souls of Black Folk*. Chicago: A. C. McClurg, 1903.

Duggan, Lisa. "Beyond Marriage: Democracy, Equality, and Kinship for a New Century." *Scholar and the Feminist Online*, nos. 10.1–10.2 (Fall 2011/Spring 2012). Accessed December 11, 2020. http://sfonline.barnard.edu/a-new-queer-agenda/beyond-marriage-democracy-equality-and-kinship-for-a-new-century/.

Dunne, Éamonn, and Michael O'Rourke. "A Pedagogics of Unlearning." In *The Para-Academic Handbook: A Toolkit for Making-Learning-Creating-Acting*, edited by

Alex Wardrop and Deborah Withers, 61–70. Bristol, UK: HammerOn Press, 2014.

Edelman, Lee. *No Future: Queer Theory and the Death Drive.* Durham, NC: Duke University Press, 2004.

Eliot, T. S. *The Waste Land, Prufrock and Other Poems.* Mineola, NY: Dover Thrift Editions, 1998.

Ellroy, James. *The Hilliker Curse: My Pursuit of Women.* New York: Vintage, 2010.

Ellroy, James. *My Dark Places: An L.A. Crime Memoir.* New York: Vintage, 1996.

Emerson, Ralph Waldo. *Journals and Miscellaneous Notebooks of Ralph Waldo Emerson.* Vol. VII: *1838–1842.* Edited by A. W. Plumstead. Cambridge, MA: Harvard University Press, 1969.

Emerson, Ralph Waldo. *Nature and Selected Essays.* Edited by Larzer Ziff. New York: Penguin, 2003.

Eng, David L., and Shinhee Han. *Racial Melancholia, Racial Dissociation: On the Social and Psychic Lives of Asian Americans.* Durham, NC: Duke University Press, 2019.

"Enoch Powell 'Rivers of Blood.'" Rivers of Blood. Accessed December 11, 2020. https://identityhunters.files.wordpress.com/2017/07/enoch-powell-rivers-of -blood-speech-1968.pdf.

Fairbairn, William Ronald Dodds. *Psychoanalytic Studies of the Personality.* 1952. New York: Taylor and Francis, 2001.

Fairbairn, William Ronald Dodds. "Theoretical and Experimental Aspects of Psycho-Analysis." *British Journal of Medical Psychology* 25, nos. 2–3 (Sept. 1952): 122–27.

Fanon, Frantz. *Black Skin, White Masks.* Translated by Charles Lam Markmann. Forewords by Ziauddin Sardar and Homi K. Bhabha. London: Pluto, 2008. Originally published in 1952 by Éditions du Seuil, France.

Fanon, Frantz. "The Fact of Blackness." In *Black Skin, White Masks,* translated by Charles Lam Markmann, forewords by Ziauddin Sardar and Homi K. Bhabha, 109–40. London: Pluto, 1986.

Fanon, Frantz. *The Wretched of the Earth.* Preface by Jean-Paul Sartre. Translated by Constance Farrington. New York: Grove, 1965.

Fausset, Richard. "What We Know about the Shooting Death of Ahmaud Arbery." *New York Times,* June 24, 2020. Accessed June 28, 2020. https://www.nytimes .com/article/ahmaud-arbery-shooting-georgia.html?referringSource =articleShare.

Federici, Silvia. "Women, Land Struggles, and the Reconstruction of the Commons." *WorkingUSA: The Journal of Labor and Society* 14, no. 1 (March 2011): 41–56.

Fink, Marty. *Forget Burial: HIV Kinship, Disability, and Queer/Trans Narratives of Care.* New Brunswick, NJ: Rutgers University Press, 2020.

Fischel, Joseph. *Sex and Harm in the Age of Consent.* Minneapolis: University of Minnesota Press, 2016.

Flatley, Jonathan. *Affective Mapping: Melancholia and the Politics of Modernism.* Cambridge, MA: Harvard University Press, 2008.

Flatley, Jonathan. "Refreshments of Revolutionary Mood." In *Literary/Liberal Entanglements: Toward a Literary History for the Twenty-First Century*, edited by Corrinne Harol and Mark Simpson, 103–47. Toronto: University of Toronto Press, 2017.

Folsom, Ed, and Kenneth M. Price. *Re-Scripting Walt Whitman: An Introduction to His Life and Work*. Malden, MA: Wiley, 2005.

Fonagy, Peter. "The Transgenerational Transmission of Holocaust Trauma: Lessons Learned from the Analysis of an Adolescent with Obsessive-Compulsive Disorder." *Attachment and Human Development* 1, no. 1 (1999): 92–114.

Fonagy, Peter, Gyorgy Gergely, Elliot L. Jurist, and Mary Target. *Affect Regulation, Mentalization, and the Development of the Self*. New York: Other Press, 2002.

Fonagy, Peter, and Mary Target. "Dissociation and Trauma." *Current Opinion in Psychiatry* 8, no. 3 (May 1995): 161–66.

Ford, Doreen. "Abolish Work!" Accessed August 1, 2020. https://abolishwork .com/.

Ford, Doreen. "Dispatches from the Ruins: Documents and Analyses from University Struggles, Experiments in Self-Education." Compiled May 2011 by 1,000 Little Hammers. Accessed July 3, 2020. https:// 1000littlehammers.files.wordpress.com/2010/02/dispatch_ruins_final3.pdf.

Ford, Tom, dir. *A Single Man*. New York: The Weinstein Company, 2009.

Forrester, John. "On Kuhn's Case: Psychoanalysis and the Paradigm." *Critical Inquiry* 33, no. 4 (Summer 2007): 782–819.

Foucault, Michel. *The Birth of Biopolitics: Lectures at the Collège de France, 1978–1979*. New York: Picador, 2010.

Foucault, Michel. "Body/Power." In *Power/Knowledge: Selected Interviews and Other Writings, 1972–1977*, translated by Colin Gordon, 54–62. New York: Pantheon, 1980.

Foucault, Michel. "Friendship as a Way of Life." In *Foucault Live: Collected Interviews, 1961–1984*, edited by Sylvère Lotringer, translated by Lysa Hochroth and John Johnston, 308–12. New York: Semiotext(e), 1996.

Foucault, Michel. "Governmentality." In *The Foucault Effect: Studies in Governmentality with two essays and an interview with Michel Foucault*, edited by Graham Burchell, Colin Gordon, and Peter Miller, 87–104. Chicago: University of Chicago Press, 1991.

Foucault, Michel. *History of Sexuality*. Volume I: *An Introduction* (1978). New York: Vintage, 1990.

Foucault, Michel. "Nietzsche, Genealogy, History." In *Language, Counter-Memory, Practice: Selected Essays and Interviews*, edited by Donald F. Bouchard, 139–64. Ithaca, NY: Cornell University Press, 1977.

Foucault, Michel. "Of Other Spaces." *diacritics* 16, no. 1 (Spring 1986): 22–27.

Freud, Sigmund. *Jokes and Their Relation to the Unconscious* (1905). Volume 8 of *The Standard Edition of the Complete Psychological Works of Sigmund Freud*, translated and edited by James Strachey. London: Hogarth, 1960.

Friedman, Jaclyn, and Jessica Valenti. *Yes Means Yes: Visions of Female Power and a World without Rape*. Berkeley, CA: Seal Press, 2008.

Fuhrmann, Arnika. *Ghostly Desires: Queer Sexuality and Vernacular Buddhism in Contemporary Thai Cinema*. Durham, NC: Duke University Press, 2016.

Gandhi, Leela. *The Common Cause: Postcolonial Ethics and the Practice of Democracy, 1900–1955*. Chicago: University of Chicago Press, 2014.

Gandhi, Leela. "The Pauper's Gift: Postcolonial Theory and the New Democratic Dispensation." *Public Culture* 23, no. 1 (January 2011): 27–38.

Gentner, Dedre. "Structure-Mapping: A Theoretical Framework for Analogy." *Cognitive Science* 7, no. 2 (April–June 1983): 155–70.

Gentner, Dedre, Brian Bowdle, Phillip Wolff, and Consuelo Boronat. "Metaphor Is Like Analogy." In *The Analogical Mind: Perspectives from Cognitive Science*, edited by Dedre Gentner, Keith J. Holyoak, and Boicho N. Kokinov, 199–253. Cambridge, MA: MIT Press, 2001.

Gibson-Graham, J. K. *A Postcapitalist Politics*. Minneapolis: University of Minnesota Press, 2006.

Gilbert, Jeremy. *Common Ground: Democracy and Collectivity in an Age of Individualism*. London: Pluto, 2014.

Gillick, Liam. *Proxemics: Selected Writings (1988–2006)*. Edited by Lionel Bovier. Zurich: JRP Ringier, 2006.

Gilmore, Ruth Wilson. *Golden Gulag: Prisons, Surplus, Crisis, and Opposition in Globalizing California*. Berkeley: University of California Press, 2007.

Gilroy, Paul. *Postcolonial Melancholia*. New York: Columbia University Press, 2005.

"Global Economic Crisis Tied to Suicide Rise." BBC.com, September 18, 2013. Accessed December 2, 2020. https://www.bbc.com/news/health-24123677.

Goffman, Erving. "Footing." In *Forms of Talk*, 124–59. Philadelphia: University of Pennsylvania Press, 1981.

Goldstein, Donna. *Laughter Out of Place: Race, Class, Violence, and Sexuality in a Rio Shantytown, with a New Preface*. Berkeley: University of California Press, 2013.

Goldstein, William. "A Clarification of Projective Identification." *American Journal of Psychiatry* 148, no. 2 (February 1991): 153–61.

Gonzales-Day, Ken. *Lynching in the West: 1850–1935*. Durham, NC: Duke University Press, 2006.

Gonzales-Day, Ken. *Profiled*. Edited by Edward Robinson. Los Angeles: Los Angeles Museum of Contemporary Art, 2011.

González-López, Gloria. *Family Secrets: Stories of Incest and Sexual Violence in Mexico*. New York: New York University Press, 2015.

Goodley, Dan. "Dis/Entangling Critical Disability Studies." *Disability and Society* 28, no. 5 (July 2013): 631–44.

Gordon, Peter E. "Why Historical Analogy Matters." *New York Review of Books*, January 7, 2020. Accessed July 3, 2020. https://www.nybooks.com/daily/2020/01/07/why-historical-analogy-matters/.

Gould, Deborah B. *Moving Politics: Emotion and* ACT UP's *Fight Against* AIDS. Chicago: University of Chicago Press, 2009.

Gramsci, Antonio. *Selections from the Prison Notebooks*. Edited by Quentin Hoare and Geoffrey Nowell Smith. London: Lawrence and Wishart, 1971.

Green, André. *The Fabric of Affect in the Psychoanalytic Discourse*. Translated by Alan Sheridan. London: Routledge, 2005. Originally published as *Le Discours vivant*. Paris: Presses Universitaires de France, 1973.

Green, André. *Key Ideas for a Contemporary Psychoanalysis: Misrecognition and Recognition of the Unconscious*. Translated by Andrew Weller. New York: Routledge, 2012.

Greenham, David. *Emerson's Transatlantic Romanticism*. New York: Palgrave Macmillan, 2012.

Grewal, Inderpal. "Authoritarian Patriarchy and Its Populism." *English Studies in Africa* 63, no. 1 (2020): 179–98.

Gunning, Tom. "Crazy Machines in the Garden of Forking Paths: Mischief Gags and the Origins of American Film Comedy." In *Classical Hollywood Comedy*, ed. Kristine Brunovska Karnick and Henry Jenkins, 87–105. New York: Routledge, 1995.

Gustafsson, Nils, and Noomi Weinryb. "The Populist Allure of Social Media Activism: Individualized Charismatic Authority." *Organization* 27, no. 3 (2020): 431–40.

Halberstam, Jack. *The Queer Art of Failure*. Durham, NC: Duke University Press, 2011.

Hall, Stuart. "The Problem of Ideology: Marxism without Guarantees." *Journal of Communication Inquiry* 10, no. 2 (June 1986): 28–44.

Halley, Janet. *Split Decisions: How and Why to Take a Break from Feminism*. Princeton, NJ: Princeton University Press, 2006.

Hardt, Michael. "Affective Labor." *Boundary 2* 26, no. 2 (Summer 1999): 89–100.

Hardt, Michael, and Antonio Negri. *Assembly*. Oxford: Oxford University Press, 2017.

Hardt, Michael, and Antonio Negri. *Commonwealth*. Cambridge, MA: Harvard University Press, 2009.

Hardt, Michael, and Antonio Negri. *Declaration*. San Francisco: Argo-Navis, 2012.

Hardt, Michael, and Antonio Negri. *Multitude: War and Democracy in the Age of Empire*. Cambridge, MA: Harvard University Press, 2000.

Hargreaves, Tracy. *Androgyny in Modern Literature*. London: Palgrave Macmillan, 2005.

Harney, Stefano, and Fred Moten. "Michael Brown." *Boundary 2* 42, no. 4 (2015): 81–87.

Harney, Stefano, and Fred Moten. *The Undercommons: Fugitive Planning and Black Study*. New York: Minor Compositions, 2013.

Harney, Stefano, and Fred Moten. "the university: last words." Personal manuscript circulated by FYPU (Fuck You. Pay Us.).

Harrington, Austin. "Lifeworld." *Theory, Culture and Society* 23, nos. 2–3 (May 2006): 341–43.

Harris, Cheryl. "Whiteness as Property." *Harvard Law Review* 106, no. 8 (June 1993): 1707–91.

Hartman, Saidiya V., and Frank B. Wilderson II. "The Position of the Unthought." *Qui Parle* 13, no. 2 (Spring/Summer 2003): 183–201.

Harvey, David. *The Enigma of Capital and the Crises of Capitalism.* Oxford: Oxford University Press, 2010.

Harvey, David. "Neoliberalism as Creative Destruction." *Annals of the American Political Economy and Social Science* 610 (March 2007): 22–44.

Hoagland, Tony. "Fear of Narrative and the Skittery Poem of Our Moment." *Poetry* 187, no. 6 (March 2006): 508–19.

Hocquenghem, Guy. *Homosexual Desire.* Translated by Daniella Dangoor, with an introduction by Michael Moon and a foreword by Jeffrey Weeks. Durham, NC: Duke University Press, 1993.

Hofstadter, Richard. "The Paranoid Style in American Politics." In *The Paranoid Style in American Politics and Other Essays*, 3–40. Cambridge, MA: Harvard University Press, 1965.

Honig, Bonnie. *Antigone, Interrupted.* Cambridge: Cambridge University Press, 2013.

Ickinger, William J. *Proxemics Research.* 2001. Accessed August 5, 2017. http://web .archive.org/web/20110716051819/http://sharktown.com/proxemics/intro.html.

Illouz, Eva. *Why Love Hurts: A Sociological Explanation.* Malden, MA: Polity, 2013.

Ingold, Tim. *Being Alive: Essays on Movement, Knowledge, and Description.* New York: Routledge, 2011.

Irigaray, Luce. *This Sex Which Is Not One.* Translated by Catherine Porter and Carolyn Burke. Ithaca, NY: Cornell University Press, 1985.

Isherwood, Christopher. *A Single Man.* New York: Avon, 1978. First published in 1964 by Simon and Schuster.

Jagoda, Patrick. *Network Aesthetics.* Chicago: University of Chicago Press, 2016.

Jagose, Annamarie. *Orgasmology.* Durham, NC: Duke University Press, 2012.

Jameson, Fredric. *The Political Unconscious: Narrative as a Socially Symbolic Act.* Ithaca, NY: Cornell University Press, 1981.

Jameson, Fredric. *Postmodernism, or, The Cultural Logic of Late Capitalism.* Durham, NC: Duke University Press, 1992.

Johnson, Barbara. *A World of Difference.* Baltimore: Johns Hopkins University Press, 1987.

Johnson, Ryan. "An Accord in/on Kantian Aesthetics (or the Sensus Communis: Attunement in a Community of Diverse Sites of Purposiveness)." *Kritike* 5, no. 1 (June 2011): 117–35.

Kael, Pauline. "The Current Cinema: *Tango*," *New Yorker*, October 28, 1972, 130–38.

Kafer, Alison. *Feminist, Queer, Crip.* Bloomington: Indiana University Press, 2013.

Kalish, Rachel, and Michael Kimmel. "Suicide by Mass Murder: Masculinity, Aggrieved Entitlement, and Rampage School Shootings." *Health Sociology Review* 19, no. 4 (2010): 451–64.

Kant, Immanuel. *Critique of Judgement*. Translated by J. H. Bernard. London: Macmillan, 1914.

Kapil, Bhanu. *Ban en Banlieue*. New York: Nightboat, 2015.

Kaplan, Suzanne, and Dori Laub. "Affect Regulation in Extreme Traumatization—Fragmented Narratives of Holocaust Survivors Hospitalized in Psychiatric Institutions." *The Scandinavian Psychoanalytic Review* 32, no. 2 (2009): 93–104.

Katz, Cindi, Sallie A. Marston, and Katharyne Mitchell, eds. *Life's Work: Geographies of Social Reproduction*. London: Blackwell, 2004.

Kelty, Christopher. "Evil Infrastructures." Generating Capitalism series. *Fieldsights: Society for Cultural Anthropology*. April 28, 2017. Accessed December 11, 2020. https://culanth.org/fieldsights/series/evil-infrastructures.

Kim, Juliana. "How the Floyd Protests Turned Into a 24-Hour 'Occupy City Hall' in N.Y." *New York Times*, June 28, 2020. Accessed June 28, 2020. https://www.nytimes.com/2020/06/28/nyregion/occupy-city-hall-nyc.html ?referringSource=articleShare.

Klausen, Jimmy Casas, and James Martel, eds. *How Not to Be Governed: Readings and Interpretations from a Critical Anarchist Left*. Lanham, MD: Lexington, 2011.

Klausner, Julie. "Cat News (Episode 1)." Accessed August 25, 2019. YouTube video, 4:02. https://www.youtube.com/watch?v=oUUdIoWLCzg.

Klein, Melanie. "A Contribution to the Psychogenesis of Manic-Depressive States." *International Journal of Psychoanalysis* 16 (1935): 145–74.

Klein, Melanie. "Mourning and Its Relation to Manic-Depressive States." *International Journal of Psychoanalysis* 21 (1940): 125–53.

Klein, Melanie. "Some Theoretical Conclusions Regarding the Emotional Life of the Infant" (1953). In *Envy and Gratitude and Other Works 1946–1963*, edited by M. Masud and R. Khan, 61–93. London: International Psycho-Analytical Library and Hogarth Press, 1975.

Koons, Cynthia. "Latest Suicide Data Show the Depth of U.S. Mental Health Crisis." June 20, 2019. Accessed December 2, 2020. https://www.bloomberg .com/news/articles/2019-06-20/latest-suicide-data-show-the-depth-of-u-s -mental-health-crisis.

Koselleck, Reinhart. *Critique and Crisis: Enlightenment and the Pathogenesis of Modern Society*. Cambridge, MA: MIT Press, 1988.

Lacan, Jacques. "The Dialectic of Frustration." In *The Seminar of Jacques Lacan: Book IV, The Object Relation, 1956–1957*, edited by Jacques-Alain Miller. Accessed September 15, 2017. https://www.scribd.com/doc/143580546/The-Seminar-of -Jacques-Lacan-Book-4-The-Object-Relation.

Lacan, Jacques. *The Ethics of Psychoanalysis: Seminar VII, 1959–60*. Edited by Jacques-Alain Miller. Translated by Dennis Porter. New York: Routledge, 1992.

Laplanche, Jean. *Essays on Otherness*. New York: Routledge, 1999.

Laplanche, Jean. *New Foundations for Psychoanalysis*. Translated by David Macey. 1987; London: Blackwell, 1989.

Laplanche, Jean. "The Theory of Seduction and the Problem of the Other." *International Journal of Psycho-Analysis* 78 (1997): 653–66.

Laplanche, Jean, and Jean-Bertrand Pontalis. "Fantasy and the Origins of Sexuality." In *Formations of Fantasy*, edited by Victor Burgin, James Donald, and Cora Kaplan, 5–34. New York and London: Methuen, 1986.

Latour, Bruno. *On the Modern Cult of the Factish Gods.* Durham, NC: Duke University Press, 2010.

Latour, Bruno. *Reassembling the Social: An Introduction to Actor-Network Theory.* Oxford: Oxford University Press, 2005.

Laymon, Kiese. *How to Slowly Kill Yourself and Others in America.* Chicago: Bolden, 2013.

Laymon, Kiese. "How to Slowly Kill Yourself and Others in America: A Remembrance." *Gawker*, July 28, 2012. Accessed August 5, 2017. http://gawker.com/5927452/how-to-slowly-kill-yourself-and-others-in-america-a-remembrance.

LeMahieu, Michael. "Robert Lowell, Perpetual War, and the Legacy of Civil War Elegy." *College Literature* 43, no. 1 (Winter 2016): 91–120.

Limon, John. *Stand-up Comedy in Theory: Or, Abjection in America.* Durham, NC: Duke University Press, 2000.

Linebaugh, Peter. *The Magna Carta Manifesto: Liberties and Commons for All.* Berkeley: University of California Press, 2009.

Linebaugh, Peter. *Stop, Thief! The Commons, Enclosures, and Resistance.* Oakland, CA: PM Press, 2014.

Litvak, Joseph. *The Un-Americans: Jews, the Blacklist, and Stoolpigeon Culture.* Durham, NC: Duke University Press, 2009.

Lloyd, David, and Paul Thomas. *Culture and the State.* New York: Routledge, 1998.

Love, Heather. *Feeling Backward: Loss and the Politics of Queer History.* Cambridge, MA: Harvard University Press, 2009.

Lowell, Robert. "For the Union Dead: A Poem." *The Atlantic*, November 1960. Accessed July 3, 2020. https://www.theatlantic.com/magazine/archive/1960/11/for-the-union-dead/308322/.

Lowell, Robert. *Life Studies and For the Union Dead.* New York: Farrar, Straus and Giroux, 2003.

Main, Mary, and Judith Solomon. "Discovery of an Insecure-Disorganized/Disoriented Attachment Pattern: Procedures, Findings and Implications for the Classification of Behavior." In *Affective Development in Infancy*, edited by T. Berry Brazelton and Michael Yogman, 95–124. Norwood, NJ: Ablex, 1986.

Malabou, Catherine. *The New Wounded: From Neurosis to Brain Damage.* Translated by Steven Miller. New York: Fordham University Press, 2012.

Manalansan, Martin. "Servicing the World: Flexible Filipinos and the Unsecured Life." In *Political Emotions*, edited by Ann Cvetkovich, Janet Staiger, and Ann Reynolds, 215–28. New York: Routledge, 2010.

Marx, Karl. *Economic and Philosophic Manuscripts* (1844). Translated and edited by Martin Milligan. Mineola, NY: Dover, 2007.

Masco, Joseph. *The Theater of Operations: National Security Affect from the Cold War to the War on Terror*. Durham, NC: Duke University Press, 2014.

Mavor, Carol. *Reading Boyishly: Roland Barthes, J. M. Barrie, Jacques Henri Lartigue, Marcel Proust, and D. W. Winnicott*. Durham, NC: Duke University Press, 2008.

Mbembe, Achille. "Necropolitics." Translated by Libby Meintjes. *Public Culture* 15, no. 1 (Winter 2003): 11–40.

McGarry, Molly. *Ghosts of Futures Past: Spiritualism and the Cultural Politics of Nineteenth-Century America*. Berkeley: University of California Press, 2008.

McGlotten, Shaka. "Ordinary Intersections: Speculations on Difference, Justice, and Utopia in Black Queer Life." *Transforming Anthropology* 20, no. 1 (March 2012): 45–66.

McGlotten, Shaka. *Virtual Intimacies: Media, Affect, and Queer Sociality*. Albany: State University of New York Press, 2014.

McCormack, Derek P. "Elemental Infrastructures for Atmospheric Media: On Stratospheric Variations, Value and the Commons." *Environment and Planning D: Society and Space* 35, no. 3 (2017): 418–37.

McRobbie, Angela. "Notes on the Perfect." *Australian Feminist Studies* 30, no. 83 (2015): 3–20.

Melley, Timothy. "'Stalked by Love': Female Paranoia and the Stalker Novel." *Differences: A Journal of Feminist Cultural Studies* 8, no. 2 (Summer 1996): 68–101.

Mendelsohn, Robert. "The Projective Identifications of Everyday Life." *Psychoanalytic Review* 96, no. 6 (December 2009): 71–894.

Mignolo, Walter D., and Catherine E. Walsh. *On Decoloniality: Concepts, Analytics, Praxis*. Durham, NC: Duke University Press, 2018.

Miller, D. A. *Jane Austen, or the Secret of Style*. Princeton, NJ: Princeton University Press, 2005.

Mills, China. "'Dead People Don't Claim': A Psychopolitical Autopsy of UK Austerity Suicides." *Critical Social Policy* 38, no. 2 (2018): 302–22.

Milosz, Czeslaw, "Gift." In *Risking Everything: 110 Poems of Love and Revelation*, edited by Roger Housden, 53. New York: Harmony Books, 2003.

Mitchell, Juliet. "Theory as an Object." *October* 113 (Summer 2005): 29–38.

Moore, Darnell L. "Premeditated Manslaughter: Notes from a Black Male Suicide Survivor." *Gawker*, December 8, 2012. Accessed August 5, 2017. http://gawker.com/5966719/premeditated-manslaughter-notes-from-a-black-male-suicide-survivor.

Moore, Darnell L. "Reflections of a Black Queer Suicide Survivor." *Prettyqueer* (blog). April 18, 2012. Accessed August 5, 2017. https://prettyqueer.tumblr.com/post/21315533500/reflections-of-a-black-queer-suicide-survivor.

Morris, Rosalind C. "Conflicts and Crisis in the Faculties: The Humanities in an Age of Identity." *Social Research: An International Quarterly* 84, no. 3 (Fall 2017): 583–615.

Morris, Rosalind C. *In the Place of Origins: Modernity and Its Mediums in Northern Thailand*. Durham, NC: Duke University Press, 2000.

Morrison, Linda L., and Deborah L. Downey. "Racial Differences in Self-Disclosure of Suicidal Ideation and Reasons for Living: Implications for Training." *Cultural Diversity and Ethnic Minority Psychology* 6, no. 4 (November 2000): 374–86.

Moten, Fred. *Black and Blur*. Durham, NC: Duke University Press, 2017.

Moten, Fred. "Blackness and Nothingness (Mysticism in the Flesh)." *South Atlantic Quarterly* 112, no. 4 (Fall 2013): 737–80.

Moten, Fred. "Black Op." PMLA 123, no. 5 (October 2008): 1743–47.

Moten, Fred. "The Case of Blackness." *Criticism* 50, no. 2 (Spring 2008): 177–218.

Moten, Fred. *In the Break: The Aesthetics of the Black Radical Tradition*. Minneapolis: University of Minnesota Press, 2003.

Moten, Fred. *Stolen Life (Consent Not to Be a Single Being)*. Durham, NC: Duke University Press, 2018.

Moten, Fred. *The Universal Machine*. Durham, NC: Duke University Press, 2018.

Mullen, Harryette. "Elliptical." In *Sleeping with the Dictionary*, 23. Berkeley: University of California Press, 2002.

Muñoz, José Esteban. *Cruising Utopia: The Then and There of Queer Futurity*. 10th anniversary edition. Foreword by Joshua Chambers-Letson, Tavia Nyong'o, and Ann Pellegrini. New York: New York University Press, 2019.

Muñoz, José Esteban. "'Gimme Gimme This . . . Gimme Gimme That': Annihilation and Innovation in the Punk Rock Commons." *Social Text* 31, no. 3 (Fall 2013): 95–110.

Nancy, Jean-Luc. "Elliptical Sense." In *A Finite Thinking*, translated by Jonathan Derbyshire, 91–111. Stanford, CA: Stanford University Press, 2003.

Negri, Antonio. "The Labor of the Multitude and the Fabric of Biopolitics." Translated by Sara Mayo, Peter Graefe, and Mark Coté; edited by Mark Coté. *Globalization Working Papers* 8, no. 3 (August 2008): 9–24.

Negri, Antonio. "N for Negri: Antonio Negri in Conversation with Carles Guerra." Translated and edited by Jorge Mestre, Ivan Bercedo, Raimon Vilatovà, Glòria Mèlich, Elaine Fradley, and Carlos Guerra. *Grey Room* 11 (Spring 2003): 86–109.

Newton, Huey P., and Herman J. Blake. *Revolutionary Suicide*. New York: Harcourt Brace Jovanovich, 1973.

Ngai, Sianne. *Our Aesthetic Categories: Zany, Cute, Interesting*. Cambridge, MA: Harvard University Press, 2015.

Ngai, Sianne. *Theory of the Gimmick: Aesthetic Judgment and Capitalist Form*. Cambridge, MA: Harvard University Press, 2020.

Ngai, Sianne. *Ugly Feelings*. Cambridge, MA: Harvard University Press, 2005.

Nguyen, Tan Hoang. *A View from the Bottom: Asian American Masculinity and Sexual Representation*. Durham, NC: Duke University Press, 2014.

Nohelani Teves, Stephanie, Andrea Smith, and Michelle H. Raheja. *Native Studies Keywords*. Tucson: University of Arizona Press, 2015.

Norton, Jack, and Cindi Katz. "Social Reproduction." In *The International Encyclopedia of Geography: People, the Earth, Environment, and Technology*, edited by D. Richardson, N. Castree, M. F. Goodchild, A. Kobayashi, W. Liu, and R. A. Marston. Wiley Online Library, March 6, 2017. Accessed December 11, 2020. https://onlinelibrary.wiley.com/doi/10.1002/9781118786352.wbieg1107.

Nyong'o, Tavia. *Afro-Fabulations: The Queer Drama of Black Life*. New York: New York University Press, 2018.

Obadia, Julienne, ed. "Special Collection: Overwhelmed by Proximity." *Anthropological Quarterly* 93, no. 1 (2020).

Ogden, Pat, Kekuni Minton, and Claire Pain. *Trauma and the Body: A Sensorimotor Approach to Psychotherapy*. New York: W. W. Norton, 2006.

Ogden, Thomas H. "On Projective Identification." *International Journal of Psychoanalysis* 60 (1979): 357–373.

Ogden, Thomas H. "Some Theoretical Comments on Personal Isolation." *Psychoanalytic Dialogues* 1, no. 3 (1991): 377–90.

O'Keefe, Victoria M., LaRicka R. Wingate, Ashley B. Cole, David W. Hollingsworth, and Raymond P. Tucker. "Seemingly Harmless Racial Communications Are Not So Harmless: Racial Microaggressions Lead to Suicidal Ideation by Way of Depression Symptoms." *Suicide and Life-Threatening Behavior* 45, no. 5 (October 2015): 567–76.

Osman, Jena, and Juliana Spahr, eds. *Chain* (1994–2005). Accessed June 1, 2020. https://jacket2.org/reissues/chain.

Paasonen, Susanna. *Many Splendored Things: Thinking Sex and Play*. London: Goldsmiths, 2018.

Panagia, Davide. *Rancière's Sentiments*. Durham, NC: Duke University Press, 2018.

Patel, Vikram. "The Burden Is Even Greater: The Solution Needs Rethinking." *Canadian Journal of Psychiatry* 65, no. 2 (2020): 99–101.

Patel, Vikram, and Pattie Pramila Gonsalves. "Suicide Prevention: Putting the Person at the Center." *PLoS Medicine* 16, no. 9 (2019): 1–4.

Patterson, Orlando. *Slavery and Social Death: A Comparative Study, with a New Preface*. Cambridge, MA: Harvard University Press, 2018. First published in 1982.

Patton, Paul. "The World Seen from Within: Deleuze and the Philosophy of Events." *Theory and Event* 1, no. 1 (1997). Accessed December 11, 2020. https://doi.org/10.1353/tae.1991.0006.

Peake, Linda J., and Beverley Mullings. "Critical Reflections on Mental and Emotional Distress in the Academy." *ACME* 15, no. 2 (2016): 253–84.

Phillips, Adam. "Close-Ups." *History Workshop Journal* 57, no. 1 (Spring 2004): 142–49.

Phillips, Adam. *Equals*. New York: Basic, 2002.

Pignarre, Philippe, and Isabelle Stengers. *Capitalist Sorcery: Breaking the Spell*. Translated and edited by Andrew Goffey. 2004; London: Palgrave Macmillan, 2011.

Pittman, Alex. "The Reserve Army of Affectivity." *Camera Obscura*, forthcoming.

Postone, Moishe. "Thinking the Global Crisis." *South Atlantic Quarterly* 111, no. 2 (Spring 2012): 227–49.

Povinelli, Elizabeth A. *Economies of Abandonment: Social Belonging and Endurance in Late Liberalism*. Durham, NC: Duke University Press, 2011.

Povinelli, Elizabeth A. *Geontologies: A Requiem to Late Liberalism*. Durham, NC: Duke University Press, 2016.

Power, Nina. *One Dimensional Woman*. Winchester, UK: Zero Books, 2009.

Power, Nina. "Which Equality? Badiou and Rancière in Light of Ludwig Feuerbach." *Parallax* 15, no. 3 (2009): 63–80.

Price, Margaret. *Mad at School: Rhetorics of Mental Disability and Academic Life*. Ann Arbor: University of Michigan Press, 2011.

Probyn, Elspeth. *Outside Belongings*. New York: Routledge, 1996.

Puar, Jasbir K. *The Right to Maim: Debility, Capacity, Disability*. Durham, NC: Duke University Press, 2017.

Rabin, Roni Caryn. "U.S. Suicides Declined Over All in 2020 but May Have Risen among People of Color." *New York Times*, April 15, 2021. Accessed April 18, 2021. https://www.nytimes.com/2021/04/15/health/coronavirus-suicide-cdc.html.

Rancière, Jacques. *Disagreement: Politics and Philosophy*. Translated by Julie Rose. Minneapolis: University of Minnesota Press, 1999.

Rancière, Jacques. *Dissensus*. London: Bloomsbury, 2007.

Rancière, Jacques. *Hatred of Democracy*. London: Verso, 2007.

Rancière, Jacques. *The Ignorant Schoolmaster: Five Lessons in Intellectual Emancipation*. Translated by Kristin Ross. Stanford, CA: Stanford University Press, 1991.

Rankine, Claudia. *Citizen: An American Lyric*. Minneapolis, MN: Graywolf Press, 2014.

Rankine, Claudia. *Don't Let Me Be Lonely: An American Lyric*. Saint Paul, MN: Graywolf Press, 2004.

Rankine, Claudia. *Just Us: An American Conversation*. Minneapolis, MN: Graywolf Press, 2020.

Reed, Anthony. *Freedom Time: The Poetics and Politics of Black Experimental Writing*. Baltimore: Johns Hopkins University Press, 2016.

Reich, Wilhelm. "The Sexual Misery of the Working Masses and the Difficulties of Sexual Reform." 1930. Translated by Kay Goodman. In *New German Critique* No. 1 (Winter, 1973): 98–110. Reich's speech, originally entitled "Sexualnot der Werktatigen und die Schwierigkeit sexueller Beratung," was published in *Sexualnot und Sexualreform*; Verhandlung der Weltliga für Sexualreform, abgehalten zu Wien am 16. bis 23. September 1930 (Vienna, 1931): 72–87.

Reid-Pharr, Robert. *Black Gay Man: Essays*. New York: New York University Press, 2001.

Richardson, Jr., Robert D. *Emerson: The Mind on Fire*. Berkeley: University of California Press, 1995.

Rifkin, Mark. *Beyond Settler Time: Temporal Sovereignty and Indigenous Self-Determination.* Durham, NC: Duke University Press, 2017.

Riggs, Marlon. *Black Is, Black Ain't.* San Francisco: California Newsreel, 1994.

Riggs, Marlon. *Tongues Untied.* San Francisco: California Newsreel, 1989.

Riley-Smith, Ben. "Was It for Real? Movie Sex Scenes They Still Talk About." *The Week,* March 25, 2011. Accessed December 11, 2020. http://www.theweek.co .uk/6735/was-it-real-movie-sex-scenes-they-still-talk-about.

Rodríguez, Juana María. *Queer Latinidad: Identity Practices, Discursive Spaces.* New York: New York University Press, 2003.

Rodríguez, Juana María. *Sexual Futures, Queer Gestures, and Other Latina Longings.* New York: New York University Press, 2014.

Rodríguez Andrés, Antonio. "Income Inequality, Unemployment, and Suicide: A Panel Data Analysis of 15 European Countries." *Applied Economics* 37, no. 4 (2005): 439–51.

Roitman, Janet. *Anti-Crisis.* Durham, NC: Duke University Press, 2013.

Rose, Jacqueline. "Feminism and the Psychic." In *Sexuality in the Field of Vision,* 1–25. London: Verso, 1986.

Rose, Jacqueline. "Where Does the Misery Come From? Psychoanalysis, Feminism, and the Event." In *Feminism and Psychoanalysis,* edited by Richard Feldstein and Judith Roof, 25–39. Ithaca, NY: Cornell University Press, 1989.

Ross, Kristin. *Fast Cars, Clean Bodies: Decolonization and the Reordering of French Culture.* Cambridge, MA: MIT Press, 1996.

Ross, Kristin. *May '68 and Its Afterlives.* Chicago: University of Chicago Press, 2002.

Rowe, John Carlos. *At Emerson's Tomb: The Politics of Classic American Literature.* New York: Columbia University Press, 1997.

Rubenstein, Michael. *Public Works: Infrastructure, Irish Modernism, and the Postcolonial.* Notre Dame, IN: University of Notre Dame Press, 2010.

Rubenstein, Michael, Bruce Robbins, and Sophia Beal. "Infrastructuralism: An Introduction." *Modern Fiction Studies* 61, no. 4 (Winter 2015): 575–86.

Sahlins, Marshall. "Infrastructuralism." *Critical Inquiry* 36, no. 3 (Spring 2010): 371–85.

Salecl, Renata. *Choice.* London: Profile, 2010.

Samuels, Ellen. "Six Ways of Looking at Crip Time." *Disability Studies Quarterly* 37, no. 3 (2017). Accessed December 12, 2020. https://dsq-sds.org/article/view /5824/4684.

Santner, Eric L., Slavoj Žižek, and Kenneth Reinhard. *The Neighbor: Three Inquiries in Political Theology.* Chicago: University of Chicago Press, 2005.

Sarlin, Paige. "Vulnerable Accumulation." *Reviews in Cultural Theory* 2, no. 3 (2008). Accessed April 22, 2020. http://reviewsinculture.com/2012/10/15/vulnerable -accumulation/.

Schneider, Nathan. "Breaking Up with Occupy." *The Nation,* September 11, 2013. Accessed June 28, 2020. https://www.thenation.com/article/archive/breaking -occupy/.

Schore, Allan. *Affect Dysregulation and Disorders of the Self*. New York: W. W. Norton, 2003.

Schumacher, Eric C. *Aristotle on the Nature of Analogy*. Lanham, MD: Lexington, 2018.

Sedgwick, Eve Kosofsky. *Epistemology of the Closet*. Berkeley: University of California Press, 1990.

Sedgwick, Eve Kosofsky. "Paranoid Reading and Reparative Reading, or, You're So Paranoid, You Probably Think This Essay Is about You." In *Touching Feeling*, 123–51.

Sedgwick, Eve Kosofsky. *Touching Feeling: Affect, Pedagogy, Performativity*. Durham, NC: Duke University Press, 2003.

Seltzer, Mark. "The Official World." *Critical Inquiry* 37, no. 4 (Summer 2011): 724–53.

Seltzer, Mark. *Serial Killers: Death and Life in America's Wound Culture*. New York: Routledge, 1998.

Sexton, Jared. "The Social Life of Social Death: On Afro-Pessimism and Black Optimism." *InTensions* 5 (2011): 1–47.

Shah, Nayan. "Forcible Feeding and the Crisis of Care in Indefinite Detention." Lecture delivered at the University of Chicago, Chicago, IL, April 2, 2015.

Shange, Ntozake. *For Colored Girls Who Have Considered Suicide / When the Rainbow Is Enuf*. 1975. New York: Scribner, 1997.

Sharpe, Christina. *In the Wake: On Blackness and Being*. Durham, NC: Duke University Press, 2016.

Shaviro, Steven. "Beauty Lies in the Eye." *symploke* 6, nos. 1–2 (1998): 96–108.

Shields, David. *Other People: Takes and Mistakes*. New York: Knopf, 2017.

Shockley, Evie. *Renegade Poetics: Black Aesthetics and Formal Innovation in African American Poetry*. Iowa City: University of Iowa Press, 2011.

Simmel, Georg. "The Metropolis and Mental Life." *On Individuality and Social Forms: Selected Writings*, edited by Donald N. Levine. Chicago: University of Chicago Press, 1972, 324–39.

Smith, Paul Chaat. *Everything You Know about Indians Is Wrong*. Minneapolis: University of Minnesota Press, 2009.

Smith, Zadie, ed. *The Book of Other People*. New York: Penguin, 2008.

Snodgrass, Mary Ellen. "Androgyny and Feminist Literature." In *Encyclopedia of Feminist Literature*, 20–22. New York: Facts on File, 2006.

Snyder, Rachel Louise. *No Visible Bruises: What We Don't Know about Domestic Violence Can Kill Us*. New York: Bloomsbury, 2019.

Somerville, Siobhan, ed. *The Cambridge Companion to Queer Studies*. Cambridge: Cambridge University Press, 2020.

Spade, Dean. *Mutual Aid: Building Solidarity during This Crisis (and the Next)*. London: Verso, 2020.

Spahr, Juliana. *This Connection of Everyone with Lungs: Poems*. Berkeley: University of California Press, 2005.

Spahr, Juliana. *The Transformation*. Berkeley, CA: Atelos Press, 2007.

Spahr, Juliana. *Well Then There Now*. Boston: Black Sparrow, 2011.

Spahr, Juliana, and David Buuck. *An Army of Lovers*. San Francisco: City Lights, 2013.

Spahr, Juliana, and Joan Retallack, eds. *Poetry and Pedagogy: The Challenge of the Contemporary*. New York: Palgrave Macmillan, 2006.

Spahr, Juliana, and Stephanie Young, eds. *A Megaphone: Some Enactments, Some Numbers, and Some Essays about the Continued Usefulness of Crotchless-pants-and-a-machine-gun Feminism*. Berkeley, CA: ChainLinks, 2011.

Spillers, Hortense J. "'Mama's Baby, Papa's Maybe': An American Grammar Book." In *Black, White, and in Color: Essays on American Literature and Culture*, 203–29. Chicago: University of Chicago Press, 2003.

Spillers, Hortense J. "Mama's Baby, Papa's Maybe: An American Grammar Book." In "Culture and Countermemory: The 'American' Connection." Special issue, *Diacritics* 17, no. 2 (Summer 1987): 64–81.

Spivak, Gayatri Chakravorty. "Can the Subaltern Speak?" In *Marxism and the Interpretation of Culture*, edited by Cary Nelson and Lawrence Grossberg, 271–313. Urbana: University of Illinois Press, 1988.

Spivak, Gayatri Chakravorty. "Can the Subaltern Speak? Speculations on Widow-Sacrifice." *Wedge*, nos. 7–8 (1985): 120–30.

Spivak, Gayatri Chakravorty. "Criticism, Feminism, and The Institution: An Interview with Gayatri Chakravorty Spivak" (1984). In *The Postcolonial Critic: Interviews, Strategies, Dialogues*, edited by Sarah Harasym, 1–16. New York: Routledge, 1990.

Spivak, Gayatri Chakravorty. "'Draupadi' by Mahasveta Devi." In "Writing and Sexual Difference." Special issue, *Critical Inquiry* 8, no. 2 (Winter 1981): 381–402. Republished in Spivak, Gayatri Chakravorty. *Other Worlds: Essays in Cultural Politics*, 179–97. London: Methuen, 1987.

Spivak, Gayatri Chakravorty. "More on Power/Knowledge." In *The Spivak Reader*, edited by Donna Landry and Gerald Maclean, 141–74. 1992. New York: Routledge and Kegan Paul, 1996.

Spivak, Gayatri Chakravorty. "The Politics of Translation." In *Outside in the Teaching Machine*, 179–200. New York: Routledge, 1993.

Spivak, Gayatri Chakravorty. "Subaltern Studies: Deconstructing Historiography." In *In Other Worlds: Essays in Cultural Politics*, 197–221. New York: Routledge, 1988.

Stacey, Jackie. "Crossing over with Tilda Swinton—the Mistress of 'Flat Affect.'" *International Journal of Politics, Culture, and Society* 28 (2015): 243–71.

Stacey, Jackie. "Wishing Away Ambivalence." *Feminist Theory* 15, no. 1 (March 2014): 39–49.

Star, Susan Leigh. "The Ethnography of Infrastructure." *American Behavioral Scientist* 43, no. 3 (November 1999): 377–91.

Star, Susan Leigh. "Infrastructure and Ethnographic Practice: Working on the Fringes." *Scandinavian Journal of Information Systems* 14, no. 2 (September 2002): 107–22.

Star, Susan Leigh, and Anselm Strauss. "Layers of Silence, Arenas of Voice: The Ecology of Visible and Invisible Work." *Computer Supported Cooperative Work* 8 (March 1999): 9–30.

Steiner, John. *Psychic Retreats: Pathological Organizations in Psychotic, Neurotic and Borderline Patients.* Foreword by Roy Schafer. New York: Routledge, 1993.

Steiner, John. *Seeing and Being Seen: Emerging from a Psychic Retreat.* New York: Routledge, 2011.

Stern, Daniel N. *The Interpersonal World of the Infant: A View from Psychoanalysis and Developmental Psychology.* New York: Basic, 1985.

Stern, Daniel N. *The Present Moment in Psychotherapy and Everyday Life.* New York: W. W. Norton, 2004.

Stevenson, Lisa. *Life beside Itself: Imagining Care in the Canadian Arctic.* Berkeley: University of California Press, 2014.

Stewart, Kathleen. *Ordinary Affects.* Durham, NC: Duke University Press, 2007.

Stewart, Kathleen. *A Space on the Side of the Road: Cultural Poetics in an "Other" America.* Princeton, NJ: Princeton University Press, 1996.

Stockton, Kathryn Bond. *Beautiful Bottom, Beautiful Shame: Where "Black" Meets "Queer."* Durham, NC: Duke University Press, 2006.

Stockton, Kathryn Bond. "Reading as Kissing, Sex with Ideas: 'Lesbian' Barebacking?" *Los Angeles Review of Books,* March 8, 2015, accessed December 12, 2020, https://lareviewofbooks.org/article/reading-kissing-sex-ideas-lesbian-barebacking/.

Stoler, Ann Laura. "Epistemic Politics: Ontologies of Colonial Common Sense." *Philosophical Forum* 39, no. 3 (Fall 2008): 349–361.

Stone, Laurie. *Everything Is Personal: Notes on Now.* Greensboro, NC: Scuppernong Editions, 2020.

TallBear, Kim. "Making Love and Relations beyond Settler Sex and Family." In *Making Kin Not Population,* edited by Adele Clarke and Donna Haraway, 147–64. Chicago: Prickly Paradigm, 2018.

TallBear, Kim. "Settler Colonial Love Is Breaking My Heart." Lecture delivered at the University of Chicago, Chicago, February 10, 2020.

Taub, Deborah J., and Jalonda Thompson. "College Student Suicide." *New Directions for Student Services* 141 (Spring 2013): 5–14.

Tavernise, Sabrina. "U.S. Suicide Rate Surges to a 30-Year High." *New York Times,* April 22, 2016. Accessed August 5, 2017. https://www.nytimes.com/2016/04/22/health/us-suicide-rate-surges-to-a-30-year-high.html?_r=0.

Taylor, Diana. "Double-Blind: The Torture Case." *Critical Inquiry* 33, no. 4 (Summer 2007): 710–33.

Terada, Rei. "Living a Ruined Life: De Quincey beyond the Worst." *European Romantic Review* 20, no. 2 (2009): 177–86.

Terada, Rei. *Looking Away: Phenomenality and Dissatisfaction, Kant to Adorno.* Cambridge, MA: Harvard University Press, 2009.

Teyssot, Georges. "Heterotopias and the History of Spaces." In *Architecture Theory Since 1968*, edited by K. Michael Hays, 296–305. 1977. Cambridge, MA: MIT Press, 1998.

Thomas, Kyla, Shu-Shen Chang, and David Gunnell. "Suicide Epidemics: The Impact of Newly Emerging Methods on Overall Suicide Rates—A Time Trends Study." BMC *Public Health* 11, no. 314 (2011). Accessed August 5, 2017. https://rdcu.be/caNni.

Thompson, A. K. *Premonitions: Selected Essays on the Culture of Revolt*. Chico, CA: AK Press, 2018.

Thompson, Chalmer E., and Helen A. Neville. "Racism, Mental Health, and Mental Health Practice." *Counseling Psychologist* 27, no. 2 (Mar. 1999): 155–233.

Thompson, David. *Last Tango in Paris*. London: British Film Institute, 1998.

Tlostanova, Madina Vladimirovna, and Walter Mignolo, eds. *Learning to Unlearn: Decolonial Reflections from Eurasia and the Americas*. Columbus: Ohio State University Press, 2012.

Tompkins, Kyla Wazana. "On the Gelatinous." Lecture delivered at the Center for the Study of Gender and Sexuality, University of Chicago, Chicago. February 4, 2016.

Trahair, Lisa. *The Comedy of Philosophy: Sense and Nonsense in Early Cinematic Slapstick*. Albany: State University of New York Press, 2007.

Tsing, Anna Lowenhaupt. *Friction: An Ethnography of Global Connection*. Princeton, NJ: Princeton University Press, 2005.

Tsing, Anna Lowenhaupt. *Mushroom at the End of the World: On the Possibility of Life in Capitalist Ruins*. Princeton, NJ: Princeton University Press, 2017.

Turner, Stephen. "Charisma Reconsidered." *Journal of Classical Sociology* 3, no. 1 (March 2003): 5–26.

uncertain commons. *Speculate This!* Durham, NC: Duke University Press, 2013.

van der Kolk, Bessel A. *The Body Keeps the Score: Brain, Mind, and Body in the Healing of Trauma*. New York: Penguin, 2014.

van der Kolk, Bessel A., and Rita Fisler. "Dissociation and the Fragmentary Nature of Traumatic Memories: Overview and Exploratory Study." *Journal of Traumatic Stress* 8, no. 4 (October 1995): 505–25.

Virno, Paolo. *A Grammar of the Multitude: For an Analysis of Contemporary Forms of Life*. Translated by Isabella Bertoletti, James Cascaito, and Andrea Casson. New York: Semiotext(e), 2004.

Warner, Michael. "The Mass Public and the Mass Subject." In *Habermas and the Public Sphere*, edited by Craig Calhoun, 377–401. Cambridge, MA: MIT Press, 1992.

Warner, Michael. *Publics and Counterpublics*. Cambridge, MA: MIT Press, 2002.

Warren, Calvin. "Onticide: Afropessimism, Queer Theory, and Ethics." Ill Will Editions (blog). 2015. Accessed December 11, 2020. https://illwilleditions.noblogs.org/files/2015/09/Warren-Onticide-Afropessimism-Queer-Theory-and-Ethics-READ.pdf.

Warren, Calvin. *Ontological Terror: Blackness, Nihilism, Emancipation*. Durham, NC: Duke University Press, 2018.

Weber, Max. *On Charisma and Institution Building*. Chicago: University of Chicago Press, 1968.

Weeks, Kathi. *The Problem with Work: Feminism, Marxism, Antiwork Politics, and Postwork Imaginaries*. Durham, NC: Duke University Press, 2011.

Welch, Tana Jean. *"Don't Let Me Be Lonely*: The Trans-Corporeal Ethics of Claudia Rankine's Investigative Poetics." MELUS 40, no. 1 (Spring 2015): 124–48.

Wellbery, David E. "Theory of Events: Foucault and Literary Criticism." *Revue Internationale de Philosophie* 41, nos. 162–63 (3/4) (1987): 420–32.

Wiegman, Robyn. "The Times We're In: Queer Feminist Criticism and the Reparative 'Turn.'" *Feminist Theory* 15, no. 1 (March 2014): 4–25.

Wilderson III, Frank B. *Red, White, and Black: Cinema and the Structure of U.S. Antagonisms*. Durham, NC: Duke University Press, 2010.

Williams, Linda. "Film Bodies: Gender, Genre, and Excess." *Film Quarterly* 44, no. 4 (Summer 1991): 2–13.

Williams, Linda. *Screening Sex*. Durham, NC: Duke University Press, 2008.

Williams, Patricia J. *The Alchemy of Race and Rights*. Cambridge, MA: Harvard University Press, 1991.

Williams, Raymond. "Ideology." In *Marxism and Literature*, 55–71. Oxford: Oxford University Press, 1977.

Williams, Raymond. *Keywords: A Vocabulary of Culture and Society*. Oxford: Oxford University Press, 1976.

Williams, Raymond. "Structures of Feeling." In *Marxism and Literature*, 128–35. Oxford: Oxford University Press, 1977.

Wilson, Ara. "The Infrastructure of Intimacy." *Signs: Journal of Women in Culture and Society* 41, no. 2 (Winter 2016): 247–80.

Winnicott, Donald W. *Playing and Reality*. London: Tavistock, 1971.

Winnicott, Donald W. "The Use of an Object." *International Journal of Psycho-Analysis* 50 (1969): 711–16.

Woodward, Keith, and Mario Bruzzone. "Touching Like a State." *Antipode* 47, no. 2 (March 2015): 539–56.

Yanagisako, Sylvia. "Immaterial and Industrial Labor: On False Binaries in Hardt and Negri's Trilogy." *Focaal: Journal of Global and Historical Anthropology* 64 (December 2012): 16–23.

Zerilli, Linda M. G. "Toward a Feminist Theory of Judgment." *Signs* 34, no. 2 (Winter 2009): 295–317.

Žižek, Slavoj. "How Did Marx Invent the Symptom?" In *Mapping Ideology*, edited by Slavoj Žižek, 296–331. London: Verso, 1994.

Žižek, Slavoj. "How to Begin from the Beginning." *New Left Review* 57 (May–June 2009): 43–55. Accessed March 27, 2016. https://newleftreview.org/issues/II57/articles/slavoj-zizek-how-to-begin-from-the-beginning.

Žižek, Slavoj. "The Spectre of Ideology." In *Mapping Ideology*, edited by Slavoj Žižek, 1–33. London: Verso, 1994.

Žižek, Slavoj. *Žižek's Jokes: Did You Hear the One about Hegel and Negation?* Cambridge, MA: MIT Press, 2014.

Zupančič, Alenka. *The Odd One In: On Comedy.* Cambridge, MA: MIT Press, 2008.

Index

Arbery, Ahmaud, 113
Arendt, Hannah, 42, 82, 145
Aristotle, 105
Arsić, Branka, 93
attachment: to the common, 80; inconvenience and, 6–7; melancholic, 119; people as, 9; reciprocity and, 76; scalability of, 97
attunement: Bertolucci's *Last Tango in Paris* and, 51; the commons and, 80, 82–83; Fleck's *Half Nelson* and, 71; mood and, 134
Augé, Marc, 55, 84
austerity, protests against, 83

Badiou, Alain, 51, 187n44
Ban en Banlieue (Kapil), 152–55, 162–70, 172
Barthes, Roland, 82, 179n16
being in life without wanting the world, 10, 123–25, 134, 137. *See also* dissociation
belonging: the commons and, 77, 81–82, 113, 116; ellipsis and, 126; Emerson and detection vs., 94; glitch and, 95; infrastructures of, 105; Johnson's *In the Air* and, 109; in Lowell's "For the Union Dead," 88; proxemics and, 143, 181n37; Spahr and, 192n56
Berardi, Bifo, 42–43
Bergson, Henri, 185n16
Bersani, Leo, 41, 96–97
Bertolucci, Bernardo: *The Dreamers*, 44; *Luna*, 64. *See also Last Tango in Paris*
"Better Off Alone" (Alice DeeJay), 110
Bion, W. R., 153, 161
biopolitics: about, 13, 197n15; dissociation and, 119–20, 122–23, 132, 141, 147; Foucault on, 65–66; of inconvenience, 4; suicidiation and, 122–23, 197n17
Bishop, Elizabeth, 181n25
Blackness, 4, 22, 113–14, 136. *See also* race and racism
Bogost, Ian, 116
Bollas, Christopher, 133, 150
Bonney, Sean, 80
Boston Common, 86–91, 87f, 115f
Bowie, David, 55
Brand, Dionne, 171
Brenkman, John, 190n13

Brennan, Teresa, 19
brokenness, 170–71
Brooks, Stephanie: *Lovely Caution*, 78–80, 79f
Buell, Lawrence, 91
Burt, Stephen, 117–18
Butler, Judith, 2
Byrd, Jodi A., 3

capitalism: about, 182nn43–44; ambivalence and, 26; Clover's genres of the dialectic and, 14; the commons and, 86–91, 115; communis sensus and, 82; Emerson on, 90, 191n33; infrastructures and, 19–20; in Rankine's *Don't Let Me Be Lonely*, 132, 136; Spahr's *Well Then There Now* and, 105
Caruth, Cathy, 132
Cattelino, Jessica, 3
Cavell, Stanley, 7, 29–30, 36, 44, 86, 92, 179n14, 185n13
Chambers-Letson, Joshua, 179n9, 180n18
Citizen (Rankine), 134, 138
Clover, Joshua, 14, 165
Cohen, Ted, 35–36
comedy: dissociation and, 130, 136–37, 145–47; Freud on, 185n15; humorless comedy in Solondz's *Happiness*, 68–70; joking in Bertolucci's *Last Tango in Paris*, 34–37, 51, 63; joking in Fleck's *Half Nelson*, 72–73; knock-knock jokes, 72, 189n62; puns, 136–37; in Rankine's *Don't Let Me Be Lonely*, 136–37; sex and the joke, 34–38; slapstick, 64, 73, 130; as tragedy plus timing, 72, 147; violence and, 73
commons and the common: about, 77–81; analogy, broken analogy, and, 92–94, 96–99, 103–6, 115–16; Boston Common, 86–91, 87f, 115f; Brooks's *Lovely Caution*, 78–80, 79f; commoning, 114–16; Emerson's "Nature" and, 90–95; Hawk's Detroit Public Schools book depository, 78, 78f; infrastructure and, 183n49; Johnson's *In the Air* and, 107–12, 107f–9f, 111f; Lowell's "For the Union Dead," 86–90; meanings of, 82; Occupy, pandemic, and crisis of "we," 112–14; poetics of infrastructure and,

93–106; sensus communis, 81–85, 98, 115; Spahr's *Connection of Everyone with Lungs*, 99–103; Spahr's *The Transformation*, 97–99; Spahr's *Well Then There Now*, 103–5; undercommons, 22, 81, 84–85; unlearning and, 80, 85, 105–16; "we are all in this together," 84, 113–14, 190n18

Connection of Everyone with Lungs (Spahr), 99–103

Cost of Living Adjustment Movement (COLA), 190n19

Cottom, Tressie McMillan, 196n6

COVID-19 pandemic, ix–x, 113–14

Cowen, Deborah, 21

crisis infrastructuralism, 24–25

Critchley, Simon, 59, 196n13

Dawdy, Shannon Lee, 13, 23

Dean, Tim, 41

de Angelis, Massimo, 114–15

de Certeau, Michel, 110

Delaney, Samuel, 41

Deleuze, Gilles, 23, 96, 125, 131, 185n23, 187n43

democracy. *See* commons and the common

Derrida, Jacques, 125

Detroit Public Schools book depository (Hawk), 78, 78f

Dewey, John, 191n34

Diaconu, Madalina, 13, 23

dissociation: biopolitics and, 119–20, 122–23, 132, 147; comedy and, 130, 136–37, 145–47; elliptical life, 120, 125–26, 137, 145–47; Isherwood's *A Single Man* and Ford's adaptation, 126–31, 127f; life, dissociative, 131–34; meanings of, 118; poetics of, 117–26; proxemics and, 143–44; psychic retreats, 7, 179n13, 195n3; Rankine's *Don't Let Me Be Lonely*, 134–42, 139f, 140f; suicidation, 121–23, 129–31, 135–36. *See also* being in life without wanting the world

disturbance: Bertolucci's *Last Tango in Paris* and, 63; the commons and, 95; dissociation and, 123, 144; Emerson's "Nature" and, 91–96; infrastructures and, 20–23; the joke and, 70, 185; in Kapil's *Ban en*

Banlieue, 166; sex and, 32–33, 38, 40–43, 67; Solondz's *Happiness* and, 70; trauma vs., 38, 40

Dobbs, Cynthia, 138, 199n56

Don't Let Me Be Lonely (Rankine), 131–32, 134–42, 139f, 140f, 162

Dreamers, The (Bertolucci), 44

Du Bois, W. E. B., 142

Duggan, Lisa, 41

Edelman, Lee, 38, 96–97

Edwards, Paul, 21

ellipsis: in Bertolucci's *Last Tango in Paris*, 65; the commons and, 94; dissociation and, 120, 125–26, 137, 145–47; in Ellroy and Kapil, 145, 153, 161; in Isherwood/Ford's *A Single Man*, 130; in Kapil's *Ban en Banlieue*, 167; in Rankine's *Don't Let Me Be Lonely*, 137; trouble and, 8

"Elliptical" (Mullens), 145–47

Ellroy, James: *The Hilliker Curse: My Pursuit of Women*, 157; Latour and, 201n8; *My Dark Places*, 152–62, 201n18

Emerson, Ralph Waldo: the commons and, 90–95, 96; "Nature," 90–95; Rowe on, 191n33; Spinoza and, 80, 191n34; Whitman and, 91

Eng, David, 119–20

entanglement, 2, 178n3

erotophobia, 33, 38–41

Fanon, Frantz, 22, 119, 142, 196n13

fantasy: ambivalence and, 26–27, 73; in Bertolucci's *Last Tango in Paris*, 46, 49, 62; commons as, 78–88; dissociation and, 130, 132; dissolution of, 8; ellipsis as unanchored to, 125; Ellroy on, 201n18; in Johnson's *In the Air*, 109; Kapil's *Ban en Banlieue* and, 164; sovereign, 3

Federici, Silvia, 80

finitude, 122, 196n13

Flatley, Jonathan, 112, 133–34

Floyd, George, 113

Fonagy, Peter, 142

For Colored Girls Who Have Considered Suicide / When the Rainbow Is Enuf (Shange), 121–22

Ford, Tom: *A Single Man*, 126–31, 127f
Forrester, John, 67
"For the Union Dead" (Lowell), 86–90, 190n27
Foucault, Michel: on biopower, 65–66, 122; on governmentality, 189n4; on heterotopias, 14, 151; on overdetermination, 183n47; on pleasure, 185n23; on sexuality, 35, 41, 47
Freud, Sigmund, 10, 35, 178n7, 179nn16–17, 185n15
friction: "being in life without wanting the world" and, 123; brokenness and, 170–71; the commons and, 80–81, 115; dissociation and, 123; inconvenience and, 2, 4, 7–10; overdetermination and, 17–18; in Spahr, 101, 106; suicidiation and, 122; Tsing on, 179n15; the unbearable and, 151
FYPU (Fuck You. Pay Us.), 190n19

"get the butter," 59–62, 188n53
Gilbert, Jeremy, 24–25
Gillick, Liam, 143, 181n37, 200n65
glitch, 24–25, 28, 95, 104
Goldstein, Donna, 145
Gonzales-Day, Ken, 113
Gopinath, Gayatri, 13
governmentality, 189n4
Green, Andrés, 115
Guattari, Félix, 23

Habermas, Jürgen, 178n7
Half Nelson (Fleck), 32, 70–74
Hall, Edward T., 143, 181n37, 200n65
Halley, Janet, 185n20
Han, Shinhee, 119–20
happiness: Bertolucci's *Last Tango in Paris* and, 43, 50, 55–59; "ha-penis," 31–32, 34, 70; sex and, 43, 73–74
Happiness (Solondz), 31–32, 68–70
Hardt, Michael, 13, 90, 96
Harney, Stefano, 5, 22, 81, 84
Harris, Cheryl, 4
Hartman, Saidiya, 196n13
Harvey, David, 95
Heidegger, Martin, 86, 133, 171
"hell is other people," 1–2

heterotopias: about, 14–17, 171; the commons and, 81, 84–85, 90, 115; dissociation and, 120–21, 126; in Ellroy's *My Dark Places*, 159, 161; embodied tactics and, 115; functional utopia and, 143; infrastructure and, 19, 22–23, 95; in Johnson's *In the Air*, 110; in Kapil's *Ban en Banlieue*, 168; overdetermination and, 18
Hilliker Curse: My Pursuit of Women, The (Ellroy), 157
Hiroshima and Nagasaki, 191n31
historical present, 14, 44, 81
Hoagland, Tony, 117–18
Hocquenghem, Guy, 41
Honig, Bonnie, 42
humor: Bertolucci's *Last Tango in Paris* and, 44; Freud on, 35, 185n15; humorlessness, 27–28, 68–69; sex, play, and, 63. *See also* comedy

inconvenience: as affect, 4; attachment and, 6–7; Bertolucci's *Last Tango in Paris* and, 63; brokenness and, 170–71; concept of, xi, 2–11; overdetermination and, 18–19; proxemics and, 143–44; sex and, 40
inconvenience drive, 6, 42, 76, 81, 121, 129
infrastructure: affective dimension of, 23–24, 25, 115; of belonging, 105; the commons and, 85–86, 92–106, 183n49; crisis infrastructuralism, 24–25; in Ellroy and Kapil, 152–53; fantasy as, 27; glitchfrastructure, 104–5; infrastructuralism, 20–21, 115, 153; infrastructuring, 183n47; institutions and, 96; mediation and, 21–23; overdetermination and, 17; poetics of, 93–106; queer infrastructuralism, 21; structure vs., 19–21, 182n44; transformational, 27, 63, 68, 86, 106–7, 112, 150, 201n8; transitional, 24–25, 55; worldmaking and, 95, 98
Ingold, Tim, 131, 199n36
inheritance: Bertolucci's *Last Tango in Paris* and, 44, 69; the commons and, 84; disinheritance, 107; Emerson on, 90; transgenerational trauma and, 141–42
In the Air (Johnson), 107–12, 107f–9f, 111f
Irigaray, Luce, 193n83

move to, 41–42; pedophilia, 69, 188n60; political radicalism and sex radicalism, 32–33, 71–72; queer commentary and zoning for, 41; sexual revolution, 43–50, 65–66; in Solondz's *Happiness*, 68–70. See also *Last Tango in Paris*

Sex and the City, 47

sexual violence and rape/murder: comedy and, 73; Ellroy's *My Dark Places*, 152–62, 201n18; intimacy and, 178n7; Kapil's *Ban en Banlieue*, 152–55, 162–70, 172; rape scene in Bertolucci's *Last Tango in Paris*, 60–62; self-evidence and, 39; sex-positivity and, 33; Solondz's *Happiness*, 69

Shange, Ntozake, 121–22

Sharpe, Christina, 13, 155, 171

Shaviro, Steven, 83

Shaw, Robert, 88–89, 89f

Shortbus (Mitchell), 47

Simmel, Georg, 132

Simondon, Gilbert, 24–25

Single Man, A (Isherwood/Ford), 126–31

Smith, Zadie, 178n5

social theory, 8, 42

Solondz, Todd: *Happiness*, 31–32, 68 70

Sommerville, Siohban, 13

Sorkin, Aaron: *The Trial of the Chicago 7*, 202n29

sovereignty: Bertolucci's *Last Tango in Paris* and weight of, 52, 76; the commons and, 80–81, 92, 95; inconvenience disturbing sovereign fantasy, 3; relationality, nonsovereign, x, 18, 21, 95

Spahr, Juliana, 93, 97, 192n56; *Connection of Everyone with Lungs*, 99–103; *The Transformation*, 97–99; *Well Then There Now*, 103–5

Spillers, Hortense, 156

Spinoza, Baruch, 90

Spivak, Gayatri Chakravorty, 28, 76, 150, 151

Star, Susan Leigh, 95

Steiner, John, 7, 170, 179n13, 195n3

Stern, Daniel, 133

Stewart, Kathleen, 144, 171

Stoler, Ann Laura, 82

Stoner, Bill, 159–60

suicidiation, 121–23, 129–31, 135–36, 196n14, 197n17, 198n34

supremacism and white supremacy: in Bertolucci's *Last Tango in Paris*, 46; in Fleck's *Half Nelson*, 71; inconvenience and, 4; in Kapil's *Ban en Banlieue*, 163–68; power and supremacist performativity, 147; in Rankine's *Don't Let Me Be Lonely*, 136. See also race and racism

Taylor, Diana, 22

Terada, Rei, 86

Transformation, The (Spahr), 97–99

transformational infrastructure, 27, 63, 68, 86, 106–7, 112, 150, 201n8

transitional infrastructure, 24–25, 55

trauma: affect theory and, 186n29; Bertolucci's *Last Tango in Paris* and, 62–63; the commons and, 85; dissociation and, 118, 123–24, 132; disturbance vs., 38–41; in Ellroy's *My Dark Places*, 163; the event and, 50; inconvenience vs., 4–5; posttraumatic stress disorder, 195n2; in Rankine's *Don't Let Me Be Lonely*, 136, 140–42, 199n56; resilience, style, and, 155; transformational infrastructure and, 150; transgenerational, 141–42

Trial of the Chicago 7, The (Sorkin), 202n29

trouble, 8

Tsing, Anna Lowenhaupt, 22, 179n15

unbearable, the, 16, 17, 150–52, 160, 170, 201n5

unlearning: in Bertolucci's *Last Tango in Paris* and, 77; the commons and, 80–82, 85, 105–16; in Ellroy's *My Dark Places*, 157–58; Emerson and, 91; governmentality and, 189n4; in Isherwood/Ford's *A Single Man*, 127–28; loosening the object, 27–29, 126, 151; sex and, 33; in Spahr, 101, 104, 106

utopia, functional, 143. See also heterotopias

violence against women. See sexual violence and rape/murder

Virno, Paolo, 83, 105

vulnerability: in Bertolucci's *Last Tango in Paris*, 45–46, 59; the commons and, 83, 112; cultural receptivity styles and, 144; dissociation and, 121; in Ellroy's *My Dark Places*, 160; entitlement and, 5; inconvenience drive and, 75; in Kapil's *Ban en Banlieue*, 163, 168; psychic retreats and, 7; sex and, 42; in Spahr's *Well Then There Now*, 103–5; "we are all in this together" and, 113

Warner, Michael, 21, 183n51
Warren, Calvin, 13
Waters, Maxine, 147

"we are all in this together," 84, 113–14, 190n18
Welch, Tana Jean, 138, 199n56
Well Then There Now (Spahr), 103–5
whiteness, 22, 45, 99
Whitman, Walt, 91
Wilderson, Frank, 196n13
Williams, Linda, 43–44
Williams, Patricia, 107, 141–42
Williams, Raymond, 20, 82, 143
Wittgenstein, Ludwig, 86
worlding, 42, 94–95, 115, 144, 153
worldmaking, 15, 95, 98, 153, 169

Žižek, Slavoj, 83, 182n39